Leading with Fierce Compassion

Bridging psychological theories on compassion with practical leadership insights, this book explores the transformative power of compassion for navigating the complexities of modern leadership and life.

In a world marked by division, burnout and uncertainty, this book offers actionable guidance on developing essential skills like self-awareness, empathy and effective communication. Through a blend of evidence-based research, therapeutic insights and real-life anecdotes from leaders, this book provides practical tools for cultivating compassion for oneself and others. It highlights the concept of Leading with Fierce Compassion and explores its profound impact on organisational culture, team dynamics and individual wellbeing. From navigating conflicts to fostering inclusive work environments and promoting collaboration, this book equips readers with the courage and skills needed to embrace compassion as a means for personal growth, resilience and authentic leadership. Readers are guided on a journey to deepen their compassion capacity, foster empathetic connections and take effective action.

This book will be a valuable resource for professionals ranging from mid-level managers to executive leadership positions within business, government and non-governmental organisations. It will be an asset to any professional interested in psychology or enhancing leadership abilities to cultivate deeper and more meaningful connections with others.

Dr Mary Miller is a clinical psychologist and executive coach helping leaders develop clarity and courage through Fierce Compassion. She brings together clinical insight and leadership coaching experience from legal, medical, academic and corporate settings across Aotearoa/New Zealand and internationally.

Leading with Fierce Compassion

Practical Wisdom for Meaningful Change

Dr Mary Miller

Routledge
Taylor & Francis Group
LONDON AND NEW YORK

Designed cover image: Mary Miller

First published 2026
by Routledge
4 Park Square, Milton Park, Abingdon, Oxon OX14 4RN

and by Routledge
605 Third Avenue, New York, NY 10158

Routledge is an imprint of the Taylor & Francis Group, an informa business

British Library Cataloguing-in-Publication Data
A catalogue record for this book is available from the British Library

ISBN: 9781032950693 (hbk)
ISBN: 9781032950686 (pbk)
ISBN: 9781003583080 (ebk)

DOI: 10.4324/9781003583080

Typeset in Sabon
by codeMantra

To all those bringing courage and care to their work.

Contents

Acknowledgements

This book started as a project during the COVID-19 pandemic at a time when many experienced fear, loss and a sense of division. I joined an online group of women from around the world, Revolutionary Women, bound together by our desire to create a bold future. Their encouragement and compassion helped this seed to grow.

I am indebted to those who have taught me directly and indirectly about compassion, including Professor Paul Gilbert, whose work in *Compassion Focused Therapy* has been inspirational.

Thank you to my publisher, Routledge, and specifically Vilija Stephens, Khadijah Ebrahim and Clare Midgley for all their help supporting me during the writing process.

I am deeply grateful to all the leaders I interviewed for this book. Whether their quotes made it into print or not, their insights and wisdom helped shape my writing. They were generous with their time and courageously shared their experiences of leading. I hope their words support others who are on the leadership path.

A special thank you to Morna MacGillivray, Katerina Daniels and Professor Bruce Arroll, interviewees who went on to provide support and encouragement. Authorship can be a lonely journey, and I am grateful for your company and guidance along the way.

I am thankful for the generosity of Angela and Rick, who let me stay in their peaceful hideaway for my solo writing retreats, where I could immerse myself in this book.

Thank you to the incisive minds of Dr Alina Pavlova and Dr Joanna MacFarlane. Your expert eyes were incredibly helpful in the editing phase.

Many thanks to Dylan Pharazyn and Aaron Hosford, whose design expertise came just at the right moment to bring my cover design into reality.

It's been an adventure to share a parallel author experience with my husband, Ruben Miller. Thank you for your encouragement and care, and for finding the time for the finest level of review possible.

To Ruben, Bibi and Miles, you've been my anchor and remind me of what really matters.

1 Navigating the age of overwhelm

Leading with Fierce Compassion

Compassionate beginnings

As a lonely only child with a vivid imagination, I escaped into the lives of others. I watched those around me and pictured myself in their world, seeing what they saw, guessing at their thoughts and feelings. I understood from an early age that there are multiple perspectives, many truths about anyone or any situation. I've always found humans fascinating.

Being rather reserved, it suited me to be a listener, to absorb myself in someone else's story, and to feel empathy for their experiences. I was a voracious reader, devouring stories, adventure and tragedy. I wished my life was exciting. I desperately wanted SOMETHING to happen.

Then something(s) happened.

I married very young, much to my friends' and family's surprise. It was a revelation to me to feel so loved and cherished. James and I were two peas in a pod. We walked down the aisle together when I was 18 and he was 19, and into the beginnings of adult life, a new city, studying at university with part-time jobs.

Shortly after we completed our studies, we went out for dinner with a friend. On the way home, we walked across a road and were hit by a drunk driver. James landed on one side of the street, and I on the other. In a moment, we were separated by a road, propelled in different directions. James never regained consciousness and died a few days later.

Our lives that were so closely entwined were severed in an instant.

I escaped with relatively minor injuries. I found myself a widow at 21, consumed with grief and terror and desperately alone. I felt so guilty for surviving, for existing.

DOI: 10.4324/9781003583080-1

Three months later, James's elderly father, Alex, died. Alex was in his late 60s when James was born, and the grief from the loss of his beloved son was too much for his frail 87-year-old body.

A few months after that, I was evicted from the flat James and I had shared and created so many memories in. The landlord tore it down to make way for a new development. I moved to London.

After attending James's funeral, my high school friend Sue was deeply saddened by the event. She went home and wrote a letter entitled "Just in case I pop my clogs", to her family and friends, sharing what an amazing life she had had and detailing her plans for her own future funeral so it would be full of love, music and funny anecdotes. Several months later, she moved to a nearby London suburb. It was such a dark time, and I had a glimmer of hope that with her nearby, there might be some moments of light. We caught up on a Tuesday night after work, and it was delightful to slip into her companionship. She could accommodate my grief in a way that many of my young friends weren't able to. That Friday afternoon, after complaining of a headache, Sue collapsed and died from a brain aneurysm. She was 22 years old.

I felt like a black widow spider, that everything that came close to me died. The world that had once seemed so safe and full of hope had become a bleak and desolate place.

My journey back to living was long.

The coping strategies I used at that time involved a lot of cigarettes and vodka, not strategies that I would recommend now! But I have a lot of compassion for that younger version of myself, doing the best she could to survive so many losses. I wish I could go back and hold her on those many nights when she was crying alone in the dark.

In my early 20s, I found that people would talk to me about the challenges in their lives, their fears and their sorrows. I could listen and be empathetic to their distress. My own experiences of grief carved out in me a capacity to sit with the suffering of others. I could get lost in the experiences of others, although later I came to understand that this was not always a helpful strategy for myself. I clung to the question my father-in-law, Alex, asked in difficult times: "What good can come from this?" I became attached to the idea that being of service to others in the short life that we have is an important guide for living. I used this as a way to manage my survivor's guilt and to make sense of a seemingly random and dangerous world.

Looking back, this period in my life marked the beginning of my lived understanding of *Fierce Compassion*; not the soft kind that offers platitudes, but a persistent drive to keep showing up in the face of difficulty. An important component of compassion is our ability to notice ourselves, our reactions and responses to different people and situations. The process of writing this book was an important moment for me to reflect. I didn't know that the difficulties I faced when I was younger would one day take me into a career as a clinical psychologist, and inform how I understand leadership and what it truly means to care for others, and ourselves. Still now, when I touch those memories, it can bring tears to my eyes. These days I can sit with myself when I am sad, hold myself and say, "I am here for you". It has taken curiosity and courage to learn how to give compassion to myself, as well as caring for others.

∞

Compassionate growth

The process of healing for me, like many others, has not been linear. I think of it more like a mixture of helpful ingredients. It took travelling halfway around the world, emigrating to a country where I didn't know anyone, therapy, long walks, deep conversations with friends, tears, online dating, meeting a wonderful man who could love all of me, yoga, beaches, sunshine, therapy, having two children who I adore and who teach me so much, journaling, studying, working as a clinical psychologist, saying "no", learning that existing does not mean I will be punished, challenging myself, listening, singing, dancing, honest conversations, mindfulness, swimming, pottery and time. The joy is found in the process, there isn't a completion point. Everyone's ingredient list is going to be different.

I am aware of my white middle-class privilege, that no matter how hard some of the challenges in my life have been, others have suffered so very greatly through systematic oppression due to their ethnicity, culture or beliefs. I believe it's our shared humanity, our experience of suffering and difficulties, that allows us to connect and empathise with each other. By sharing our vulnerabilities and listening to others' experiences, we can move to reduce suffering wherever possible and avoid the perpetuation of further harm.

In Aotearoa/New Zealand, where I now live, I deepened my respect for the indigenous culture and ways of knowing that are different from Western conceptualisations. I was touched by a metaphor used by Māori to describe how the long, fibrous leaves of the flax plant can be woven together to make a kete (basket) for knowledge. The basket metaphor stuck in my mind. The ideas I share in this book come from different strands of my life – my clinical experience, the wisdom of clients I have worked with, my many teachers and the research and theories of all those who have come before me. I am grateful to those who shared their experiences of compassion with me during the interviews I undertook for this book. We learn so much from each other's stories. *Fierce Compassion* is a basket for this knowledge, woven together in a new way, with an opportunity for you to use it in ways that are helpful to you.

As I deepened my understanding of compassion in my client work, I also deepened my use of compassion for myself. We have a saying as psychologists that "we are all on our own mountain".[1] From where I am, I can see your mountain, and where the path might be difficult, and together we can explore some options to help you get to where you want to be. But, I am on my own mountain too, and my own mountain is hard for me to see myself. Sometimes the path ahead is unclear, and I can stumble just like you.

During my upbringing, first in Scotland and then in the very south of England, being a "good girl" was very important. Be polite, courteous, think of others' needs first and don't EVER be a bother. I often joke with my closest friends that my epitaph could have been "she was never a bother!" I learnt to please others as a way of validating my existence. Attaining pleasure from their pleasure. If they were happy, I would feel happy.

Later, these patterns would show up when I was presenting. I became more aware of the anxiety I experience when speaking, the fear of getting it "wrong" or being a "bad" psychologist. I know I am not alone in slipping into self-doubt and criticism.

Of course, as soon as I sat down to write this book, imposter syndrome showed up. And it's sneaky! Hiding in plain sight by asking legitimate-sounding questions. "Who am I to write about compassion?", and "What do I know?".

But these types of questions that on the surface appear to show concern are rhetorical ones. The answers are waiting in the shadows.

I'm sure that variations of this response have been experienced by nearly anyone who has ever sat down to write anything. It's a common human experience to feel vulnerable when we speak out. It's taken a lot of practice for me to notice and name these self-critical thoughts. They are good at sounding convincing and demanding my attention. Over the years,

I learnt to turn the volume down on my inner critic; although I have to practise it every day and I can still get hooked by its scare tactics. It took me much longer to realise that when the inner critic became quieter, it left in its wake a kind of void, an absence, nothingness. What was lacking was self-compassion. And this is something I now actively cultivate every day, whether in my thoughts or actions.

What would I say to a friend when they are sitting down to write the opening to a book they are creating?

I know they have some interesting ideas to share with the world, and they are passionate about what they do. But they are feeling uncertain, they are nervous about putting pen to paper. I take them out for a coffee at their favourite cafe. "I can understand that it's daunting to start writing. I'm so glad you are going to share what you know with the world. You've got this. Just start and see where it takes you".

∞

Leading with Fierce Compassion in a complex world

We live in turbulent times, where it seems that outrage grows while human connection frays. The term "polycrisis" captures the compounding challenges we face, including globalisation and protectionism, climate and social justice issues and rapid technological advances.[2,3] When we hear of the challenges facing the political, environmental and work systems that we live in, we can find ourselves tuning out because they are too overwhelming. During a time when we are experiencing increasing change, uncertainty and volatility, people are more stressed and isolated than ever before. Instead of caring more, it can appear that people are caring less, and that we may be heading for a compassion crisis.

Those in leadership positions face the prospect of navigating these challenges personally, as well as supporting and managing those they work with and the systems they work in. Businesses and organisations need to be increasingly nimble to address changing economic, social and environmental conditions. Leaders have to respond to these challenges in their decision-making while holding empathy for those impacted by changes. Flexible work arrangements and shifting priorities of employees bring the importance of clear and effective communication by leaders to the fore. Leaders must explore both how to support staff with mental health challenges, as well as train managers in emotional intelligence skills to ensure functional team dynamics. Yet those in leadership positions can find themselves isolated at the top. In organisations, they may be sandwiched between the expectations of their board or senior management and the staff they lead, or in the entrepreneurial or activism space, they may be forging ahead alone.

We are experiencing unprecedented technological sophistication and digital connectivity, yet society is becoming increasingly fragmented, and individuals are feeling more isolated. We live in the "age of outrage",[4] where comments and opinions are thrown about the internet like never before. While in some areas technology can provide amazing ways for people to connect, learn and express, it has also brought with it a shadow side, where there is an increasing sense of disconnection, "othering" and division. Research shows that fostering a sense of connection brings physical and psychological health benefits, but social connection has been falling in American society over the past few decades, with similar trends seen in developed countries across the world.[5–7] Instead of technology bringing people together, it seems to be pushing people apart and driving polarisation.

While we are "connected" 24/7, most of us have lost touch with our own experiences in the busyness and rush of the modern 21st-century world. We feel more anxious, we get more depressed, we are stressed and unhappy. While there has been a steady increase in levels of mental distress over the past few decades, these trends were accelerated by the experience of the COVID-19 pandemic.[8] We are driven to succeed, to acquire, to produce, all with the nagging feeling that we aren't enough, that we are failing, that doom and disaster loom around every corner. Fed by the continuous news cycle, social media algorithms and the advertising industry, we are kept in a state of chronic crisis living. We now live in a so-called "attention economy",[9–12] which preys on our inbuilt overfocus on danger to keep us doom-scrolling. We compare ourselves to others unfavourably and chase external representations of our success, while our stress levels continue to rise. If we aren't struggling ourselves, we likely know someone who is. When we notice others are suffering, we may find ourselves shutting down, or perhaps blaming others for their predicament, or disconnecting from people we find too unlike ourselves, our values or our lives.

Challenges usually bring difficulty and distress. While this can be a helpful part of the process of change and growth, we may also find ourselves impacted by our suffering or the suffering of those around us. As a clinical psychologist and leadership consultant, I've worked closely with individuals navigating these tensions between success and meaning, resilience and burnout.

Compassion offers us a way to navigate the suffering. The Dalai Lama defines compassion as meaning "an awareness of suffering in others (*or in ourselves*), and the deep commitment to try to alleviate that suffering".[13] Compassion calls us to develop our ability to notice suffering and to respond to it with a sense of warmth and care and then to take wise action to help reduce the distress. At the heart of compassion lies an intent towards helpfulness and connection to others, ourselves and the world around us. For those in leadership positions, increasing our capacity for compassion allows us to respond more effectively to our suffering, and this, in turn, increases the authenticity of our leadership and our ability to connect and respond to the difficulties of others and the systems in which we operate.

When we think of a leader, especially a leader for challenging times, we may think of the need for strength. I use the word *Fierce* as a reminder that compassion takes strength, too. An inner kind of strength, guided by wisdom and courage. Strong leadership isn't immiscible to compassion, in fact it is an important component of the inner motivation towards helpfulness.

The way to compassion and connection isn't more information, more noise.

It's about learning a process: the ability to tolerate our own emotional experiences with grace, and to be able to extend that grace to others who are having their own experiences. As differentiated selves, we are then free to work together collaboratively, or to tolerate the existence of others who aren't.

∞

The direction of Fierce Compassion

When I was working with clients, especially the ones from senior leadership or other positions of responsibility, I noticed just how hard they could be on themselves. Self-criticism and shame are known to be transdiagnostic risk factors, which is a fancy way of saying these responses are unhelpful and tend to cause lots of secondary problems.

Sometimes the compassion challenge was reversed. Clients felt good about themselves, but expected the highest standards from their colleagues and were critical and blaming when they fell short. They found themselves facing complaints of bullying or being overlooked in favour of younger staff. The rules of the "harden up" world in which they had risen through the ranks are changing, and they found themselves frustrated, misunderstood and uncertain. Failure was not something they were used to, and "trying harder" wasn't working.

I witnessed just how effective developing their capacity for compassion was for changing their relationship to difficulties and how it unlocked new ways for them to approach previously seemingly insurmountable challenges. Through study, training and research, I learnt that compassion can look like care (gentle) and it can also be *Fierce* (strong), calling on our inner courage and wisdom. There is an interplay between self-compassion, compassion for others, receiving compassion and how the systems we find ourselves in support or hinder compassion.

In preparation for writing this book, I undertook interviews with people in senior leadership positions in business, government, medicine, law, entrepreneurship and activism. I am indebted to their generosity in sharing their insights and wisdom about their experiences of compassion (and sometimes lack of compassion) in the workplace and their lives. The key themes of leadership challenges that came from these interviews shaped the areas addressed in this book. Quotes from some interviewees share their insights on specific topics, and some names have been changed for confidentiality purposes at their request.

The word leader might bring to mind a strong and charismatic person in charge of a large group of people, but we can all be leaders in our own way. I use the word "leader" as "a person who rules, guides, or inspires others".[14] While this book focuses on leadership challenges typically experienced in the workplace, we can be leaders anywhere we interact with others – at work, home and in our communities and society. Challenges can be an opportunity for growth and success, yet they also often bring stress, uncertainty, worry and sleepless nights.

In Chapters 2 and 3 look into what we mean by compassion and how it can be helpful in our lives. We delve into the emotional regulation systems that influence our reactions as we navigate overwhelm and explore the theories and research behind *Fierce Compassion*. Chapter 4 explains that it is helpful to think of compassion as a skill with definable parts that can be developed with practice. We may have a sense that we need to BE more compassionate, but may not know HOW. It is important to recognise that being compassionate is often not supported by the systems we live in, yet research shows how effective these skills are for tangible "bottom line" results. This chapter introduces the core reflective learning cycle of *Fierce Compassion* – the ability to *Notice*, *Empathise* and take *Wise Action*. The reflective learning cycle brings together theory and practice in a process that encourages continual adaptation, critical thinking and the establishment of new behaviours.[15–17]

In chapters 5–10, we look at how to put the reflective learning cycle into practice in the key areas identified by the leaders who were interviewed. Themes emerged when there was a compassion challenge: the dominance of working hard to achieve success where rest is seen as a luxury; when high expectations lead not to perfection but to self-criticism and procrastination; the challenges of supporting others and the burnout that comes from not having healthy boundaries; the benefit of clear feedback and courageous conversations; the dangers of increasing division; and the difficulty of existing within challenging work systems. While these themes emerged from leaders' reflections on their work, they also include personal experiences from their home lives; we can't cleave our workplace selves from our personal selves.

We can think of compassion as having three directions: to others, to ourselves and from others to ourselves.[18] We may find one of these expressions of compassion easier to slip into – the compassion flows. But our capacity may vary – perhaps we find it is easier to give compassion than to receive it. Or sometimes we may be able to extend compassion to ourselves, but realise that it is hard to find for others with different views or backgrounds. The key themes identified from the interviews are split into the three directions of compassion – Chapters 5 and 6 explore issues of self-compassion, Chapters 7 and 8 compassion for others and Chapters 9 and 10 examine how the systems we live and work in affect our compassion capacity.

In certain organisations or for particular individuals, showing compassion may seem like a pipe dream. Compassion may appear naive when we need to be street-smart, or soft when we need to be tough. *Fierce Compassion* seeks to challenge these assumptions. By increasing our compassion capacity, we can make immediate helpful changes for both ourselves and others. This book explores ways to put this idea into practice.

Sometimes we may be working in a step-wise manner towards a larger change. It may be helpful to extend our perspective, to take a wider lens, to understand that some changes take decades or generations. As the saying goes, sometimes "we plant a seed so that future generations can sit in the shade of the tree". Large societal shifts have required individual effort and collective action, and these have previously been possible – women winning the right to vote, the civil rights movement and the decriminalisation of homosexuality. These were driven by individuals who never lost the hope that change was possible, even in the face of insurmountable odds. And they continued because of the connected, collective movement: community. Of course, there is still much work to be done. But we are TOLD that change isn't realistic by the system we are trying to change. Isn't it in the interest of the status quo to have us believe we have less power than we do?

Compassion is an act of resistance to a worldview where individualism and competition are heralded as the only pathway to success. Compassion offers a revolutionary experience of how we connect with ourselves, others and the world around us. Developing compassion is both an inward and outward journey that requires patience, practice and grace. It takes effort to cultivate; it does not always come naturally, and it requires both gentleness and a fierceness to reveal its full potential. But in a time of increasing pessimism and uncertainty, compassion offers hope and optimism: the experience that when we connect, we are more than the sum of our parts.

∞

Compassion is an act of resistance.

I refuse to harden, to divide, to ignore the suffering of others.

I will feel deeply, cry often, be sensitive, listen to others, say when I don't know, face the vulnerability of taking action and stay open to change.

These are fierce qualities, not because they dominate, but because they endure. It takes strength to sit with suffering. Strength to lead with humility. Strength to listen when you feel like shouting.

I notice the inner cringe of sharing my personal experiences, as the edges of shame try to creep in. But I know the power of vulnerability, of sharing our humanity. That is how we make connections within ourselves and with others, and these connections are at the heart of compassion.

In a world full of despair, it is so important to hold the hope that things can and will change. I strive for a more connected, creative, and compassionate future, for myself, for others and the systems we live in.

Bring your own lens, adapt these *Fierce Compassion* ideas so they make sense to you. We are more similar than we are different, AND there are differences in our experiences and views of ourselves, others and the world. My invitation to you is to come curious and open-hearted. What would a more compassionate, connected and creative world be like?

References

1. Hayes, S. C. (2004). Acceptance and commitment therapy, relational frame theory, and the third wave of behavioral and cognitive therapies. *Behavior Therapy, 35*(4), 639–665. https://doi.org/10.1016/s0005-7894(04)80013-3
2. Morin, E., & Kern, A. B. (1993). *Terre-patrie*. Seuil.
3. Helleiner, E. (2024). Economic globalization's polycrisis. *International Studies Quarterly*, *68*(2), 1–9. https://doi.org/10.1093/isq/sqae024
4. Ramanna, K. (2024). *The Age of Outrage: How to Lead in a Polarized World*. Harvard Business Press.
5. Kannan, V. D., & Veazie, P. J. (2023). US trends in social isolation, social engagement, and companionship – nationally and by age, sex, race/ethnicity, family income, and work hours, 2003–2020. *SSM - Population Health*, *21*(21), 101331. https://doi.org/10.1016/j.ssmph.2022.101331
6. Holt-Lunstad, J. (2024). Social connection as a critical factor for mental and physical health: Evidence, trends, challenges, and future implications. *World Psychiatry*, *23*(3), 312–332. https://doi.org/10.1002/wps.21224
7. Ortiz-Ospina, E. (2020). Loneliness and social connections. *Our World in Data*. https://ourworldindata.org/social-connections-and-loneliness
8. Daniali, H., Martinussen, M., & Flaten, M. A. (2023). A global meta-analysis of depression, anxiety, and stress before and during COVID-19. *Health Psychology*, *42*(2), 124–138. https://doi.org/10.1037/hea0001259
9. Burkeman, O. (2019, November 22). "The attention economy is in hyperdrive": How tech shaped the 2010s. *The Guardian*. https://www.theguardian.com/culture/2019/nov/22/attention-economy-in-hyperdrive-how-tech-shaped-2010s-oliver-burkeman
10. The battle for consumers' attention. (2017). *The Economist*. https://www.economist.com/special-report/2017/02/09/the-battle-for-consumers-attention
11. Crawford, M. B. (2015). *The World Beyond Your Head*. Farrar, Straus and Giroux.
12. Davenport, T. H., & Beck, J. C. (2002). *The Attention Economy: Understanding the New Currency of Business*. Harvard Business School.
13. Dalai Lama (1995). *The Power of Compassion*. HarperCollins.
14. Collins English Dictionary. (n.d.). *Leader Definition and Meaning*. https://www.collinsdictionary.com/dictionary/english/leader
15. Schön, D. A. (1983). *The Reflective Practitioner: How Professionals Think in Action*. Basic Books.

16. McBrien, B. (2007). Learning from practice – Reflections on a critical incident. *Accident and Emergency Nursing*, *15*(3), 128–133. https://doi.org/10.1016/j.aaen.2007.03.004
17. Paterson, C., & Chapman, J. (2013). Enhancing skills of critical reflection to evidence learning in professional practice. *Physical Therapy in Sport*, *14*(3), 133–138. Science Direct. https://doi.org/10.1016/j.ptsp.2013.03.004
18. Gilbert, P. (2010). *The Compassionate Mind: A New Approach to Life's Challenges*. Constable.

2 Beyond nice and kind

Revealing the power of compassion

Compassion is often confused with other terms like kind or nice. In this chapter, we explore the components of compassion and examine how to fully utilise this capacity. *Fierce Compassion* calls us to gather our inner wisdom and courage to guide us towards helpful actions. We will look at the emerging field of compassion research, which highlights why we can feel hopeful about the helpfulness of building compassion for ourselves as leaders and for those around us.

Often, compassion brings to mind a sense of gentleness; people relate it to words like kindness, or empathy, and it is commonly thought of as a more "feminine" trait, something that women have naturally, a "soft skill". However, this is a limited view of compassion, where it is misunderstood, and therefore, underutilised.

There isn't one agreed-upon definition, and the meaning of the word varies between languages; some cultures don't have a directly translatable word that means compassion. The English word compassion comes from the Latin word Compati: *com* "with/together"; *pati* "to suffer".[1] We can get a sense of compassion as being to do *with* (others or ourselves), and suffering. In Buddhist teachings, which go back thousands of years, there is an emphasis on the importance of compassion. Many people refer to the Dalai Lama's definition of compassion as "an awareness of suffering in others (or in ourselves), and the deep commitment to try to alleviate that suffering"[2] Suffering sometimes comes from the choices we make, like working extra hours or taking on debt. But sometimes it is unchosen suffering arising from circumstances beyond our control, such as being the victim of abuse or

DOI: 10.4324/9781003583080-2

experiencing loss. While we may not choose our suffering, it can be made more bearable in a "landscape of compassion".[3]

When we consider compassion for the suffering of others, we may experience compassion for those who suffer but have not done anything wrong (victims of war or abuse), or the suffering caused through doing something wrong (crime). Some people question why we would extend compassion to those who have chosen to do something wrong. The answer to this question is twofold. Firstly, making mistakes and causing others pain is part of being human, and sometimes this comes as a result of the trauma we have experienced. Secondly, receiving compassion when we have done something wrong makes it more likely that we can learn from the suffering, repair any damage we have caused and then avoid repeating the same mistakes.[4,5] Compassion can help us embrace suffering so we learn from it, rather than avoid it. This is likely part of the reason why those who have had adversity in their lives are more likely to extend compassion to others.[6]

There are many different ways to increase our compassion. While there are religious and spiritual practices that have compassion cultivation as a central tenet, in all psychotherapies there is an emphasis on the importance of compassion within the therapeutic relationship. Compassionately supporting a client and building therapeutic rapport is an effective component for recovery from mental distress.[7] More recently, Eastern practices of mindfulness and compassion have been secularised for a Western audience and incorporated in therapeutic approaches, such as Mindfulness-Based Cognitive Therapy (MBCT), Mindfulness-Based Stress Reduction (MBSR), Acceptance and Commitment Therapy (ACT) and Compassion-Focused Therapy (CFT). Paul Gilbert, who developed CFT, drew on evolutionary neuroscience and social psychology perspectives on compassion to help treat those with mental health difficulties, particularly those involving shame and self-criticism. Programmes that have been shown to improve self-reported measures of compassion and wellbeing include:[8]

- Mindful Self-Compassion (Dr Kirsten Neff and Christopher Germer)
- Compassion Cultivation Training (Stanford University)
- Cognitively Based Compassion Training (Emory University)
- Compassionate Mind Training (Paul Gilbert)

∞

The evolution of compassion

When trying to understand compassion, it can be helpful to view it through an evolutionary lens. If you think back to a time when we were all living in caves, in small family and tribal communities, there was a need for us to be able to share, communicate and understand one another for our survival. For instance, in contrast to the stereotype of Neanderthals as unintelligent and violent, there is growing research that highlights their ability to care for the sick or injured.[9] The discovery of a six-year-old child who most likely suffered from Down syndrome suggests that care was given in an altruistic manner, as it would have required much more than just their mother's help to allow them to survive to this age, given the mobility and challenges of Neanderthal life.[10] Neanderthals are part of our family tree, classified as a different species due to biological differences. But more recent research has shown that there was also interbreeding between Neanderthals and humans, and shared behaviours, such as the use of tools, hunting techniques, art and caring for those who are injured.[11] Early humans looked after each other, tending to injuries such as broken bones, and offering dental care, with some researchers suggesting that the ability to care was the foundation of humanity.[12] These affiliative (feeling socially connected and safe with others) capabilities were subject to evolutionary pressures, as those who could form strong social and emotional bonds were more likely to survive.

We are all human and are all capable of great acts of compassion, and, conversely, great acts of violence. There may be differences between genders because of our physical strength, reproductive capabilities and how we are socialised. For example, women should be good, nice and caring; boys should be tough, brave and not show their feelings. But, for the survival of the species, we developed neurophysiological systems to enable us to share resources to endure sufficiently for our offspring to mature. We needed to be able to communicate, collaborate and care about each other. We became hard-wired for compassion.

∞

Compassion challenges

If we are hard-wired to be compassionate, what gets in the way?

As well as affiliative pathways associated with compassion, we also developed other neurophysiological systems to help keep us alive, respond to threats, dangers and motivate us towards essential resources. These systems are easily stimulated by modern life. Western modern culture is often associated with the idea that working harder equals success. We live in an increasingly individualised meritocracy, where we are told we are only as valuable as what we achieve. There is a competitive vision of society, where to be "kind" can be perceived as both naive and dangerous; you will get eaten by a bigger dog. These ideas stimulate the areas of our brain associated with survival (even in the absence of immediate danger to our survival). We are living in the paradigm of Darwin's survival of the fittest. Interestingly, his comments on co-operation weren't so vigorously disseminated! He noticed the paradox that species with high levels of co-operation also thrived, even though altruism would not necessarily promote the continuation of the individual's genes.[9] The discussion around the benefits of selfishness compared to co-operation has rumbled on for decades, with Hamilton's work in the 1960s demonstrating a relationship in altruistic acts between the relatedness of the individuals involved, the cost to the bearer and the benefit to the recipient.[13] Disagreement about the benefits of individual versus group approaches continues, and this book looks at the evidence for the benefits of compassionate co-operation.

As we grow up, we become influenced by our cultural beliefs concerning human behaviour, and these shape our assumptions and beliefs in ways that we are often not conscious of. If we have absorbed (mostly unconsciously) ideas about the adversarial and competitive nature of humans, this will also influence how we conceptualise compassion. While most people agree that compassion is a helpful thing to do or be, deeper questioning reveals some of the underlying beliefs held about compassion. Often, therapy clients initially agree that being more compassionate (to themselves or others) would be a useful goal. However, we soon encounter common worries that being self-compassionate means:

- I will be lazy
- It's indulgent
- I'm spoilt
- I will never get anything done
- I don't deserve it

*This is not a comprehensive list, please feel free to add your own worries

When thinking about being more compassionate to others, common objections are:

- It will make them soft
- They are too sensitive
- It's being permissive
- It's living in "la la land"
- That's not the REAL world

*This is not a comprehensive list, please feel free to add your own objections

If we are going to be really aware of our own suffering, or the suffering of others, it takes courage. We might not like the feelings we encounter or the less-than-desirable (and very human) aspects of ourselves that we might meet. We may need to build a tolerance for our distress and that of others. It can take us out of our comfort zone or mean that we have to draw healthy boundaries, or that we need to have challenging conversations (with others and ourselves). In fact, there is a lot about compassion that doesn't on the surface seem particularly nice or kind! Acting with compassion can be uncomfortable, challenging, upsetting, confronting and full of uncertainty (in the short term). For example, if we are trying to help someone who is an alcoholic, they may desperately want a drink. This may take away their immediate distress in the short term, but indulging them is going to keep them addicted with all the associated impacts in the long term. A compassionate approach would support them in managing their feelings and physical responses while they work their way out of addiction. Going through this process is likely to bring up lots of different thoughts and feelings for both people. To be compassionate requires an acceptance of our whole self, and a relationship with others that allows a full range of human experience.

∞

The skill of compassion

As we explored earlier, the Dalai Lama's definition of compassion involves two core components: the awareness of suffering and a commitment to alleviate it. We can understand compassion through its component parts. The awareness of suffering requires us to be able to connect with the emotional experience of ourselves and others, to tune in, to notice. Blessed with imagination, our minds often find themselves rushing off into the future or dwelling on the past, creating stories and interpretations, hopes and fears. To be aware, we are required to bring the focus of the mind to the present, to notice what is actually happening, which can be challenging. The awareness of how we really are can clash with our idea of how we are, were or want to be. We often have contradictory thoughts, emotions and reactions even about a single event.

To notice the suffering of others requires that we have a "Theory of Mind". This is the ability to imagine that someone else has thoughts, feelings or experiences that are different from our own and to be able to "put ourselves in someone else's shoes". This capacity generally begins to develop around the age of 18 months.[14] This is a crucial ability that aids compassion (noticing and understanding) and helps us to make predictions. We can manage the uncertainty about what is coming by predicting alternative futures. Our ability to make these future-based predictions typically develops around the ages of four to five.[15]

We can easily feel overwhelmed by what others might be going through. You may hear people say, "I can't imagine how it must feel to [...insert tragedy]". What we actually mean is we can touch the appropriate emotion in ourselves – horror, grief, fear – but we are worried about being overwhelmed by our emotions. We don't want to feel it. When we start to consider where compassion takes us, it is easy to see that awareness of suffering requires us to be honest, to show vulnerability, to sit with difficult, unwanted emotions and to have the courage to do so.

Once we've tuned into suffering – our own or others' – the next step is what sets compassion apart from sympathy: the willingness to act (or consciously not act). To be willing to take action is to be willing to take a risk. We may have to step out of our comfort zone, to have an uncomfortable conversation, to draw a boundary, to say no, to face a situation we have been avoiding. It requires us to be brave, to step into the unknown.

The qualities required for practising compassion – honesty, vulnerability, tolerating challenging emotions, courage and bravery – are skills we can develop, which require strength. This is where "*Fierce*" comes in. Some have argued against the use of the word *fierce* because of connotations of violence, which is antithetical to compassion. However, the dictionary definition of *Fierce* includes characteristics of "*strong and powerful*" or "*showing strong feeling or energetic activity*",[16] and, especially for women, "*having or expressing bold confidence or style*".[17] I use the word *Fierce* to highlight the strength and energy required to be vulnerable, honest and brave. Buddhist traditions have long spoken of the "fierce sword of compassion". As Jack Kornfield writes,

> There is a yes in compassion, and there is also a no, said with the same courage of heart. No to abuse, no to violence, both personal and worldwide. The no is said not out of hate but out of unwavering care. Buddhists call this the fierce sword of compassion.[18]

But, if you find the word *Fierce* brings you difficulty or discord, please feel free to replace it with a word that works for you.

Commonly, people understand compassion as something we have or don't have, viewing it as a quality or a personality trait. We may tell ourselves that we should "be" more compassionate to a loved one or colleague, assuming that compassion should just be there on demand. We should just feel compassionate in certain situations. Or not. If it just isn't there, we move on. These ways of viewing compassion can keep us stuck. It positions compassion as a stable and enduring state, rather than a skill that can be developed over time, which may vary depending on our internal and external conditions. Instead, to increase our capacity to respond to suffering effectively, we can see compassion as a capacity, a skill we can choose to learn and develop.

When we develop a new skill (or improve an existing skill), we will make mistakes as we grow and develop. This view permits us to begin, and then to refine our skills as our capabilities increase. Notice how different this is from searching for a perfect version of compassion, or simply expecting compassion to arise. Think of a sporting analogy – if we want to learn how to swim, we don't expect ourselves to put in an Olympic performance off the dive board and glide through the water to the end of the pool in record time. We may start off exploring the water, dipping our heads under. We may think we are not truly swimming. While this may technically be correct, a desire to only "truly swim" may stop us learning to swim at all. Sometimes we wait for motivation to show up when we want to try something new. Therapists have a handy little phrase – "action first, motivation later". This summarises that by starting to take action, the ground is laid for motivation to come online. I think compassion is like that, too. By starting to make compassionate acts – then, over time, the motivation deepens and the compassion comes more easily.

∞

The benefits of compassion

If we have the evolutionary systems to support compassion, but our modern-day culture gets in the way, why should we bother to practice reconnecting with this capacity? For a start, altruism, which is part of the ability to demonstrate compassion to others, has been found to be more attractive than either good looks or a sense of humour![19] If we think back to that cave-person experience, it was probably a very useful trait that if we were suffering, our partner would stick around to help us out.

Apart from helping us attract a partner, it appears that compassion brings many benefits. The dynamic and growing field of research shows a wide range of improvements from practising compassion, including emotional regulation, mental wellbeing, physiological health and improved workplace culture.

The ability to regulate our emotional experiences supports improved mental wellbeing. Practising compassion skills appears to support psychological flexibility, which helps us adapt to different challenges in everyday life.[20] Compassion may improve mental health outcomes through its impact on our ability to regulate our emotions.[21] Compassion's ability to help us adapt and regulate emotions reduces depressive symptoms,[22–24] anxiety,[22] shame[22] and self-criticism.[22,25] Shame and self-criticism have particularly damaging consequences for our mental health, and these transdiagnostic risk factors for psychopathology seem to be improved by a compassionate approach. Our brain has a tendency towards negativity,[26] and when we turn this negativity on ourselves, it has a significant impact on our brain functioning.[27] Practising compassion helps reduce activation in the areas of the brain associated with the threat response, whereas those who speak to themselves in a self-critical manner experience increased activation in these areas.[28] Compassion-based therapeutic approaches appear to help reduce psychopathology generally,[29] and they even help reduce symptoms for those who hear psychotic voices.[30]

It's not just our mental wellbeing that is impacted by compassion. Our ability to respond to stress can be measured in terms of heart rate variability, which is the capacity for change in the frequency of heartbeats. Higher variability shows a better stress response and a healthier autonomic nervous system. The sympathetic nervous system is responsible for the fight/flight response, whereas the parasympathetic nervous system acts as a brake to slow down the heart rate. Both systems are needed for good health. Practising compassion increases heart rate variability[31–34] showing an improved physiological response to stress. With higher heart rate variability, we respond to stress more openly, seeing a broader perspective, which helps reduce anger. The parasympathetic system response can be strengthened through compassion.[34–38] As well as impacting our hearts' response to stress, it seems that compassion practice may also have positive effects on immune response.[39–41] For leaders navigating uncertainty and change, the ability to regulate emotion, reduce reactivity and respond with care can improve outcomes.

In the workplace, there are benefits in using compassionate approaches for leaders, their teams and the workplace culture as a whole. As with compassionate benefits for general wellbeing, the practice of compassion at work can help reduce stress responses,[42] improve emotional regulation[29] and increase workplace resilience.[43] When compassion is practised in workplace relationships, it can help improve collegiality and decrease a key indicator of psychological distress – loneliness.[44] Compassion can facilitate a more open and supportive workplace environment that helps to improve learning and creativity as people are free to take appropriate risks,[44,45] as opposed to the constricting effects of a fear-based work culture. Compassionate ability is a key component of leadership styles that focus on generating a supportive workplace culture for the benefit of the business, employees and customers.[46–48]

There are benefits in growing compassion for ourselves on our leadership journey, for our own mental and physical wellbeing, as well as for those around us. Compassion can also support us to create workplace cultures that foster vital attributes for success in the increasingly competitive work environment: creativity and connection. To gain these benefits, it is helpful to understand that compassion is not something that we just "have" but rather a set of skills that can be learnt and practised. The compassionate leadership journey requires strength, the inner fierceness to understand ourselves and others deeply, and the ability to transform this understanding into helpful action. In the next chapter, we will take a deeper look at the systems underlying compassion so that we can understand how to work with them to harness their power.

∞

Summary – beyond nice and kind

This chapter challenges common misconceptions and shows that compassion is:

- Much more than being kind or nice
- Both *Fierce* and *Gentle*, requiring courageous action
- Grounded in evolutionary, neurobiological and cultural foundations
- Commonly mistaken for indulgent, weak or unrealistic
- A skill that can be learned and practised
- A powerful force for leadership, wellbeing and social change

References

1. *Compassion | Origin and Meaning of Compassion by Online Etymology Dictionary*. (2019). Etymonline.com. https://www.etymonline.com/word/compassion
2. Dalai Lama. (1995). *The Power of Compassion*. HarperCollins.
3. Feldman, C., & Kuyken, W. (2011). Compassion in the landscape of suffering. *Contemporary Buddhism*, *12*(1), 143–155. https://doi.org/10.1080/14639947.2011.564831
4. Breines, J. G., & Chen, S. (2012). Self-compassion increases self-improvement motivation. *Personality and Social Psychology Bulletin*, *38*(9), 1133–1143. https://doi.org/10.1177/0146167212445599
5. Inzlicht, M., Shenhav, A., & Olivola, C. Y. (2018). The effort paradox: Effort is both costly and valued. *Trends in Cognitive Sciences*, *22*(4), 337–349. https://doi.org/10.1016/j.tics.2018.01.007
6. Lim, D., & DeSteno, D. (2019). Past adversity protects against the numeracy bias in compassion. *Emotion*. https://doi.org/10.1037/emo0000655
7. Rogers, C. (1957). The necessary and sufficient conditions of therapeutic personality change. *TACD Journal*, *17*(1), 95–103. https://doi.org/10.1080/1046171x.1989.12034347
8. Kirby, J. N., Tellegen, C. L., & Steindl, S. R. (2017). A meta-analysis of compassion-based interventions: Current state of knowledge and future directions.*Behavior Therapy*, *48*(6), 778–792. https://doi.org/10.1016/j.beth.2017.06.003
9. Galway-Witham, J., Cole, J., & Stringer, C. (2019). Aspects of human physical and behavioural evolution during the last 1 million years. *Journal of Quaternary Science*, *34*(6), 355–378. https://doi.org/10.1002/jqs.3137
10. Spikins, P. (2015). *How Compassion Made Us Human - The Evolutionary Origins of Tenderness, Trus*. Pen & Sword Books Ltd.
11. Ekman, P. (2010). Darwin's compassionate view of human nature. *JAMA*, *303*(6), 557. https://doi.org/10.1001/jama.2010.101
12. Conde-Valverde, M., Quirós-Sánchez, A., Diez-Valero, J., Mata-Castro, N., García-Fernández, A., Quam, R., Carretero, J. M., García-González, R., Rodríguez, L., Sánchez-Andrés, A., Arsuaga, J. L., Martínez, I., & Villaverde, V. (2024). The child who lived: Down syndrome among Neanderthals? *Science Advances*, *10*(26). https://doi.org/10.1126/sciadv.adn9310

13. Hamilton, W. D. (1964). The genetical evolution of social behaviour. *Journal of Theoretical Biology*, *7*(1), 1–16. https://doi.org/10.1016/0022-5193(64)90038-4
14. Rogers, C. (1957). The necessary and sufficient conditions of therapeutic personality change. *TACD Journal*, *17*(1), 95–103. https://doi.org/10.1080/1046171x.1989.12034347
15. Redshaw, J., & Suddendorf, T. (2016). Children's and apes' preparatory responses to two mutually exclusive possibilities. *Current Biology*, *26*(13), 1758–1762. https://doi.org/10.1016/j.cub.2016.04.062
16. Cambridge Dictionary. (2025, February 26). *Fierce*. CambridgeWords. https://dictionary.cambridge.org/dictionary/english/fierce
17. *Merriam-Webster Dictionary*. (2024, October 25). *Fierce*. Merriam-Webster.com. https://www.merriam-webster.com/dictionary/fierce
18. Kornfield, J. (2009). *The Wise Heart: A Guide to the Universal Teachings of Buddhist Psychology*. Bantam Books.
19. Arnocky, S., Piché, T., Albert, G., Ouellette, D., & Barclay, P. (2016). Altruism predicts mating success in humans. *British Journal of Psychology*, *108*(2), 416–435. https://doi.org/10.1111/bjop.12208
20. Sirois, F. M., Nauts, S., & Molnar, D. S. (2018). Self-compassion and bedtime procrastination: An emotion regulation perspective. *Mindfulness*, *10*(3), 434–445. https://doi.org/10.1007/s12671-018-0983-3
21. Inwood, E., & Ferrari, M. (2018). Mechanisms of change in the relationship between self-compassion, emotion regulation, and mental health: A systematic review. *Applied Psychology: Health and Well-Being*, *10*(2), 215–235. https://doi.org/10.1111/aphw.12127
22. Gilbert, P., & Procter, S. (2006). Compassionate mind training for people with high shame and self-criticism: overview and pilot study of a group therapy approach. *Clinical Psychology & Psychotherapy*, *13*(6), 353–379. https://doi.org/10.1002/cpp.507
23. Ehret, A. M., Joormann, J., & Berking, M. (2015). Examining risk and resilience factors for depression: The role of self-criticism and self-compassion. *Cognition and Emotion*, *29*(8), 1496–1504. https://doi.org/10.1080/02699931.2014.992394
24. Diedrich, A., Grant, M., Hofmann, S. G., Hiller, W., & Berking, M. (2014). Self-compassion as an emotion regulation strategy in major depressive disorder. *Behaviour Research and Therapy*, *58*, 43–51. https://doi.org/10.1016/j.brat.2014.05.006
25. Vidal, J., & Soldevilla, J. M. (2022). Effect of compassion-focused therapy on self-criticism and self-soothing: A meta-analysis. *British Journal of Clinical Psychology*, *62*(1), 70–81. https://doi.org/10.1111/bjc.12394
26. Baumeister, R. F., Bratslavsky, E., Finkenauer, C., & Vohs, K. D. (2001). Bad is stronger than good. *Review of General Psychology*, *5*(4), 323–370.
27. Kim, J. J., Parker, S. L., Doty, J. R., Cunnington, R., Gilbert, P., & Kirby, J. N. (2020). Neurophysiological and behavioural markers of compassion. *Scientific Reports*, *10*(1), 1–9. https://doi.org/10.1038/s41598-020-63846-3

28. Neff, K. D., & McGehee, P. (2010). Self-compassion and psychological resilience among adolescents and young adults. *Self and Identity*, *9*(3), 225–240. https://doi.org/10.1080/15298860902979307
29. Wilson, A. C., Mackintosh, K., Power, K., & Chan, S. W. Y. (2019). Effectiveness of self-compassion related therapies: A systematic review and meta-analysis. *Mindfulness*, *10*(6), 979–995. https://doi.org/10.1007/s12671-018-1037-6
30. Mayhew, S. L., & Gilbert, P. (2008). Compassionate mind training with people who hear malevolent voices: A case series report. *Clinical Psychology & Psychotherapy*, *15*(2), 113–138. https://doi.org/10.1002/cpp.566
31. Di Bello, M., Carnevali, L., Petrocchi, N., Thayer, J. F., Gilbert, P., & Ottaviani, C. (2020). The compassionate vagus: A meta-analysis on the connection between compassion and heart rate variability. *Neuroscience & Biobehavioral Reviews*, *116*, 21–30. https://doi.org/10.1016/j.neubiorev.2020.06.016
32. Petrocchi, N., & Cheli, S. (2019). The social brain and heart rate variability: Implications for psychotherapy. *Psychology and Psychotherapy: Theory, Research and Practice*, *92*(2), 208–223. https://doi.org/10.1111/papt.12224
33. Petrocchi, N., Ottaviani, C., & Couyoumdjian, A. (2016). Compassion at the mirror: Exposure to a mirror increases the efficacy of a self-compassion manipulation in enhancing soothing positive affect and heart rate variability. *The Journal of Positive Psychology*, *12*(6), 525–536. https://doi.org/10.1080/17439760.2016.1209544
34. Luo, X., Qiao, L., & Che, X. (2018). Self-compassion modulates heart rate variability and negative affect to experimentally induced stress. *Mindfulness*, *9*(5), 1522–1528. https://doi.org/10.1007/s12671-018-0900-9
35. Costello, J. F. (2001). Methylation matters. *Journal of Medical Genetics*, *38*(5), 285–303. https://doi.org/10.1136/jmg.38.5.285
36. Porges, S. (2009). The polyvagal theory: New insights into adaptive reactions of the autonomic nervous system. *Cleveland Clinic Journal of Medicine*, *76*(Suppl_2), S86–S90. https://doi.org/10.3949/ccjm.76.s2.17
37. Thayer, J. F., & Lane, R. D. (2000). A model of neurovisceral integration in emotion regulation and dysregulation. *Journal of Affective Disorders*, *61*(3), 201–216. https://doi.org/10.1016/s0165-0327(00)00338-4
38. Gerritsen, R. J. S., & Band, G. P. H. (2018). Breath of life: The respiratory vagal stimulation model of contemplative activity. *Frontiers in Human Neuroscience*, *12*(12), 1–25. https://doi.org/10.3389/fnhum.2018.00397
39. Bellosta-Batalla, M., Ruiz-Robledillo, N., Sariñana-González, P., Capella-Solano, T., Vitoria-Estruch, S., Hidalgo-Moreno, G., Pérez-Blasco, J., Romero-Martínez, Á., & Moya-Albiol, L. (2017). Increased salivary IgA response as an indicator of immunocompetence after a mindfulness and self-compassion-based intervention. *Mindfulness*, *9*(3), 905–913. https://doi.org/10.1007/s12671-017-0830-y
40. Breines, J. G., Thoma, M. V., Gianferante, D., Hanlin, L., Chen, X., & Rohleder, N. (2014). Self-compassion as a predictor of interleukin-6 response to acute psychosocial stress. *Brain, Behavior, and Immunity*, *37*, 109–114. https://doi.org/10.1016/j.bbi.2013.11.006

41. Ghodrati Torbati, A., Nejat, H., Toozandehjani, H., Samari, A. A., & Akbari Amarghan, H. (2020). Effect of Compassion-Focused Therapy (CFT) on blood cortisol and cognitive-emotion regulation in drug abusers. *Jundishapur Journal of Health Sciences*, *12*(1), 1–6. https://doi.org/10.5812/jjhs.100148
42. Zessin, U., Dickhäuser, O., & Garbade, S. (2015). The relationship between self-compassion and well-being: A meta-analysis. *Applied Psychology: Health and Well-Being*, *7*(3), 340–364. https://doi.org/10.1111/aphw.12051
43. Chatterjee, S., Chakraborty, S., Fulk, H. K., & Sarker, S. (2021). Building a compassionate workplace using information technology: Considerations for information systems research. *International Journal of Information Management*, *56*, 102261. https://doi.org/10.1016/j.ijinfomgt.2020.102261
44. Peng, J., Chen, Y., Xia, Y., & Ran, Y. (2017). Workplace loneliness, leader-member exchange and creativity: The cross-level moderating role of leader compassion. *Personality and Individual Differences*, *104*, 510–515. https://doi.org/10.1016/j.paid.2016.09.020
45. de Zulueta, P. (2015). Developing compassionate leadership in health care: An integrative review. *Journal of Healthcare Leadership*, *8*(8), 1–10. https://doi.org/10.2147/jhl.s93724
46. Jit, R., Sharma, C. S., & Kawatra, M. (2017). Healing a broken spirit: Role of servant leadership. *Vikalpa: The Journal for Decision Makers*, *42*(2), 80–94. https://doi.org/10.1177/0256090917703754
47. van Dierendonck, D., & Patterson, K. (2014). Compassionate love as a cornerstone of servant leadership: An integration of previous theorizing and research. *Journal of Business Ethics*, *128*(1), 119–131.
48. Crosweller, M. (2022). Disaster management and the need for a relational leadership framework founded upon compassion, care, and justice. *Climate Risk Management*, *35*, 100404. https://doi.org/10.1016/j.crm.2022.100404

3 Awakening the Soothe system

Fierce Compassion's role in leadership

In Chapter 2, we explored what *Fierce Compassion* means and what benefits can be gained from increasing our skills with it. In this chapter, we will take a "peek under the lid" at the systems influenced by compassion. Knowledge of these forces can support those in leadership positions to understand themselves and their reactions, as well as those of their colleagues and teams. Increasing our awareness of forces that can influence our behaviour, thoughts and feelings is helpful before we start engaging with skills in compassion. We can have a great box of tools, but if we don't understand why we might use a particular tool for a certain situation, we aren't getting the maximum benefit.

There are mental processes that influence our thoughts, feelings and behaviours that we are not always aware of. Different therapeutic modalities have different theories to help understand our motives. Unconscious motives and desires were called archetypes by Carl Jung.[1] Aaron Beck, the founder of Cognitive Behavioural Therapy (CBT), referred to unconscious forces that drive the way we think, feel and act as core beliefs.[2] In Dialectical Behaviour Therapy (DBT), the regulation of rational and emotional impulses is referred to as creating our "wise mind" – a state that draws on the strengths of both systems.[3] Paul Gilbert, who developed Compassion-Focused Therapy (CFT), describes social mentalities, which drive us to seek out different types of relationships and interact with others.[4] The ability to switch between mentalities appropriately for the situation is an indication of psychological health. The relationship between different areas and functions in our brains and our physiology is complex, and we function at our optimum when there is an integration of our various capabilities.

We have a brilliant brain, but it is also complicated. Sometimes this complication produces contradictory thoughts and feelings.[4] Given different

DOI: 10.4324/9781003583080-3

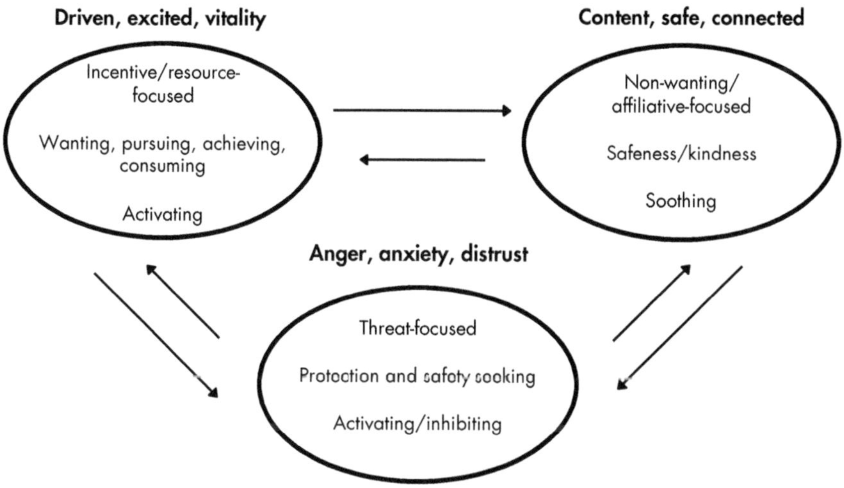

Figure 3.1 Three types of affect regulation systems. Reproduced from Gilbert, The Compassionate Mind (2009), with permission from Little, Brown Book Group.[5]

circumstances and states of mind, we can feel, think and act quite differently in the same situation. How often do we rationally think that there is no need to worry about an upcoming event, but find ourselves feeling anxious along with the associated physiological responses: butterflies in our stomach, running to the toilet? We can understand these contradictory experiences as functions of three main systems underlying human behaviour that developed as we evolved, which Paul Gilbert describes as *Threat*, *Drive* and *Soothe*[4] (see Figure 3.1). The *Threat* system is primarily involved in our safety, noticing and responding to dangers. The *Drive* system helps motivate us towards the resources needed for survival. The *Soothe* system helps us develop caring relationships to enable a sharing of resources andS skills to support our survival and development.

∞

Our alarm system

We are probably most familiar with our *Threat* system, and have likely heard it described as our fight, flight or freeze response to danger; a "do not get killed machine" as Russ Harris, the creator of the Acceptance and Commitment Therapy (ACT), termed it.[6] If we think about when we lived in caves, it made sense when we came across a danger to fight it if we thought we could win, or to run away from it if we thought we couldn't, or to freeze. A fourth response has also been suggested: that sometimes in reaction to danger, we may adopt a fawn response, where we appease others to reduce conflict and avoid harm. You have likely experienced your *Threat* system in action and understand how it feels. There is a strong physiological response as our system floods with adrenaline and cortisol: our heart races, we sweat and feel nauseous.

As we evolved, our brain became increasingly sophisticated, with the ability to imagine the future and reflect on the past. Now we could anticipate future danger – "careful, this is where the saber-tooth tigers like to hang out" – and reflect on past experiences – "that was a close one, I'm not walking there at dusk again!" However, our social and technological evolution has outpaced our neurophysiological evolution. Historically, a *Threat* may have meant death in the literal sense. In the modern world, our "death" happens in a more abstract manner.

We fear:

- Losing our job or promotion
- Being overweight or old or ugly
- Being laughed at, criticised or shamed
- Being late
- Not getting likes on our social media post

*This is not a comprehensive list, please feel free to add your own fears

We are likely to fight, flee, freeze or fawn in a more modern way, too. We argue, stonewall, criticise and become passive-aggressive. We may avoid the meeting, speaking engagement or party we are dreading. We quit, change jobs, towns, relationships. We procrastinate and delay. We twitch with anxiety, feel nauseous and take antacids. We have panic attacks that we try to hide. We stay up late watching mini-series. We drink to forget. We scroll on our phone, watching the lives of others or post only the highlights of our day.

∞

The real drive to survive

We have two other systems that we are likely not so familiar with. Firstly, our *Drive* system is best understood as a motivational system that aims to move us towards desired resources. From an evolutionary perspective, this meant resources to keep us alive, such as food, shelter and to find other humans for procreation, protection and collaboration. It wasn't any use sitting around all day admiring the beauty of nature, we had to get out there and fend for ourselves. When we reached our desired resource, it would trigger the release of dopamine in our reward centre, and it felt good. This helped us learn to seek out resources that were helpful to our survival. There was an evolutionary pressure towards those who took action and whose brains were rewarded and learnt from their previous experiences. We also developed competitive responses to secure the best resources, partnerships or tribal affiliations.

In our modern society, we find ourselves driven to all sorts of diverse resources: a new job, a new car, the latest mobile phone, the latest season's clothes and more friends. The list of things we need to survive, or think we need, has grown long. We set ourselves goal after goal, and each time we achieve them, we get a hit of dopamine. It isn't just the big things, though; we write ourselves to-do lists and power through our chores, most of the time barely even registering that we are doing them. We can find ourselves competing and comparing ourselves with others.

Western society, with an emphasis on individualism and meritocracy, has strong messages associated with the *Drive* system:

- Hard work equals success
- You get what you deserve
- If you put your mind to it, you can do anything

And equally critical messages when we aren't achieving:

- You're lazy, spoilt, self-indulgent, stupid

The Threat–Drive loop

Both our *Threat* and *Drive* systems are easily stimulated and over-reactive in our modern world, and, unfortunately for us, they also reinforce each other (see Figure 3.2).

When *Threat* is overstimulated, we see problems everywhere, our view narrows, we become anxious, negative and irritable. We either try even harder or begin avoiding and procrastinating. When *Drive* is overstimulated,

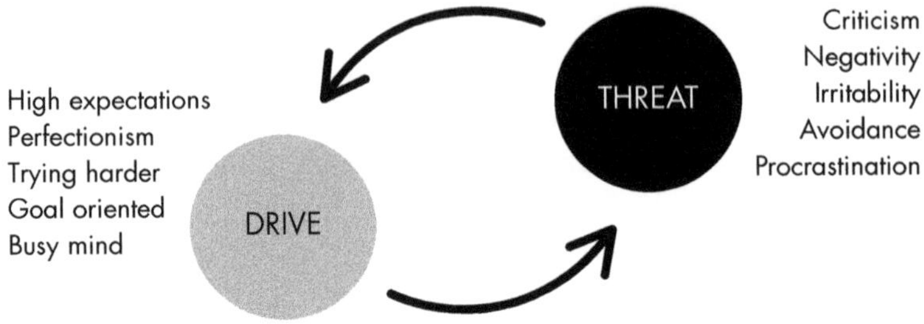

Figure 3.2 The Threat–Drive loop.

we become a slave to the next goal, rushing and so busy we over-ride our limits and boundaries (and other people's too!). We are caught in a tug of war in the *Threat–Drive* loop, reacting to and stimulating each other until we end up stressed, anxious and keyed up.

∞

The soothed child

We have a third system that is often undervalued in our modern society – the *Soothe* system, which supports states of calm, contentment and social connection. Unlike the satisfaction derived from achievement in the *Drive* system, *Soothe* states are associated with oxytocin and endorphins, which bring a sense of warmth and safety.

From an evolutionary perspective the *Soothe* system helped ensure the survival of human infants, who require long periods of care from adults to reach maturity. Harry Harlow, an American psychologist in the 1950s, demonstrated that when infant monkeys were separated from their mothers, they preferred soft surrogate "mothers" over wire ones.[7] Even though both surrogates provided food, they chose comfort. This highlighted an innate need for warmth and comfort, beyond survival essentials. While this experiment wasn't very compassionate to these poor young monkeys, his research provided groundbreaking evidence for the importance of maternal touch in the parent-child relationship.[7]

A lack of warmth and care also impacts humans. Romanian orphans who were deprived of physical touch and emotional connection, whilst still receiving the basics needed for survival, developed smaller brains in adulthood.[8]

Family environments that are safe, warm and predictable are a powerful foundation for better life outcomes.[9] To receive or give a *Soothe* response can involve care through facial expressions, tone of voice, touch and behaviours. In a soothed state, we may experience relaxation, or feel safe enough to redirect our attention to explore the environment around us. Asense of safety and comfort can be created by physical touch from a loved one,[10] and touch improves outcomes for premature babies.[11] Children who receive care and compassion are more likely to give compassion to others in the future.[12,13] Secure and safe attachments to parental figures improve mental health outcomes.[14]

While it might sound as though the responsibility is being laid at the feet of parents, it is important to remember that many parents today face unprecedented pressures. Historically, the care given to children came from a wider group of adults rather than just parents. Whereas, in modern society we are currently experiencing increasing levels of disconnection and loneliness.[15] Around a third of new mothers report chronic feelings of loneliness.[16,17] Isolation impacts caregivers' capacity to offer warmth and care to their children. Living close to family may help you have happy children,[18] but not everyone has this option. Compassionate parenting is related to improved prosocial behaviour in children,[19] but being able to parent compassionately also depends on our social and economic systems to support parents, children and families.

When people don't experience soothing care early in life, their *Soothe* system may be underdeveloped. Those who received low parental warmth often struggle with shame, reduced self-compassion and receiving care.[8] Traumatic childhoods can alter the Hypothalamic-Pituitary-Adrenal (HPA) axis, which mediates the stress response and may lead to heightened stress reactivity even when in safe environments.[8] Therefore, for those with a childhood history of trauma, developing the *Soothe* state may take additional support and practice with the help of a registered mental health professional.[11]

The *Soothe* system continues to benefit us in adulthood. In one study, women threatened with electric shock had lower brain activity related to *Threat* responses when holding a partner's hand, and the benefits were larger for those in secure relationships.[20] But not everything that appears to be care creates calm. When under *Threat*, we may seek a sense of control, social dominance and the avoidance of rejection in an attempt to find safety. But these motivations are associated with *Threat* system activation. In comparison, when we feel safe, we can view ourselves and the world in a state of relaxed attention. A quick way of checking in with ourselves is: when we are feeling safe, we are in our *Soothe* system; if we are seeking safety, we are in our *Threat* system.[4]

A warm disposition is an important attribute of compassion and is associated with prosocial behaviours, better academic performance and increased wellbeing.[21] Warmth may include verbal and non-verbal signals of caring and kindness, sharing of positive affect and related feelings of increased connectedness, liking and affection.[22] These states induce a sense of calm and manage emotions and behaviours that originate from *Threat* and *Drive* systems, such as anger, anxiety, sadness, aggression, striving, running away and submission. This ability to care is at the heart of compassion.

We can practise bringing compassion to ourselves and others when compassion is hard to find. It's not our fault, but rather the interaction of our physiological systems and the conditions we find ourselves born into. It is possible to "rewire" our systems due to the neuroplasticity of the brain, to provide a more soothing, emotionally regulated response to stressors. But this takes practice and support. We may not have received optimal care as a child, or we may not have been able to give this care ourselves, yet we can find compassion for these experiences: we are doing the best we can with the resources available to us. As leaders, we need to understand how our own history influences our ability to *Soothe* ourselves and others. This is not about blame, but about taking responsibility for the brain we have and how we lead with it.

Pause here for a moment to reflect…

- What were the social and environmental factors that influenced the development of your Soothe system?
- How have they impacted your ability to self-soothe as an adult?
- How do they impact your ability to Soothe others as a leader?

∞

Compassion and the Threat, Drive and Soothe systems

Holding in mind an understanding of these systems and how they are activated can help those in leadership positions. Compassion brings the systems into balance and lets us access the most helpful aspects of each system. As leaders, it is important to know how to do this for ourselves, to maintain optimal performance. But also so that we aren't walking around with over-active *Threat* and *Drive* reactions, which inevitably trigger these responses in those around us. Compassion can help us act from a more regulated place and help others to do the same. It can also help us recover from times when we have caused or received distress.

Take a moment for yourself and imagine your *Threat*, *Drive* and *Soothe* systems. Consider what actions, feelings, thoughts, and physical sensations might relate to each system.

- *Over the last week, on average, how active have each of these systems been for you?*

You might like to draw each of the systems as a circle, with the size of the circle representing how active that system is.

For more of us in our modern world, the *Threat* and *Drive* systems are dominant, and typically our circles will look something like the diagram shown in Figure 3.3.

We can use this check-in as a quick way of connecting with these underlying systems, and it can be helpful to know our patterns and tendencies at different times of the day/week/year.

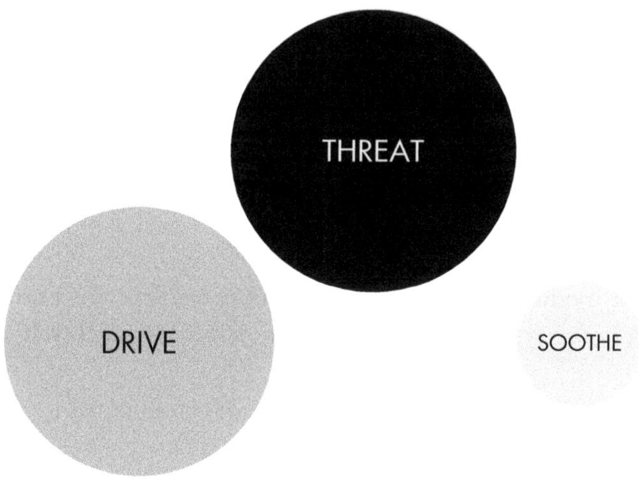

Figure 3.3 An example showing the proportions of the Threat, Drive, and Soothe systems.

Our modern life easily stimulates the *Threat* and *Drive* systems – unstable employment, poverty, advertising, news media and under-emphasises our need for affiliation with others, where we don't want or need more. The cultural shift to increasing materialism, individualism and seeking extrinsic goals is linked to the recent rise in mental health difficulties, particularly in young people.[23] We get sold the idea of contentment by being consumers and purchasing more products and services. Yet true contentment is not so easily commodified. Activating our *Soothe* state regulates the *Threat-Drive* system and regulates our motivation to acquire. We can use compassion as the key to unlocking the potential of our *Soothe* system. There are a variety of ways to explore our compassion skills. For instance, compassion meditation stimulates the *Soothe* system and makes us less reactive to stressors[24] and reduces the *Threat* response.[25] We explore compassion meditation in the next chapter.

Many of the factors that influence our thoughts, feelings and behaviours are not our fault. Recognising these factors can be hugely destigmatising for those who feel that their distress is because they are mad, bad or wrong. Depending on our early childhood experiences, we may find it easier or harder to access a *Soothe* response than others. However, we are the only ones who can take responsibility for the brain we have. As leaders, we must raise our skills so that we can use our power and influence in a prosocial manner. In the next chapter, we will explore how to put these ideas into practice using the *Fierce Compassion* reflective learning cycle.

∞

Chapter 3 Summary – awakening the Soothe system

This chapter explores how compassion helps regulate the brain's *Threat*, *Drive* and *Soothe* systems, which shape our behaviour and wellbeing:

- The *Threat* and *Drive* systems are easily overstimulated in modern life, fuelling stress and reactivity
- The *Soothe* system brings balance, connection and emotional regulation, but is often undervalued

- Early caregiving experiences shape our capacity to access the *Soothe* system and show compassion
- Leaders benefit from recognising these internal systems to avoid reactive patterns and support others
- Compassion enhances leadership by restoring balance and promoting a more grounded, prosocial response
- Even those with difficult pasts can strengthen their *Soothe* system through practice and neuroplasticity

References

1. Jung, C. G., & Hull, R. F. C. (2014). *Collected Works of C.G. Jung, Volume 6: Psychological Type*. Princeton University Press.
2. Beck, A. T. (2019). A 60-year evolution of cognitive theory and therapy. *Perspectives on Psychological Science*, *14*(1), 16–20. https://doi.org/10.1177/1745691618804187
3. Eeles, J., & Walker, D. (2022). Mindfulness as taught in Dialectical Behaviour Therapy: A scoping review. *Clinical Psychology & Psychotherapy*, *29*(6), 1843–1853. https://doi.org/10.1002/cpp.2764
4. Gilbert, P. (2010). *The Compassionate Mind: A New Approach to Life's Challenges*. Constable.
5. Reproduced from Gilbert, *The Compassionate Mind* (2009), with permission from Little, Brown Book Group.
6. Harris, R. (2008). *The Happiness Trap*. Robinson.
7. Harlow, H. F., Dodsworth, R. O., & Harlow, M. K. (1965). Total social isolation in monkeys. *Proceedings of the National Academy of Sciences*, *54*(1), 90–97. https://doi.org/10.1073/pnas.54.1.90
8. Mackes, N. K., Golm, D., Sarkar, S., Kumsta, R., Rutter, M., Fairchild, G., Mehta, M. A., & Sonuga-Barke, E. J. S. (2020). Early childhood deprivation is associated with alterations in adult brain structure despite subsequent environmental enrichment. *Proceedings of the National Academy of Sciences*, *117*(1), 641–649. https://www.pnas.org/content/117/1/641
9. Kirby, J. N. (2019). Nurturing family environments for children: Compassion-focused parenting as a form of parenting intervention. *Education Sciences*, *10*(1), 3. https://doi.org/10.3390/educsci10010003
10. Montagu, A. (1971). *Touching: The Human Significance of the Skin: The Human Significance of the Skin*. Columbia Univ. Pr.
11. Campbell-Yeo, M., Disher, T., Benoit, B., & Johnston, C. (2015). Understanding kangaroo care and its benefits to preterm infants. *Pediatric Health, Medicine and Therapeutics*, 6(6), 15. https://doi.org/10.2147/phmt.s51869

12. Hintsanen, M., Gluschkoff, K., Dobewall, H., Cloninger, C. R., Keltner, D., Saarinen, A., Wesolowska, K., Volanen, S.-M., Raitakari, O. T., & Pulkki-Råback, L. (2019). Parent–child-relationship quality predicts offspring dispositional compassion in adulthood: A prospective follow-up study over three decades. *Developmental Psychology*, *55*(1), 216–225. https://doi.org/10.1037/dev0000633
13. Miller, J. G., Kahle, S., Troxel, N. R., & Hastings, P. D. (2020). The development of generosity from 4 to 6 years: Examining stability and the biopsychosocial contributions of children's vagal flexibility and mothers' compassion. *Frontiers in Psychology*, *11*, 1–10. https://doi.org/10.3389/fpsyg.2020.590384
14. Cassidy, J., Jones, J. D., & Shaver, P. R. (2013). Contributions of attachment theory and research: A framework for future research, translation, and policy. *Development and Psychopathology*, *25*(4pt2), 1415–1434. https://doi.org/10.1017/s0954579413000692
15. Beutel, M. E., Klein, E. M., Brähler, E., Reiner, I., Jünger, C., Michal, M., Wiltink, J., Wild, P. S., Münzel, T., Lackner, K. J., & Tibubos, A. N. (2017). Loneliness in the general population: Prevalence, determinants and relations to mental health. *BMC Psychiatry*, *17*(1), 1–7.
16. *A Report Looking into the Impact of Loneliness in Children, Young People and Families. It Starts with Hello.* (n.d.). Retrieved May 13, 2025, from https://homestart-kirklees.org.uk/wp-content/uploads/2024/08/action_for_children_it_starts_with_hello_report__november_2017_lowres.pdf
17. Luoma, I., Korhonen, M., Puura, K., & Salmelin, R. K. (2018). Maternal loneliness: Concurrent and longitudinal associations with depressive symptoms and child adjustment. *Psychology, Health & Medicine*, *24*(6), 667–679. https://doi.org/10.1080/13548506.2018.1554251
18. Buettner, D., Nelson, T., & Veenhoven, R. (2020). Ways to greater happiness: a Delphi study. *Journal of Happiness Studies*, *21*(8), 2789–2806. https://doi.org/10.1007/s10902-019-00199-3
19. Viet, T. H., Nanthamongkolchai, S., Munsawaengsub, C., & Pitikultang, S. (2022). Positive parenting program to promote child development among children 1 to 3 years old: A quasi-experimental research. *Journal of Primary Care & Community Health*, *13*, 215013192210897. https://doi.org/10.1177/21501319221089763
20. Luo, H., Liu, Q., Yu, C., & Nie, Y. (2021). Parental warmth, gratitude, and prosocial behavior among Chinese adolescents: The moderating effect of school climate. *International Journal of Environmental Research and Public Health*, *18*(13), 7033. https://doi.org/10.3390/ijerph18137033
21. Schrage, K. M., Maxwell, J. A., Impett, E. A., Keltner, D., & MacDonald, G. (2020). Effects of verbal and nonverbal communication of affection on avoidantly attached partners' emotions and message receptiveness. *Personality and Social Psychology Bulletin*, *46*(11), 014616722091031. https://doi.org/10.1177/0146167220910311
22. Coan, J. A., Schaefer, H. S., & Davidson, R. J. (2006). Lending a hand: Social regulation of the neural response to threat. *Psychological Science*, *17*(12), 1032–1039. https://doi.org/10.1111/j.1467-9280.2006.01832.x

23. Twenge, J. M., Gentile, B., DeWall, C. N., Ma, D., Lacefield, K., & Schurtz, D. R. (2010). Birth cohort increases in psychopathology among young Americans, 1938–2007: A cross-temporal meta-analysis of the MMPI. *Clinical Psychology Review*, *30*(2), 145–154. https://doi.org/10.1016/j.cpr.2009.10.005
24. Hofmann, S. G., Grossman, P., & Hinton, D. E. (2011). Loving-kindness and compassion meditation: Potential for psychological interventions. *Clinical Psychology Review*, *31*(7), 1126–1132. https://doi.org/10.1016/j.cpr.2011.07.003
25. Kim, J. J., Parker, S. L., Doty, J. R., Cunnington, R., Gilbert, P., & Kirby, J. N. (2020). Neurophysiological and behavioural markers of compassion. *Scientific Reports*, *10*(1), 1–9. https://doi.org/10.1038/s41598-020-63846-3

4

Cultivating compassionate capacity

The path of Fierce Compassion

We've looked at what systems operate beneath the surface of our thoughts, emotions and behaviours, and how compassion can help to support the *Soothe* system. In this chapter, we build on this understanding and explain why compassion can be a helpful attribute for leaders. Now we look into the "how", with a reflective learning cycle for compassion. This leadership tool helps to develop compassionate skills and navigate challenges through a compassionate lens. *Fierce Compassion* doesn't offer one answer, it provides a process for exploring possible approaches to suit whatever situation you are facing. This chapter explains the reflective learning cycle in detail. In the second half of the book, we look at how these skills can be put into practice for common leadership challenges.

∞

NEW – a reflective learning cycle

I want to be more compassionate!

Alright then. But how? Is it just a decision? Do we just raid the compassion cupboard and get some more?

As mentioned earlier in this book, it helps to think of compassion as a skill, a muscle we can strengthen and grow through practice.

As we've explored, compassion involves three essential elements: awareness, empathic attunement and action, in order to reduce suffering. Researchers in the field of compassion have similarly characterised compassion as having three components: noticing, feeling and responding.[1–3]

DOI: 10.4324/9781003583080-4

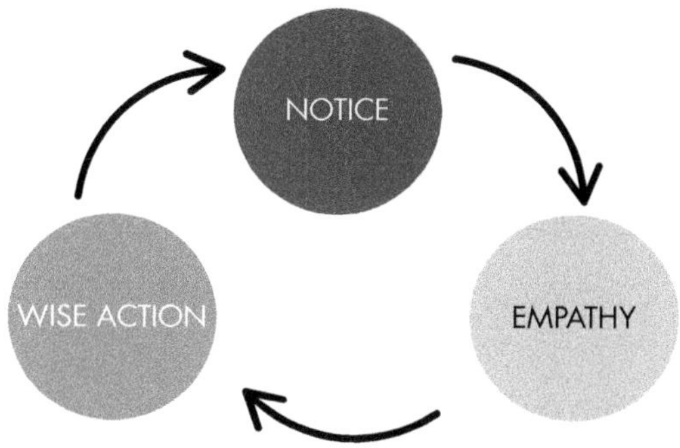

Figure 4.1 The NEW reflective learning cycle.

Fierce Compassion conceptualises compassion as containing three core steps – *Notice*, *Empathise* and *Wise Action* (*NEW*) (see Figure 4.1).

When we think about compassion in this way, we can start to see areas where we can increase our skills. The *NEW* reflective learning cycle gives us a practical way to strengthen these skills in ourselves and for leadership. *Fierce Compassion* uses these core areas for both others and ourselves. The relationship between compassion for ourselves and others is explored later in this chapter.

Step 1: Notice

First, we explore how to *Notice* situations and our responses, bringing awareness to any suffering in ourselves or others. It's easy to get stuck in the *Threat–Drive* loop, especially when we are facing the pressures of leadership. The first step to unhooking from this loop is to increase skills at noticing.

Step 2: Empathise

We then shift the focus to cultivating a sense of warmth and care towards ourselves and others – we are priming our *Soothe* system. You may be more familiar with the noun "empathy", but I've chosen to use the verb "*Empathise*" deliberately to keep the cycle dynamic and to reinforce that compassion in leadership is a way of showing up.

Both Steps 1 and 2 help stimulate your *Soothe* system, bringing the *Threat–Drive–Soothe* systems closer towards balance (see Figure 4.2).

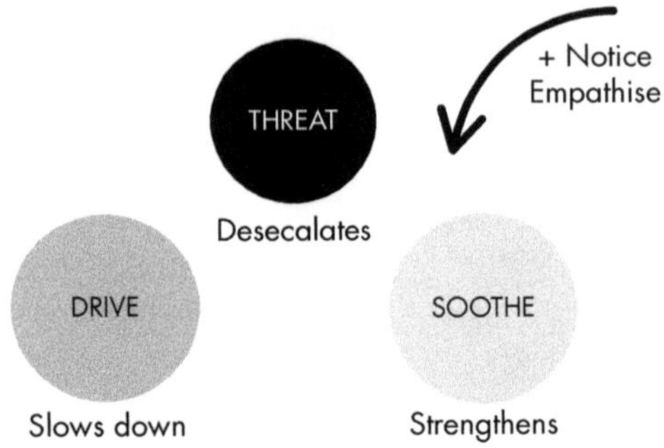

Figure 4.2 Notice and empathise strengthen the Soothe system.

Step 3: Wise Action

In Step 3, we draw on the helpful attributes of our three systems to consider protection, motivation and connection that generate our next *Wise Action* (see Figure 4.3).

This *NEW* approach helps us gain a sense of space and perspective, where we can learn to generate understanding of ourselves (even those bits we are ashamed of) and of others. From here we cultivate empathy for our own and others' foibles, challenges, failures and inadequacies – touching the vulnerability of our common human experience.

These important steps of noticing, understanding and empathy are the foundation from which we can consider what our *Wise Action* will be. Action, that this time includes the whole picture, so that solutions are broader, richer, more holistic and thorough.

The reflective learning cycle is an important approach in *Fierce Compassion* as it helps us shift from theoretical knowledge to putting ideas into practice.[4,5] By reflecting on our experiences we can iteratively improve our skills and increase our flexibility to adapt to different situations.[6] This style of experiential learning leads to a deeper and richer understanding. The step-wise iterative change is akin to agile implementation strategies that propose that successful solutions require a repeated learning cycle – of piloting, adjusting and monitoring in real time.[7] For leaders, this critical reflection helps to avoid acting from assumptions and habits that may otherwise limit their potential.[8]

∞

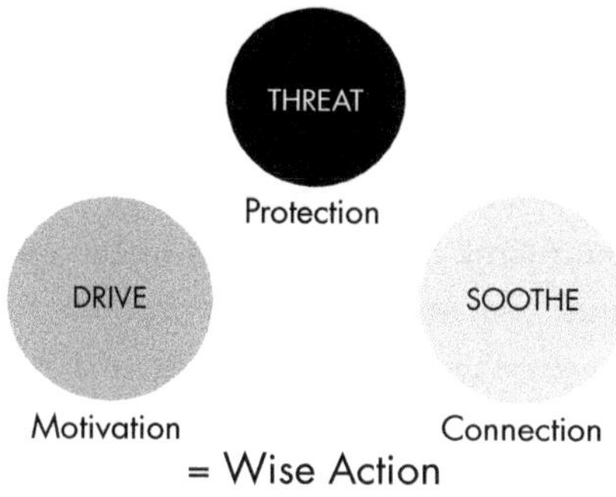

Figure 4.3 Protection, motivation and connection lead to wise action.

Step 1: Noticing

General benefits of mindfulness

The first bit sounds straightforward enough – noticing suffering. We can consider several components: present moment awareness, the observer perspective, non-judgement and curiosity. Using these mindfulness-based techniques helps improve our ability to *Notice*, and also leads to reductions in stress, anxiety and depression.[9]

Our mind is really like a time-travelling machine that can transport us into the future or the past. We have imagination, which helps us to predict what might happen or creatively engage with future possibilities. From an evolutionary perspective, this capability was a game-changer. Learning from past mistakes helped us prepare for future dangers and opportunities. Dreaming of something that didn't exist meant we could create solutions for problems. You could say that the mind evolved to become a problem-solving machine.

However, this ability to imagine can cause problems when it is exposed to the chronic stress of modern living. Our minds can constantly live in the future, worrying about what might happen. We no longer only respond to possible future threats that might exist, but also to any future threats that our imagination can dream up. Conversely, we get dragged back into the past, ruminating over what we could or should have done, brewing our feelings of disappointment, frustration and regret.

Fierce Compassion is a process that helps us unhook from the *Threat–Drive* loop. Our ability to *Notice* and bring awareness to ourselves and the situation is the foundation for developing our compassion capacity. To be aware of suffering, we need to be able to attend to what is happening right now.

Present moment

Pause here for a moment to reflect… How are you right now? No, really, how are you? How are you really, right now?

To unhook from the racing mind, we need to be able to focus our minds on the present moment. Our mind tends to wander for almost half of the day, and some of this time can be a space for processing and creativity.[10] Yet we are often happiest when focused on what we are doing in the present moment.[11] To unhook from our time-travelling machine, it is helpful to learn how to press pause.

I often imagine that the mind is like a bunch of naughty monkeys playing around and causing mischief. If we try to focus on the present moment and have an idea about our mind being completely calm and peaceful, we may turn to the monkeys and say "shhhhhh". Sometimes – ok, most of the time – this doesn't work so well. Have a go and see what happens when you ask your monkeys to just shut up for a while. In my experience, the monkeys are extremely naughty and they tend to get even louder. Thankfully, I know from hearing many other people's experiences that this happens to others too! So sometimes it is helpful to give the monkeys a task to focus on, which can help them start to settle down.

There are many ways to practice bringing our attention to the present moment, and I will outline some of them here. You may already have ways of doing this that work for you. If you aren't yet sure, then I would encourage you to experiment and *Notice* without judgement what it is that helps you bring your focus to the present.

Focusing on the breath is a simple and portable way to anchor the mind. It is always there. Breathing in and out, we can be present right now, as it is happening. By asking our mind to follow this rhythm, it can help our mind focus on the "now" rather than being in the future or the past. But some people don't find breathing exercises helpful, experiencing them physically uncomfortable, boring or irritating. If that's you, there are some alternatives.

Another approach is to gently scan your internal world, observing and naming sensations as they arise in the body. Focusing on how we are right now.

You might like to try pairing a physical task with mindful attention that can enhance body awareness. One exercise is to focus on our feet and notice and name the sensations that we feel. We can sway and stand on one leg and take small steps, just noticing what changes in the sensation in our feet. This is a really great one for when you are standing in line waiting for coffee.

At times, it can be uncomfortable to focus on our inner world. Perhaps what we notice is distressing or uncomfortable, which our monkeys then complain about loudly. It may be helpful to shift our attention to the world around us. Try noticing and naming five things you see, hear and feel to bring yourself into the present moment. Name and notice five things we can see, five things we can hear, five things we can feel… and then four things… and then three… and so on.

Anything that is currently occurring can be used as a focal point for the present moment. Any task that we undertake can be focused on in detail – we can notice and name the actions and sensations from tapping our fingers on the keyboard or walking around the office.

This is different from distraction, where we use external activities to take us away from the present moment. When distracted, we are taken away from the reality of how we are, and into an alternative reality – watching TV, listening to a podcast, scrolling on the phone, daydreaming.

- *Which method of pressing pause works best for you?*
- *Does how you are feeling or where you are affect which method you choose?*

Staying on the platform

You may start to notice that as soon as you connect with the present moment, it is gone, and you have to connect with the next present moment. Each moment is like the carriage of a train passing us by as we stand on the platform, and as it moves past, another carriage appears in front of us, and together they make the train.[12] But what happens if we end up getting on a carriage? We get caught up in a particular present moment – a thought, a sensation – and it carries us away. Suddenly, we find ourselves *on* the train, rather than on the platform. Our focus wanders, and we find ourselves once again in the future or the past. This is normal and natural, and our minds do it thousands of times each day.

We are trying to increase our ability to stand on the platform AND to notice when we have got on a train carriage AND then choose to get off again at the next station.

Many people get disheartened with present moment practice because they expect to feel a lovely sense of calm and emptiness. Sometimes this might happen, but when we make it the goal, we are missing the point. If our mind is busy and our emotions are raging when we contact the present moment, this is what we will notice. We aren't doing anything wrong. But if we notice the rushing thoughts and the strong emotions and then engage with them – "Urgh, I am doing this wrong!", "It isn't working!", "Why don't I feel calm?!" – then we got on a carriage of the train and we were taken away from the present. It may help to name the category of thought – busy mind, critical thoughts, planning, problem-solving – naming and noticing the train carriage as it passes us by. Compassion isn't about feeling nice or calm, but about growing the awareness of how things really are (instead of being distracted or worried about the past or the future).

Observer perspective

The purpose of present moment awareness is to step out of our future worry or past rumination and instead develop our capacity for the observer perspective.

Think of it this way. We have a mind that thinks and feels (does), and a mind that can watch us thinking and feeling and doing (observes). We can have a thought – "I am a stupid, lazy person who will never become anything in my life" – and we can notice we are having that thought.

If this is all getting a bit abstract, try this exercise from Acceptance and Commitment Therapy.[11] Bring to mind a thought that you have about yourself in the form "I am…". Whether it is a helpful or unhelpful thought, just allow it to run through your mind and repeat it in your head a few times. Now change the phrase to "I am having the thought that I am….". Let this run through your mind and repeat it over a few times. Now repeat to yourself, "I am noticing I am having the thought that I am…".

- *What did you experience?*

Most people report that they get a sense of distance or observation of the original thought, "I am…". This is a taste of the observer perspective.

Another way to think about the observer perspective is to imagine that your life is a movie and you are the star of the show. Your movie is playing at the local cinema and you go along to watch it. Your thinking, feeling or doing mind is like the actor in the movie – saying the lines, reacting to what is happening around them. But you can also be a member of the audience, watching the movie, noticing what the actor is doing and how they are feeling. When we cultivate awareness, it requires a shift from being the actor in the movie to being a member of the audience. The observer perspective.

We are watching, noticing and curious about what is going to happen next. However, sometimes when we are watching the movie, we may notice that we aren't just any old member of the audience, we are also the movie critic! Commenting on what the actor is doing badly, the stupid things they say, every mistake they make and how they SHOULD or COULD have been doing so much better. Sometimes it turns out that the cinema is full of movie critics.

Judgement kicks in and takes us away from present moment awareness. We are ruminating on the past, thinking of the mistakes and what could be done better, and pulled into the future, worried about what might happen next.

Now imagine this is a magic movie theatre, where there is always another row at the back of the room. Wherever the movie critic is, you can always take a seat behind them. From this vantage point, you can now see the movie AND the movie critic. You can notice and name what the actor in the movie is doing AND what the movie critic is doing.

Sometimes the monkeys in our minds are very clever. When we notice the movie critic, we become the critic of the movie critic. "Oh, there I go again! Why do I do this to myself? Haven't I learnt by now? What's wrong with me!!!?". I'm pretty sure this isn't only happening in my mind, that most of us can get caught up in this meta-level criticism. Just know you can always move a row behind and notice the movie critic's critic too.

It can help us to stay as an audience member watching the movie, if we come in a spirit of curiosity and non-judgement. Being curious and just noticing and observing the movie. We can think of our observer mind like a curious scientist, noticing, naming and observing with no judgement or interference.

Of course, sometimes we get caught up in the movie, we just love it. We feel the same emotions as the actor. We can't wait for that happy ending. Even pleasant and happy thoughts and feelings can take us out of the present moment. Can we come back to being curious audience members, just noticing and observing what is happening?

As we move further and further back in the cinema, noticing the movie and the movie critics, our perspective broadens. We can take in more details of what is occurring around the actor, the scenes, the situations and the conditions in which they are existing. Some people like to think of this broader perspective as if they are up in a helicopter or as though they are a bird high up above, looking down and noticing. We begin to move from a state of present moment awareness to contemplating – a steady observation with attention to thoughts, feelings, physical sensations, reactions/actions, patterns and the situation in which it is all occurring.

Now that we've explored the theory, we can turn inward. The following reflective practice invites you to pause, *notice* and gently observe your own experience, just as it is, without needing to change it.

Notice

Reflective exercise

Find a quiet space. Some people find it helpful to jot down notes or reflections as they go, or read the questions first and then close your eyes as you ask yourself them in your mind.

Begin by pressing pause. Using whatever practice suits you best, you may like to take a few slower breaths, or focus on your feet, or actions that you are doing. Imagine you are a scientist exploring the issue you are currently focusing on with curiosity and openness.

Describe the situation in which the distress is occurring, and try using a few short, factual sentences.

Notice what is happening in your body. Scan from your toes up your body to your head and notice any physical sensations. Name anything you notice without further comment or analysis. Just observe how you are right now.

Notice what is happening in your mind. When you think about this issue, notice where your mind goes. What thoughts do you have about this situation? Once you have noticed what you are thinking, bring your attention to how you are thinking. Notice the style or pattern of thinking. Perhaps your thoughts are critical, worrying or negative? Notice the tone of voice that these thoughts have. There is no need to change your thoughts or to get carried away by them, just notice them as they come and go.

Notice what is happening to your emotions. How do you feel regarding the situation? Can you name the emotion(s) that arise in response to this situation? If you are having difficulty naming the emotion, you may like to notice where you experience this feeling in the body instead. You are not trying to change how you feel, but rather to become curious and make space for whatever feelings arise.

Notice how you act. Tune into how this situation changes what you do. Perhaps you start acting differently, or maybe you stop or postpone doing something? Becoming aware, without judgement, of how this situation affects your behaviour.

Become aware of the bigger context in which this situation occurs – the work environment, your family environment, your society and culture. Notice what this broader perspective reveals.

Patterns might begin to emerge. Perhaps you are responding in a familiar way that may feel like a habit, or perhaps this response is new to you.

You have been finding the observer perspective, noticing and naming your experience. If you notice that the mind gets caught up in the story of what is happening or it begins to self-criticise, just come back to your breath. There is no right or wrong way, you are just observing what happens.

Take a few moments to write down what you have noticed. Practice using neutral language without judgement or comment.

Each of the following chapters explores an area of challenge to leaders, using the *NEW* framework. In each *Notice* section, there is a reminder to practice this exercise of pausing and tuning in to your own experience.

When our *Threat* and *Drive* systems are activated, we can get stuck in patterns of behaviours, which often are driven by our innate repertoire of safety strategies, our childhood conditioning and the habitual responses we form over time. We may react to a situation based on our ancient automatic defence and safety system, and then explain these responses through a lens of our cognitive understanding of ourselves, others and the world around us. Psychodynamic therapists refer to these conceptualisations as self-objects, and cognitive therapists call them schema. It is useful to understand that sometimes our automatic, habitual responses that seem helpful in the short term can actually be prolonging or maintaining our distress in the long term. Short-term solutions can become long-term problems. It is an act of great compassion to ourselves to recognise that our unhelpful actions are often an attempt to manage distress and difficulty in the best way we can at the time. If you've experienced trauma, tuning into the body or present moment can bring up distressing symptoms. Be kind to yourself and try other grounding techniques that work for you, or consider additional support from a registered mental health professional.

As we develop the capacity to reflect on the emotional states of others (and ourselves), this is referred to as mentalisation. How well we can mentalise is negatively affected by a range of factors, including a lack of reflection or awareness, avoidance of emotional states or a lack of language to describe emotions. We may at times overly focus on one particular emotion to avoid noticing other emotions that are less acceptable to us. When our *Threat* system is stimulated, we switch to a more reactive state and a tendency to think in black and white, or all-or-nothing, terms. This is great for responding to immediate danger, but it inhibits our ability to mentalise, as it is a higher-level competency of our frontal cortex and therefore slower and more effortful. By increasing our mindful awareness and feelings of safety in a therapeutic context, we can increase our mentalisation capacity. Practising this component of compassion helps us to move out of the reactive, narrow view of the situation and into a state where it is easier to feel, understand and *Empathise* with ourselves and others. This means we are better placed to *Notice*, observe, take in new information, broaden our perspective and think in creative and novel ways about the situation.

∞

Step 2: Empathise

Empathy is defined as "the action of understanding, being aware of, being sensitive to, and vicariously experiencing the feelings, thoughts and experiences of another"[13] It is the ability to put ourselves in the shoes of another person and to feel what we imagine they are feeling. I also use the term empathy to refer to self-empathy, which is described elsewhere as introversive empathy, or impathy.[14,15] In Step 1, we looked at skills to begin to *Notice* our own experience. Self-empathy extends this experience to include a warm and caring attitude towards our own experiences. Self-empathy means noticing and recognising what is happening in you with a sense of care and non-judgement. Many people in the Western world find it easier to generate empathy for others than for themselves.[16] But with practice, we can build this warm stance towards our own experiences; the self-validation that it is ok that we feel how we feel. This doesn't mean we always act on these feelings – that wouldn't always be wise. But the first step is to acknowledge that they are there, even those feelings that we find harder to accept about ourselves – jealousy, rage, bitterness and so on.

When we become more aware of our reactions to situations that are causing us difficulty, we may naturally find ourselves feeling more caring towards ourselves. However, especially if we have had cold and critical experiences in our childhood or if our inner critic is well developed, we may find instead that the harsh inner dialogue is too strong. We find ourselves caught in judgement, self-criticism and shame. For the development of self-compassion, it is essential to follow awareness with exercises to cultivate feelings of self-empathy – being sensitive to our own feelings and thoughts, with a warm and kind disposition.

Some of us may find developing skills in empathy and compassion easier than others. Neurodiverse people have been described as having deficits in empathy and compassion. But more recent studies show that those with a specific type of neurodiversity, autism, can experience a strong sense of "felt" empathy, but may struggle more with "thinking" empathetically.[17] More recently, researchers have found that neurotypical people may have difficulty understanding neurodiverse people and vice versa,[18] while neurodiverse people may more easily understand others with neurodiversity.[18] Therefore, a perceived lack of empathy may be better understood as difficulties in understanding and communication.[18] Those with a history of trauma or who find it particularly difficult to engage with these feelings of warmth towards oneself may require extra support to help develop this capacity. While it is wonderful to learn and develop compassion on one's own, remember that connection is at the heart of compassion. Sometimes we need to connect with a mental health professional to enable us to engage with ourselves with compassion. Reaching out for support is a tremendous act of self-compassion. So don't be disheartened if you find the empathy exercises challenging and the warmth elusive. You aren't broken, you just need some support and care; a spark to start your own compassion fire.

Empathy is a component of compassion. But empathy on its own can pose two problems: it can cause distress, and it can be used for harm. If we dwell on the suffering of others (or ourselves) for too long, we may end up in empathic distress, where we feel overcome by our own experience of suffering.[19] On the other hand, empathy doesn't always mean care, as empathic understanding can be used for negative purposes. A limitation of empathy is that it can be used against someone in a harmful way.[20] If you want to cause someone maximum harm, you can use your empathic skills to figure out how to hurt them the most.[21] Compassion helps overcome the difficulties with empathy. Compassion requires empathy but goes further with the additional step of alleviating suffering.[22] When we move into action to reduce suffering, it is more likely that we experience positive emotional states – it feels good to be compassionate.[23] The inherent imperative in compassion is to be helpful, and this can guide empathy towards beneficial outcomes. In the following examples in this section, for ease of reading, I use the term "empathy" as a component of compassion, and at times "compassion" when referring to the felt component of compassion.

There are different pathways by which we can increase our level of empathy – through the *emotional* experience of empathy or a *cognitive* experience (thinking empathically).[24] We often don't consider how to actively engage our empathy. At times, we find ourselves moved by a beautiful piece of music, crying at a movie, or calmed by a warm cup of tea. It can help to experiment to see what works for us, and use an emotional connection, or our thoughts, actions and physical sensations to assist us. Something that stimulates our *Soothe* system might be irritating for someone else. We also have the ability to regulate our experience of empathy, which is important when there are conflicting experiences to navigate.[24] Think of the nurse who has to restrain an aggressive patient to administer essential medical help.

Below is an overview of approaches that we can use to engage our empathy in order to support our compassion capacity. In the second part of this book, each chapter includes a different practice to support our empathic response. It will be helpful to bring your curious scientist's perspective with you, to experiment and see what truly works for you (and this may change over the course of the day or week or years).

Feel the feels

It probably makes intuitive sense to access empathy through feeling the emotional state. Our imagination, which can cause us so many troubles when it is driven by our *Threat–Drive* system, can be of great assistance when we employ it in the service of stimulating our *Soothe* system.

When we imagine something or actually experience it, the same neural pathways in the brain light up. If I ask you to think about your favourite meal, and describe it in detail – the colours, textures, smell, where you would eat it and with whom – you will likely experience a physiological response – your mouth may water or your tummy rumble in anticipation. Our minds are not actually very good at differentiating between "real" experiences and imagined ones. This can cause us great distress when we think of something that terrifies us (something moving under the bed!), but we can also use this capability to our advantage: it can be used in therapeutic approaches to imagine the feared situation in detail, and a successful outcome can help prepare us for facing the same challenge in real life.

To increase our feelings of empathy and compassion, we can visualise somewhere that we have felt a sense of being warm and safe, or create an imagined ideal version of a compassionate image where we feel that way.[25] Most people find it helpful to close their eyes when they want to bring something from their imagination to mind, as the same areas involved in imagination are also used for looking and may be otherwise occupied.[26] Connecting deeply with this visualisation helps to stimulate the parasympathetic nervous system and increase our *Soothe* response. Research shows that compassion-focused imagery can stimulate the *Soothe* system and decrease activity in the hypothalamic-pituitary-adrenal axis, although those with high self-criticism or insecure attachment styles may need professional support to develop these capabilities.[27] Visualisations are a type of thought; some of us will "see" these images in our mind's eye, while for others they may "see" words, or a felt sense. Others find visualisation difficult to connect to and gain more benefit from other approaches.

Emotions are closely related to physical sensations in the body. We often describe emotions using physical metaphors – butterflies in our stomach, the weight of the world on our shoulders. So if we are struggling to connect with an emotion, it can help to access it via our physical sensations. We may be able to generate the feelings of warmth and connection through engaging in activities that stimulate our parasympathetic response – we may try soaking in warm water, walking, being in nature, hugging our loved ones and pets or using smells to transport us to times where we have felt calm and at ease. It often takes some gentle experimentation to discover what truly feels restful for us. As we enter these calmer states of being, we are more likely to be able to generate empathic responses.

Warm thoughts

When we consider the *Threat*, *Drive* and *Soothe* systems, we often end up exploring what we are feeling or doing. But it is important to remember that our emotional regulation is also affected by our thinking style. Try telling yourself that you are a useless failure who is going to amount to nothing a few times, and see what happens to your mood. We tend to have a running commentary in our mind, which is mostly like the radio playing in the background. But our inner dialogue may be activating our *Threat* or *Drive* system.

An empathic style, with self-compassionate thinking, can act as an emotional regulation strategy as it appears to increase activity in the prefrontal cortex and heart rate variability.[28] Cultivating a warmer, more caring inner voice can gradually shift our emotional tone. This may be especially important if you have internalised a strong critical voice. Generating alternative, more helpful thoughts can be useful, but they can be of limited help unless they come with a felt sense of warmth and compassion. A limitation of Cognitive Behavioural Therapy is that sometimes clients share "I rationally understand that it's not my fault, but I still FEEL self-critical". Generating warmer, more caring thoughts can take time and may require other techniques that stimulate the *Soothe* system when the self-critic is strong. One option is to try writing self-compassionate letters, which can be regularly reread to strengthen the association with self-compassionate thought.

Behaviours

The way we think about a situation often changes our behaviour. It also works the other way around – if we change our behaviour, it can change how we think about a situation. Sometimes it can be hard to stimulate the emotional pathway towards compassion for several reasons, including depression or loss of feeling (anhedonia). If this is the case, it can be helpful to switch instead to behavioural strategies, which can lead to positive emotional experiences.

At times, we may not be able to access the feeling, empathy or compassion, but we can commit to undertaking the behaviour regardless. Occasionally it's necessary to act first, and the empathic or compassionate feelings are likely to follow later on. This is because we are activating the pathways related to compassion through our behaviours. For example, if we are struggling to feel compassionate towards ourselves, we can still commit to acting in a self-compassionate way. These may be *Gentle* acts of compassion, like making ourselves something nourishing to eat or giving ourselves a break. Or they may be *Fierce*, requiring our inner strength to set a limit on our phone time, or say no to an unhelpful commitment. Doing small, compassionate acts for others often helps awaken these feelings within us, too – small, thoughtful actions like letting someone know how much they mean to us, or thanking someone for an everyday task. We may want to be wary of over-giving to our own exclusion, but if we come from a place of compassion for both the self and others, we are likely to experience the *Soothe* state. Soothing behaviours help us regulate and can easily be confused with *Wise Action*, which is how we act *after* we have self-regulated, which we explore in Step 3.

∞

Step 3: Wise Action

Notice and *Empathise* act to slow down the *Threat* response, moderate the *Drive* tendency, and support the *Soothe* system, which begins to bring our systems into balance, or closer towards balance (see Figure 4.4)

As this happens, we are then in a position to more easily access what would be helpful to reduce suffering – our compassionate response. I call this *Wise Action*, to differentiate it from acting from a place of fear or scarcity, which tends to mean problem-solving, quick fixes, rescuing or impulsive short-term solutions.

Figure 4.4 Protection, motivation and connection lead to wise action.

Sometimes the most helpful action is to not act. This is the action of conscious non-action, which is different from *Threat*-based responses of avoidance, procrastination or disengagement. Wisdom comes from being able to make our best judgement based on the information we have available. When we are emotionally regulated we are better able to see the bigger picture and respond to complexity.

After we have engaged our *Soothe* system, our *Threat* system may still be appropriately stimulated. Consider a situation where someone was getting bullied at work – when *Threat* is overstimulated and there is no *Soothe*, they may react habitually to situations of danger by appeasing or avoiding taking action. This may have been helpful at certain times in the past to keep them safe. If they are now in a place where there are more options available, first engaging *Soothe* and regulating the *Threat* and *Drive* may help them to organise the actions necessary to address the bully, report the bullying behaviour, seek support or leave the situation.

When our systems are more in balance, we can access the beneficial aspects of our *Drive* system to motivate us towards resources that are necessary for our survival. We may default into habitual responses. For instance, an evolutionary desire to accumulate resources may be intensified by a childhood where there was deprivation, resulting in an overfocus on financial security beyond what is necessary, leading to overwork and stress. It is implicit in compassion work that we act from an orientation of helpfulness rather than harm. It may be helpful at this point to remember our personal values – what truly matters to us, what we want to be known for, and how we wish to engage with the world around us. Prioritising external goals (achievement, money, fame, status) is correlated with poorer mental health outcomes than prioritising intrinsic values (a sense of purpose and meaning in what we do). Intrinsic values are correlated with reduced levels of stress, anxiety, depression and physiological indicators such as heart rate and blood pressure.[29]

Our *Wise Actions* draw on our inner wisdom – our experiences of ourselves, others and the world. *Wise Action* doesn't mean perfect action. We can only respond from our best understanding at that moment. *Wise Action* is an iterative process. We do the best we can to try to alleviate suffering with the humility of knowing that we make mistakes and may have misunderstood in some way. This is why *Fierce Compassion* is not a linear process. We do not increase our ability to *Notice, Empathise,* take *Wise Action*, then tick the box and move on. The cycle continues (see Figure 4.5).

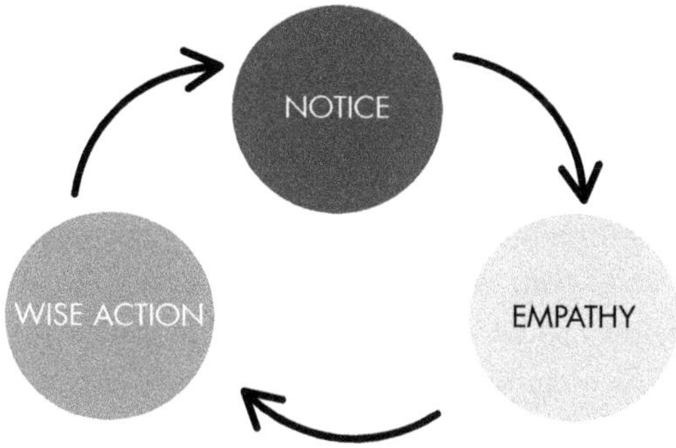

Figure 4.5 The NEW reflective learning cycle.

After we take *Wise Action*, we return to awareness, either for the same situation or other challenges. Compassion becomes a skill, a learning journey where there is no destination. It is not possible to be perfect, and it's not a helpful aim. Instead, we embrace our imperfections, the imperfections of others and the imperfections of the systems we live in. *Fierce Compassion* is a process to come back to time and time again, to help us navigate this experience of caring and creating, of being human.

You are the expert in your life, you understand the situation, the conditions in the present and past that have informed you, and what may be most useful for you going forward. After first noticing and empathising, the emphasis in *Wise Action* is to draw on your inner wisdom. When we reflect on what might be helpful, we may become aware of an area where we want to develop new skills or benefit from some suggestions. In the following chapters, I give some ideas for *Wise Action* that may be useful guides, but the focus remains on self-reflection and your inner wisdom.

Differentiating between Soothe and Wise Action

Sometimes, empathising and soothing activities are so pleasant that we can get stuck there. We mistake taking behavioural action to stimulate our *Soothe* system for *Wise Action*, and we may be overly *Soothe*-focused. Conversely, if our *Soothe* system is very depleted our next *Wise Action* may very well be to engage in more *Soothe* activities. It is a fine differentiation and we may not always know if we are in *Soothe* behavioural activation or *Wise Action*. Here are some reflective questions to help differentiate between the two.

- **Sketch your own Threat, Drive and Soothe systems** – Sometimes a useful check-in is to draw our *Threat*, *Drive* and *Soothe* circles to reflect how active these systems are at the time. This can give us an insight into whether we need more *Soothe* or are ready to take *Wise Action* (or the *Wise Action* of knowing we need more *Soothe*!).
- **Consider Fierce/Gentle** – We may like to reflect on the *Gentle-Fierce* continuum (below) to check if we are getting stuck in habitual patterns of avoidance. For instance, avoiding the "*Fierce*" action called for by the situation we find ourselves in.
- **Notice how you feel about your chosen action** – Remember that a classic *Threat* response is to freeze. Here we may find ourselves in procrastination or avoidance, which can look similar to *Soothe*. A way to explore which system we are in is to check in with our physiological response. Do we feel at ease and a sense of warmth and connection (indicating the *Soothe* system is activated) or do we feel distracted, restless or numb (indicating the *Threat* system is activated)?

Wise Action

Reflective exercise

Given the awareness you have brought and the empathy that you have cultivated, what Wise Action would be helpful for yourself or others at this time?

Sometimes in challenging situations, we respond with habits that are helpful in the short term, but that may harm us in the long run. Can we also bring compassion to these responses, understand that it is a very common human experience to want to avoid suffering, and that we are managing the best we can? In these situations, it may be wise to remind ourselves that if the situation is objectively safe, we can try to act the opposite of what our threat system is telling us to do.

If we feel resistance to the action, we might like to ask ourselves, is the step too big? Are we slipping into rescuing, fixing or avoidance? Is our action wise? Can we bring compassion to the acceptance that perhaps it can help to scale our action back or to take small steps for it to be wise, or remind ourselves of a longer timeline?

Sometimes we may not know what to do – the wise action may be unclear. We may need to tolerate this uncertainty. Sometimes the most helpful action is the action of non-action. This is an active non-action that includes continuing to observe ourselves and others, rather than practising avoidance. When our wise action is unclear or our capacity for compassion for ourselves or others is low, we may need to focus first on resourcing ourselves. We may like to consider how to call on both gentleness and fierceness to help guide our wise action.

We may make a mistake. With all our best intentions in heart, sometimes we take an action that doesn't work out as we hoped it would. After taking an action, we go back to Notice and Empathise, to bring compassion for being human and making mistakes and learning as we go. It helps to generate compassion for ourselves that we are doing our best with what we know right now, and that our understanding may change in the future.

Considering the awareness you have generated, the understanding and empathy that you have connected with, what is the wise action that is helpful in this current situation?

∞

Fierce and Gentle

Compassion can be *Gentle* and *Fierce*. Remember, *Fierce* represents characteristics of "strong and powerful" or "showing strong feeling or energetic activity". This is the overt reminder that compassion requires strength, courage, bravery and wisdom. It is helpful to see it as a continuum between the qualities of fierceness and gentleness (see Figure 4.6). Depending on the situation, we may need more gentleness or more fierceness. We may not know what we need. One way forward is to play, to experiment, to hold it lightly. While we are aiming for *Wise Action*, there should not be a burden of getting it "perfect" or "right". We can only be where we are right now, our view is always limited by our capabilities at that moment. Hold

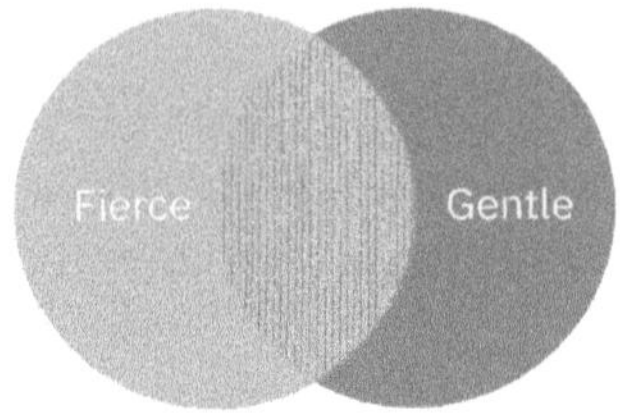

Figure 4.6 The Fierce and gentle aspects of compassion.

compassion for yourself, know that you are trying your best, that it's ok to make a mistake – this is how we learn and grow our compassion. Compassion is not risk-free. We are engaging, connecting and relating to ourselves and others. There is potential for hurt and upset, but this is also where the richness and joy lie.

∞

Self:Other:System

Self and other

There is a relationship between compassion for others and self-compassion. While the mechanisms involved are not yet fully understood, research shows that compassion for others and self-compassion are, on one hand, distinct capabilities, yet there is also an association between the two[30–35] (see Figure 4.7). It may be that when we practice self-compassion we also experience a sense of connection to something greater than ourselves, and that these self-transcending experiences help us to connect more compassionately to others.[36]

It is often said that to be truly compassionate, one must first learn to be self-compassionate. But what I frequently notice in clients is a tendency to be much more compassionate to others than to ourselves (see Figure 4.8). Research supports that this is common and that we are less likely to be self-compassionate when our mental wellbeing is poorer.[35,37,38] Yet, when we are self-compassionate, it reduces our psychological distress.[35,37,38] What I've seen over and over again is that people are often aware of the suffering of others and are motivated to help them (compassion for others), but are not aware of their own suffering, or minimise it or criticise themselves for it (non-self-compassion

Figure 4.7 The relationship between compassion for the self and others.

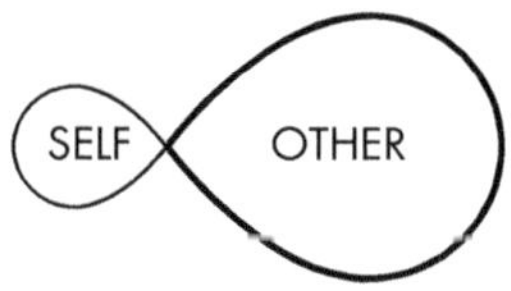

Figure 4.8 Sometimes compassion is easier to give to others than ourselves.

or self-criticism). For people who have difficulties receiving compassion from others, they may work overly hard to improve their self-worth but end up lacking a sense of success and feel that no one cares about them.

We can use the association between compassion for others and self-compassion to help strengthen our overall compassion capacity. If we are finding it hard to access self-compassion, we can use our ability to give compassion to others and mirror this back to ourselves. For instance, when we speak to ourselves compassionately like we would speak to a friend, the area of the brain activates that would normally do so if our friend were actually speaking to us.[39]

As we increase our capacity for self-compassion, there is a deepening of our empathic connection with others, increasing our ability to show them compassion too. Many therapists report that after they have had a mental health difficulty, they are more able to *Empathise* with their clients' struggles. While originally they may have been able to share empathy and compassion, it is our learning from ourselves and one another that deepens these capabilities.[40] We are then able to be differentiated selves, separate from, but also connected to, those around us.

Systems

As our compassionate perspective deepens, our awareness allows us to notice that we are also operating in systems that may affect our or others' abilities to be compassionate, or cause us to react in a habitual way (see Figure 4.9).

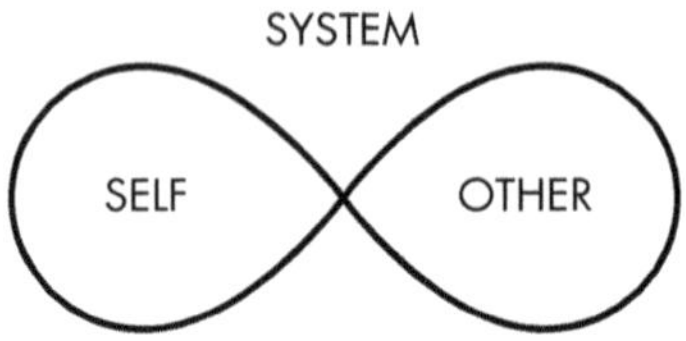

Figure 4.9 There is a relationship between the system, ourselves and others.

Many people would agree that suffering is inevitable at work. Whether it is as a result of our challenges, illnesses, losses, relationships or financial stress, or from factors to do with the organisation itself – redundancy, restructuring or mistreatment[41] – systems can support or impede our ability to access or receive compassion.

The three components of compassion to *Notice*, *Empathise* and take *Wise Action* to reduce suffering are important relationship functions that also support collective compassion at work.[42] Ordinary everyday practices at work can create conditions that support compassion. Having compassionate practices in place can also ensure that it is appropriate to the need and doesn't negatively impact work functioning.[42] While systems can interfere with these components, they can also support them, and there are good reasons why we should bother. When individuals at work receive compassion, they feel more committed to their workplace,[1,43] they see their colleagues in a more positive light, and it helps them recover more quickly from painful or traumatic experiences.[1,44] Compassionate leadership can help people recover after a traumatic experience at work[45]. Given that grief-related absences cost more than $72 billion annually,[46] there is also a compelling financial incentive to develop a more compassionate workplace.

As discussed in Chapter 2, while Charles Darwin is best known for his view that evolution involved a battle for the "survival of the fittest", his view on the benefits of co-operation has not been so well shared. In 1871, he wrote that communities that included the greatest number of the most sympathetic members would flourish best and rear the greatest number of offspring.[47] Those of us who value compassion and co-operative ways of being can perhaps take some comfort from the fact that if there wasn't an evolutionary advantage to being warm, kind and caring, these traits would have likely disappeared long ago. Creating compassionate systems requires "care and share" approaches rather than "control and hold" strategies.[48]

As we use the *NEW* reflective learning cycle for developing *Fierce Compassion*, it can be helpful to reflect on the relationship between ourselves, others and the systems we work in to understand how these factors are impeding or supporting our compassion capacity. These three areas of the self, others and the systems we work in are explored in the next six chapters, using examples from leaders who were interviewed to explore common compassion challenges. Where the primary focus of a chapter is on one of these areas, such as the self, you can also reflect on how the same issue affects others; for instance, reflecting on your own perfectionism, the perfectionism of others, or how the work system may encourage perfectionism.

∞

This chapter introduced the *NEW* reflective learning cycle, which helps us focus on how to build skills in the three core components of compassion. It is helpful to reflect on the balance between *Gentle* and *Fierce Compassion*, which will vary depending on the circumstances and our internal resources. We can view challenges by thinking about them at three different levels – for ourselves, others and the systems we work in. As leaders, the *NEW* process becomes a supportive tool we can lean into when we want to develop our compassion capacity generally, or in response to specific areas of challenge. Leaders from a range of disciplines – business, government, legal, medical, activist and entrepreneurial – generously shared their insights about compassion, and the themes that emerged from these interviews give the focus for the areas discussed. In the second part of this book, we look at how to put *NEW* into action. Chapters 5 and 6 explore challenges for the self, Chapters 7 and 8 focus on our interactions with others, while Chapters 9 and 10 look at factors involved in the systems we work and live in. While the skills in each chapter build on one another, each chapter can also stand alone if a particular area feels most relevant. You may find it helpful to return to chapters at different points in time. Different situations often reveal new layers of understanding, and you're likely to engage with the ideas in fresh ways each time.

Fierce Compassion is a process; there isn't a destination. Instead, it is a flexible system of reflection and learning aimed to support us to develop compassion. As we grow our ability to be compassionate we access the benefits that it can bring – a sense of greater connectedness, increased creativity, improved physiological health and hopefulness.

∞

Summary – cultivating compassionate capacity

This chapter introduces a practical framework for strengthening *Fierce Compassion* in real-world leadership:

- The *NEW* reflective cycle – *Notice*, *Empathise* and *Wise Action* – gives practical steps for developing *Fierce Compassionate* leadership
- Compassion involves both *Gentle* and *Fierce* responses, depending on the situation
- Leadership requires navigating compassion for ourselves, others and the wider systems we live and work in
- The capacity to lead with compassion grows through ongoing, reflective practice

References

1. Lilius, J. M., Worline, M. C., Maitlis, S., Kanov, J., Dutton, J. E., & Frost, P. (2008). The contours and consequences of compassion at work. *Journal of Organizational Behavior*, *29*(2), 193–218. https://doi.org/10.1002/job.508
2. Kanov, J. M., Maitlis, S., Worline, M. C., Dutton, J. E., Frost, P. J., & Lilius, J. M. (2004). Compassion in organizational life. *American Behavioral Scientist*, *47*(6), 808–827. https://doi.org/10.1177/0002764203260211
3. Strauss, C., Lever Taylor, B., Gu, J., Kuyken, W., Baer, R., Jones, F., & Cavanagh, K. (2016). What is compassion and how can we measure it? A review of definitions and measures. *Clinical Psychology Review*, *47*(1), 15–27. https://doi.org/10.1016/j.cpr.2016.05.004
4. Schön, D. A. (1983). *The Reflective Practitioner: How Professionals Think in Action*. Basic Books.
5. McBrien, B. (2007). Learning from practice – Reflections on a critical incident. *Accident and Emergency Nursing*, *15*(3), 128–133. https://doi.org/10.1016/j.aaen.2007.03.004
6. Paterson, C., & Chapman, J. (2013). Enhancing skills of critical reflection to evidence learning in professional practice. *Physical Therapy in Sport*, *14*(3), 133–138. Science Direct. https://doi.org/10.1016/j.ptsp.2013.03.004
7. Omonije, A. (2024). Agile methodology: A comprehensive impact on modern business operations. *International Journal of Science and Research*, *13*(2). ResearchGate. https://doi.org/10.21275/SR24130104148
8. Helsing, D., Howell, A., Kegan, R., & Lahey, L. (2008). Putting the "Development" in professional development: Understanding and overturning educational

leaders' immunities to change. *Harvard Educational Review*, 78(3), 437–465. https://doi.org/10.17763/haer.78.3.888l759g1qm54660
9. Clark, C. (1997). *Misery and Company*. University of Chicago Press.
10. Gonçalves, Ó. F., & Rachel, M. (2023). The time has come to be mindwanderful: Mind wandering and the intuitive psychology mode. In P. S. Boggio, T. S. H. Wingenbach, M. L. da Silveira Coêlho, W. E. Comfort, L. M. Marques, & M. V. C. Alves (Eds.), *Social and Affective Neuroscience of Everyday Human Interaction: From Theory to Methodology* (pp. 145–160). Springer. https://doi.org/10.1007/978-3-031-08651-9_9
11. Khoury, B., Sharma, M., Rush, S. E., & Fournier, C. (2015). Mindfulness-based stress reduction for healthy individuals: A meta-analysis. *Journal of Psychosomatic Research*, *78*(6), 519–528. https://doi.org/10.1016/j.jpsychores.2015.03.009
12. Harris, R. (2008). *The Happiness Trap*. Robinson.
13. Merriam Webster. (2025). *Empathy*. Merriam-Webster.com. https://www.merriam-webster.com/dictionary/empathy
14. Jordan, J. V., & Stone Center for Developmental Services and Studies. (1991). *Women's Growth in Connection: Writings from the Stone Center*. Guilford Press.
15. Neubrand, S., & Gaab, J. (2022). The missing construct: Impathy. *Frontiers in Psychology*, *13*, 1–13. https://doi.org/10.3389/fpsyg.2022.726029
16. Thupten Jinpa. (2016). *A Fearless Heart: How the Courage to Be Compassionate Can Transform Our Lives*. Avery Publishing Group.
17. Baron-Cohen, S. (2013). Empathy deficits in autism and psychopaths: Mirror opposites? In M. R. Banaji & S. A. Gelman (Eds.), *Navigating the Social World: What Infants, Children and Other Species Can Teach Us* (pp. 212–215). Oxford University Place.
18. Milton, D., Gurbuz, E., & López, B. (2022). The 'double empathy problem': Ten years on. *Autism*, *26*(8), 1901–1903. https://doi.org/10.1177/13623613221129123
19. Dowling, T. (2018). Compassion does not fatigue! *PubMed*, *59*(7), 749–750.
20. Bloom, P. (2016). *Against Empathy: The Case for Rational Compassion*. Vintage.
21. Kohut, H. (2010). On Empathy 1. *International Journal of Psychoanalytic Self Psychology*, *5*(2), 122–131. https://doi.org/10.1080/15551021003610026
22. Goetz, J. L., Keltner, D., & Simon-Thomas, E. (2010). Compassion: An evolutionary analysis and empirical review. *Psychological Bulletin*, *136*(3), 351–374. https://doi.org/10.1037/a0018807
23. Fernando, A. T., Arroll, B., & Consedine, N. S. (2016). Enhancing compassion in general practice: It's not all about the doctor. *British Journal of General Practice*, *66*(648), 340–341. https://doi.org/10.3399/bjgp16x685741
24. Decety, J. (2011). Dissecting the neural mechanisms mediating empathy. *Emotion Review*, *3*(1), 92–108. https://doi.org/10.1177/1754073910374662
25. Maner, S., Morris, P. G., & Flewitt, B. I. (2022). A systematic review of the effectiveness of compassion focused imagery in improving psychological outcomes in clinical and non-clinical adult populations. *Clinical Psychology & Psychotherapy*, *30*(2), 250–269. https://doi.org/10.1002/cpp.2801

26. Reddan, M. C., Wager, T. D., & Schiller, D. (2018). Attenuating neural threat expression with imagination. *Neuron, 100*(4), 994–1005.e4. https://doi.org/10.1016/j.neuron.2018.10.047
27. Maratos, F. A., & Sheffield, D. (2020). Brief compassion-focused imagery dampens physiological pain responses. *Mindfulness, 11*, 2730–2740. https://doi.org/10.1007/s12671-020-01485-5
28. Di Bello, M., Carnevali, L., Petrocchi, N., Thayer, J. F., Gilbert, P., & Ottaviani, C. (2020). The compassionate vagus: A meta-analysis on the connection between compassion and heart rate variability. *Neuroscience & Biobehavioral Reviews, 116*, 21–30. https://doi.org/10.1016/j.neubiorev.2020.06.016
29. Morris, L. S., Grehl, M. M., Rutter, S. B., Mehta, M., & Westwater, M. L. (2022). On what motivates us: A detailed review of intrinsic v. extrinsic motivation. *Psychological Medicine, 52*(10), 1–16.
30. Ari, E., Cesur-Soysal, G., Basran, J., & Gilbert, P. (2022). The compassionate engagement and action scales for self and others: Turkish adaptation, validity, and reliability study. *Frontiers in Psychology, 13*, 1–9. https://doi.org/10.3389/fpsyg.2022.780077
31. Gu, J., Baer, R., Cavanagh, K., Kuyken, W., & Strauss, C. (2020). Development and psychometric properties of the Sussex-Oxford Compassion Scales (SOCS). *Assessment, 27*(1), 3–20. https://doi.org/10.1177/1073191119860911
32. Neff, K. D. (2003). The development and validation of a scale to measure self-compassion. *Self and Identity, 2*(3), 223–250. https://doi.org/10.1080/15298860309027
33. Pommier, E., Neff, K. D., & Tóth-Király, I. (2019). The development and validation of the compassion scale. *Assessment, 27*(1), 107319111987410. https://doi.org/10.1177/1073191119874108
34. Tendhar, T., Marcotte, M. A., Saikia, M. J., & de Mesquita, P. B. (2022). Relationship of compassion for self and others to sense of well-being of college students. *Journal of American College Health*, 72, 1246–1254. https://doi.org/10.1080/07448481.2022.2074276
35. García-Campayo J., Barceló-Soler, A., Martínez-Rubio, D., Navarrete, J., Pérez-Aranda, A., Feliu-Soler, A., Luciano, J. V., Baer, R. A., Kuyken, W., & Montero-Marín, J. (2023). Exploring the relationship between self-compassion and compassion for others: The role of psychological distress and wellbeing. *Assessment, 31*(5), 1038–1051. https://doi.org/10.1177/10731911231203966
36. Cha, J. E., Serlachius, A., Cavadino, A., Kirby, J. N., & Consedine, N. S. (2023). Self-compassion and compassion for others: A multiple mediation study of personal values. *Mindfulness, 14*(10), 2417–2429. https://doi.org/10.1007/s12671-023-02202-8
37. Zessin, U., Dickhäuser, O., & Garbade, S. (2015). The relationship between self-compassion and well-being: A meta-analysis. *Applied Psychology: Health and Well-Being*, 7(3), 340–364. https://doi.org/10.1111/aphw.12051

38. Gilbert, P. (2023). An evolutionary and compassion-based approach to yearning and grief. In D. L. Harris & A. H. Y. Ho (Eds.), *Compassion-Based Approaches in Loss and Grief* (pp. 1–10). Routledge.
39. Kim, J. J., Henderson, T., Best, T., Cunnington, R., & Kirby, J. N. (2020). Neural and self-report markers of reassurance: A generalized additive modelling approach. *Frontiers in Psychiatry*, *11*, 1–7. https://doi.org/10.3389/fpsyt.2020.566141
40. Lim, D., & DeSteno, D. (2019). Past adversity protects against the numeracy bias in compassion. *Emotion, 20*(8), 1344–1356. https://doi.org/10.1037/emo0000655
41. Driver, M. (2007). Meaning and suffering in organizations. *Journal of Organizational Change Management*, *20*(5), 611–632. https://doi.org/10.1108/09534810710779063
42. Lilius, J. M., Worline, M. C., Dutton, J. E., Kanov, J. M., & Maitlis, S. (2011). Understanding compassion capability. *Human Relations*, *64*(7), 873–899. https://doi.org/10.1177/0018726710396250
43. Grant, A. M., Dutton, J. E., & Rosso, B. D. (2008). Giving commitment: Employee support programs and the prosocial sensemaking process. *Academy of Management Journal*, *51*(5), 898–918. https://doi.org/10.5465/amj.2008.34789652
44. Frost, P. J., Dutton, J. E., Worline, M. C., & Wilson, A. (2000). Narratives of compassion in organizations. SAGE Publications Ltd EBooks, 26–45. https://doi.org/10.4135/9781446219850.n2
45. Powley, E. H. (2013). The process and mechanisms of organizational healing. *The Journal of Applied Behavioral Science*, *49*(1), 42–68. https://doi.org/10.1177/0021886312471192
46. Dutton, J. E., Frost, P. J., Worline, M. C., Lilius, J. M., & Kanov, J. M. (2002, January 1). Leading in times of trauma. *Harvard Business Review*, 54–61. https://hbr.org/2002/01/leading-in-times-of-trauma
47. Ekman, P. (2010). Darwin's compassionate view of human nature. *JAMA*, *303*(6), 557. https://doi.org/10.1001/jama.2010.101
48. Gilbert, P. (2021). Creating a compassionate world: Addressing the conflicts between sharing and caring versus controlling and holding evolved strategies. *Frontiers in Psychology*, *11*, 1–38. https://doi.org/10.3389/fpsyg.2020.582090

5 Redefining success Fierce Compassion for achievement

In the next two chapters, we explore *Fierce Compassion* for ourselves in two areas that emerged from the interviews that commonly affect leaders: overworking for achievement and perfectionism. In Chapter 5, we discuss working overly hard to achieve, which can happen for several reasons. We are living in a time of busyness, where there is a focus on productivity and a blurring of the lines between work and home life. When we set ourselves a goal and work towards it, it can be an incredibly satisfying and enriching experience. However, a tendency to focus on achievement can tip us over into working more and more. When we find ourselves overworking or linking our sense of self-worth to achievement, we also start to experience increasing levels of stress and burnout. In this chapter, we focus on the tendency to overwork driven by our own demands, while overworking due to demands from the workplace is explored in Chapter 10.

∞

Notice

> Well, number one, I'm exhausted, and I'm not performing right now. I'm not at my best because I'm tired. Just flat-out tired. The last year, on top of the previous year, has been tough – it's been a huge emotional roller coaster. I have become resentful in my fatigue, instead of giving myself a break. I am at this point where I'm like, listen, I work

DOI: 10.4324/9781003583080-5

> and work to make this place a better place, but nobody appreciates it, and nobody notices, or tries to help.
>
> – Karma Metzler Fitzgerald, Collaborative Community Builder, Grant Writer, Consultant

To begin, we explore the broader cultural messages about achievement, how they influence our behaviour and shape our inner dialogue, before turning inward to *Notice* our own patterns and responses.

Stress can be helpful. Eustress refers to a level or type of stress that is motivating and helps us feel a sense of growth and accomplishment. We can become "stress-blind", used to high levels of stress that feel normal to us. But high levels of stress or chronic stress are related to a wide range of negative health outcomes: decreased brain size, reduced cognitive functioning, decreased immunity, increased heart rate and blood pressure, gastrointestinal and hormonal issues.[1] Stress also impacts our mental wellbeing across our lives. Adverse events in childhood lead to higher levels of mental health difficulty later in life.[2–11] As adults, chronic stress can cause insomnia,[12] increase the likelihood of developing anxiety and depression[13] and worsen existing mental health conditions.[14,15] We are more at risk of overworking if our organisation has effort-reward imbalances, low organisational justice and high job demands.[16] High job strain and long work hours are associated with an increased risk of cardiovascular disease, and job insecurity leads to higher levels of depression.[17]

We can all list healthy choices we *could* be making, but sometimes we don't take helpful actions. We may have habits and patterns of resistance that we are unaware of. If we live with high stress levels a lot of the time, there is a risk that we begin to normalise the stress, which numbs us to the potential consequences.[18] In this chapter, we explore our tendencies to work hard to see what would happen if we readjusted our beliefs about work, achievement and productivity through a compassionate lens.

The curse of the high-functioning individual

Our biological disposition towards achieving things for our survival is impacted by the conditions in which we live. Living in modern culture, which puts an emphasis on productivity, meritocracy and individuality, may mean we link achievement to our self-worth. But meritocracy ignores the impact of privileges, connections, community, collective support... and luck.

We absorb implicit and explicit rules or beliefs about achievement and success from the culture, family and society we grow up in. You may have had messages such as:

- "If you work hard, you can achieve anything"
- "Hard work equals success"
- "Nothing in life is free"

Karma, who has worked tirelessly for her community, including running for the House of Representatives seat for Idaho in 2022, narrowly losing out by 85 seats, reflects on her tendency to overwork:

> I think – you didn't earn it. You haven't returned enough. It's a sin on a farm, you know, if there is still light, you should be at work. There is still stuff to be done. I have a constant battle in my head about what I should be doing. I call it the 'should monster'. What should you be doing? What it means to be a good woman, a good wife, a good mother. Who made that rule that I have to work myself into an early grave to be seen as valuable? I made that rule.
>
> – Karma Metzler Fitzgerald, Collaborative Community Builder, Grant Writer, Consultant

Our *Drive* system knows how to push for the attainment of a goal, but it becomes both a master and a slave to increased demands, driving us on towards the next dopamine hit. Achieving can become our dominant coping tool and habitual response to stress – *"if there is a problem, just try harder"*. The motivational force from the *Drive* system acts as arousal (not the fun kind, but a measure of the level of stress on our system). Stress in itself is not a bad thing; the gap between what we have and what we need is the basic motivational force to get us to do anything. Without it, we wouldn't eat, find shelter or seek loved ones. But how much stress is helpful?

More than a hundred years ago, academic psychologists, Yerkes and Dobson, proposed a relationship between stress and performance,[19] and, since then, many studies also show an inverted U relationship.[20,21] "Stress" is a complex idea, which includes psychological and physiological reactions, and the breadth of research makes it harder to answer the simple question – how does stress affect performance? Overall, it appears that performance does fall as stress increases past a certain point, depending on the type of stress and mitigating factors.[22–30]

The relationship between productivity and hours worked has been explored for over 150 years – since the start of the industrial revolution.[30] In 1926, Henry Ford famously reduced the time worked by his employees, introducing the eight-hour work day and five-day working week, and found that productivity increased while production costs fell.[31] A wide range of research shows that overwork reduces productivity both at the individual and organisational level.[32–39] Overwork leads to increased mental and physical fatigue, an increase in accidents, decreased efficacy and increased errors, and these are particularly pronounced when related to a lack of sleep.[33,38] For leaders, it is important to reflect on both their own tendency to overwork and how helpful it is to encourage overwork in their staff.

If our basic needs are met when stress levels are low, we may find that our *Soothe* system is naturally stimulated and we feel rested and at peace. But sometimes we may also experience boredom from a lack of purpose or meaning. As the level of stress rises, we enter a phase of increasing performance, and this feels good. We are in our growth zone, our *Drive* system is activated, we are motivated to move towards a goal or outcome, and we are rewarded with hits of dopamine. However, at a certain point, the amount of stress we are experiencing overly stimulates our *Threat* response, and our performance begins to fall. As the stress continues to increase our performance drops away. Most people agree that the pattern makes intuitive sense, but there is often a disconnect between the intellectual understanding of this idea and the experience of what it feels like when we are on the curve and how it influences our behaviour.

I have renamed the relationship between stress and performance as "The curse of the high-functioning individual", which, you must admit, is a lot more catchy (see Figure 5.1). I have observed over and over again what happens with my clients when they are on the curve. If you are used to achieving at a high level, you are used to relying on your *Drive* system to deliver you hits of dopamine. Consider what happens to you when your performance starts to fall. The most likely automatic response is to try harder. If you are on the lower end of the curve, this is helpful. But when you are on the other side of the curve, inadvertently, when you work harder, you increase your stress, and your performance goes down even more. This is confusing and tends to induce anxiety and thoughts

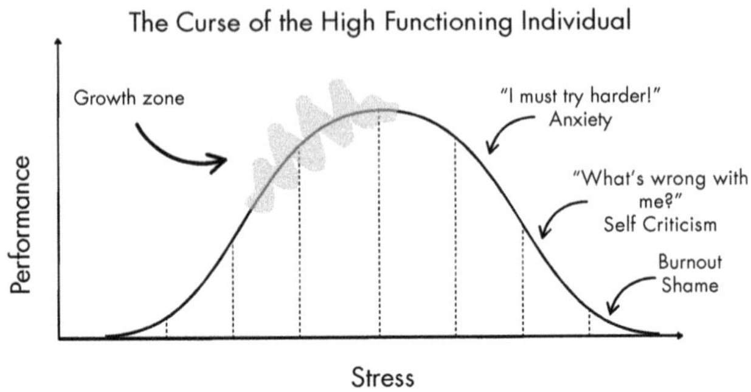

Figure 5.1 The curse of the high-functioning individual.

such as *"what is wrong with me?"*. To cope with this discomfort, you try even harder, your performance continues to fall, and anxiety, depression, self-criticism and shame creep in. I've seen so many clients in burnout who just kept trying harder and harder.

There is nothing wrong with the *Drive* system – it is an essential motivational system that we would suffer without. However, when "work harder" is the only tool in our toolbox, it is not helpful in all situations. It is like we are all accelerator with no brake. We would never dream of buying a car like that, it would be too dangerous. We often cause ourselves more suffering because we don't know where we are on the curve, and we apply the wrong strategy.

When we overly rely on our *Drive* system as a coping mechanism, we also stimulate our *Threat* system with the perceived danger of failing to reach our goals, meet our deadlines, or "letting people down". The two systems become over-developed, stuck in a *Threat–Drive* feedback loop. Like a weightlifter who only concentrates on one arm, the *Soothe* system meanwhile isn't exercised and it atrophies. As we use it less, it becomes harder to access a state of calm, connection and rest. I have heard many clients say some version of *"I can't stop, so I just have to keep going"*. We can end up feeling too wired to rest. Anyone who has been around a young toddler can recognise this *"tired and wired"* state. They are exhausted, but they are also winding themselves up (perhaps into a tantrum) rather than settling down to rest. Often this ends in tears (sometimes parents as well as the child!). Interestingly, tears help release oxytocin, which is a key hormonal modulator of the *Soothe* system. So maybe those toddlers are onto something. But when we say we are *"too tired to rest"*, it is like saying we are *"too dirty to have a shower"*. We desperately need the rest, we just haven't practised how to access it.

If we can't switch off, it's a sign of overstimulated *Drive* and *Threat* systems. Can we extend empathy, that we are suffering and we need to care for ourselves? We can't just expect to be able to switch on an underdeveloped *Soothe* system overnight, but we can be gentle yet persistent with ourselves as we learn how to grow this ability.

Pause here for a moment to reflect...

- *How do you respond if you are not achieving at the level you wish to?*
- *When do you get caught in the Threat–Drive loop?*
- *In what situations might you find yourself "wired and tired"?*

The productivity cost

We may end up focusing on achievement for a variety of reasons, like the pressure from our education and employment systems, parental and peer influences, or economic pressures. Achievement per se is not a bad thing; however, our responses when trying to achieve can cause us difficulties. Especially when they result in self-criticism and attempts to work even harder. We may overlook the costs and pitfalls of this focus on achievement. Bruce, an expert in healthcare education and leadership, notices that in the medical profession the focus on achievement to bolster a sense of self-worth can prevent people from sharing that they are struggling:

> People like to look good in this profession, which can mean there is an avoidance and stigma around acknowledging symptoms of depression and anxiety. Ambitious parents and medical school training push out people who are focused and ambitious, but narrow. There are many who feel unloved unless they are doing exceptionally well.
>
> – Professor Bruce Arroll, Faculty of Medical and Health Sciences

When I am exploring the concept of optimal stress and the impact on performance, clients will often describe colleagues who seem to be able to cope with higher levels of stress. It is unhelpful to compare our own stress-performance curve with someone else's, because it ignores inherent differences. We don't acknowledge what we can't see, such as the hidden supports and privileges that a person may have, be they genetic, financial or familial.

At other times, we aren't witnessing the hidden costs of their achievement. Sometimes we can maintain our performance in one domain, beyond the normal peak position. We do this by "borrowing" from another domain – we spend less time with our friends and family, we stop going to the gym, we become irritable, hollow versions of ourselves, sacrificed on the altar of performance. We compare our insides to other people's outsides. How often do we present a glossy exterior to our colleagues, editing out the stressors and impact that the role is having on us and our loved ones?

We tend to be attracted to professions that suit our strengths or meet the expectations of those around us. Certain professions suit a particular set of core schema (ways of seeing ourselves, others and the world), and then the system enshrines those characteristics. For instance, studying law tends to attract perfectionists who pay attention to details, who can argue a point and do not display any weakness. While these may be great attributes for becoming a lawyer, they don't always transfer that well to other areas of life, such as personal relationships. Our strengths can also cast a shadow. We accentuate certain skills and habits, but may fail to notice their detrimental effects or strengthen other abilities.

Take a moment to consider...

- *What do you notice when you compare yourselves to how others seem to manage high levels of stress?*
- *What other domains do you "borrow" from to maintain a level of performance at work?*
- *What characteristics does your role encourage, and how might these help or not help you in other areas of your life?*

Helpful amounts of stress

Something I hear consistently from people more advanced in their career about younger staff is a frustration with what they perceive as a *"lack of resilience"* or not so kindly as *"snowflake"* oversensitivity. But the younger generation faces challenges. For Gen Z there is increased uncertainty about job and financial security, with worries about their ability to afford to buy a home or pay for retirement, and a strong sense of economic pessimism.[40] They experience higher rates of mental illness than their older colleagues: 55% of Gen Z compared to 31% for those aged 55–64.[40] There can be a sense from senior professionals that younger staff should be prepared to suffer in the same way they did. It can be challenging to let go of the belief that working exceptionally hard is a good thing. We can also end up wearing a *"badge of busyness"* as a sign of success and importance, and worry what people will think of us if they don't witness us striving.

What I mean by working too hard can be easily misconstrued. Sometimes we may need to engage in a short burst of hard work, and that may be helpful in our lives. What I am talking about is chronic overwork, the over-reliance on "working hard" as a coping strategy, with an out-of-balance emphasis on working harder no matter what the cost. If we find ourselves denying that chronic overwork is an issue, we may be engaging in a defence mechanism against the grief that comes with recognising in ourselves what "success" has cost – the hours lost with family and friends, the sleepless nights, health impacts and a hollow sense of achievement. It can feel easier to perpetuate an unhealthy norm than face difficult feelings. The fierceness of compassion can help us stay with these uncomfortable realisations.

To change systems that perpetuate chronic overwork, we must be willing to explore what the cost was. On the other hand, I can hear people saying *"But the next generation really aren't resilient"*, and I wonder if both can be partly true? We need a certain level of challenge and stress in our lives to grow and learn, and removing these stressors can have a paradoxical effect of increasing anxiety. We learn to doubt our own capabilities and miss opportunities to develop helpful coping strategies. The positions represent opposite ends of a spectrum – make no changes because surviving a toxic system is part of a *"toughen up"* learning process, or remove all challenges because all stress is toxic. *Fierce Compassion* encourages a nuanced exploration of the grey between these spaces, asking the question, *"What is a healthy and helpful amount of stress and challenge?"* There isn't one answer; rather, it is an ongoing conversation, a negotiation, which creates space to explore and learn.

Pause here for a moment to reflect…

- *What do you think about others who you perceive to work less hard than you do?*
- *What do you notice about the impact of striving for achievement in your life?*

Notice

Reflective exercise for achievement and overworking

Find a quiet space. Some people find it helpful to jot down notes or reflections as they go, or you can read the questions first, then close your eyes and reflect on them and note your reflections afterwards.

Begin by pressing pause. Using whatever practice suits you best. You may like to take a few slower breaths, or focus on your feet, or actions that you are doing. Imagine you are a scientist exploring the issue you are currently focusing on with curiosity and openness.

Describe the situation in which overworking is occurring, using a few short, factual sentences.

Notice what is happening in your body. Scan from your toes up your body to your head and notice any physical sensations. Name anything you notice without further comment or analysis. Just observe how you are right now.

Notice what is happening in your mind. When you think about this issue, notice where your mind goes. What thoughts do you have about this situation? Once you have noticed what you are thinking, bring your attention to how you are thinking. Notice the style or pattern of thinking. Perhaps your thoughts are critical, or worrying, or negative? Notice the tone of voice that these thoughts have. There is no need to change your thoughts or to get carried away by them, just notice them as they come and go.

Notice what is happening to your emotions. How do you feel regarding the situation? Can you name the emotion(s) that arise in response to this situation? If you are having difficulty naming the emotion, you may like to notice where you experience this feeling in the body instead. You are not trying to change how you feel, but rather become curious and make space for whatever feelings arise.

Notice how you act. Tune into how this situation changes what you do. Perhaps you start acting differently, or maybe you stop or postpone doing something? Becoming aware, without judgement, of how this situation affects your behaviour.

Become aware of the bigger context in which this situation occurs – the work environment, your family environment, your society and culture. Notice what this broader perspective reveals.

Patterns might begin to emerge. Perhaps you are responding in a familiar way that may feel like a habit, or perhaps this response is new to you.

You have been finding the observer perspective, noticing and naming your experience. If you notice that the mind gets caught up in the story of what is happening or it begins to self-criticise, just come back to your breath. There is no right or wrong way, you are just observing what happens.

Take a few moments to write down what you have noticed. Practice using neutral language without judgement or comment.

∞

Empathise

If we have developed a way of being that overly relies on our *Drive* system, the ability to access the *Soothe* system can be underdeveloped. For those of us who are used to pushing through difficulties to get results, when we first start to consciously access the *Soothe* system, we may find it difficult, and that can be frustrating. The answer is not to overwork and push through the challenge, criticising ourselves as we go! Imagine an arm – for whatever reason, this arm isn't very strong. If you go to the gym and try to lift a heavy weight, you are at risk of causing damage. Better to start with small movements, little and often, practise the technique and don't focus too much on the outcome to start with. The chances are you are going to ache, and it might feel like you aren't getting anywhere. Can you bring empathy that it can be a hard and frustrating process to build up strength in a helpful way? Practising little and often will be helpful in the long term. So when you start trying to access the *Soothe* system, be kind and *Gentle* to yourself. But not too kind and

Gentle. You need firm persistence, a commitment to yourself, which is worth the investment.

There are many ways to start playing with the *Soothe* system. Get curious and explore, try out and see what works for you. I suggest one exercise below for overworking from focusing on achievement, but you can use any of the empathy-generating exercises from the following chapters. It can be helpful to start with something easier for you, where there is at least a little spark and curiosity. This isn't the time to pick an exercise that feels like a challenge and to persevere even if you are finding it fruitless (hello *Drive* system!). As you start to build capacity, try to revisit previously discarded techniques that may now be accessible.

Empathise reflective practice

Creating a compassionate haven

The best time to practice this exercise is when you are already feeling somewhat relaxed and are in a comfortable position. Allow your eyes to become heavy and loosely focused on these words. Read a sentence or two at a time and close your eyes in between (or softly focus on one point in front of you).

Begin by noticing the flow of air into and out of your body. There is no need to change it, just allow your focus to notice the gentle inhalation and exhalation.

You might be aware that the air is slightly cooler as you breathe in and slightly warmer as you breathe out.

Start to gently lengthen your exhale, allowing the lungs to completely empty before beginning the inhale. Slower, longer, deeper exhale; slower, longer, deeper inhale.

We are going to use our imagination to create an image of compassion – this is a place you can come back to in the future to reconnect with a sense of compassion. You may find it easy to create an image straight away, or it may be something that develops and changes over time. Today, allow yourself to be curious with a sense of play.

When you think about compassion, what comes to your mind?

Allow yourself a few moments to explore what compassion looks like – perhaps it reminds you of a colour, a shape, a person, an animal or a place in nature.

What comes to mind may be something in real life, or it may be something from your imagination.

For this image to be really compassionate, it would come with a sense of being completely understood and accepted just as you are. A sense of a greater wisdom holding you with warmth and care.

Allow your mind to wander. You may experience several images in your mind, or it may take a while for one option to come. Whatever happens, just hold the question with curiosity – when you think about compassion, what comes to mind?

Now, allow your mind to settle on one image that represents compassion to you.

Notice the colours, sounds, smells and textures associated with this mental picture. Is there a sense of movement or stillness?

Imagine this image conveying to you a feeling of warmth, love and deep care. A sense of feeling completely understood and accepted, just as you are.

Surrounded by compassion in this way, imagine that as you breathe in you can breathe in this feeling of compassion, and that as you exhale the compassion washes over you.

Notice how you feel in your body when you bring this compassionate image to mind.

If this compassionate image had a voice, what would it sound like?

What compassionate words might it say to you?

What might this compassionate image want to do for you?

Notice again the air moving into and out of the body. Become aware of your body and where it is touching the seat or the ground. Bringing your awareness back to your body, slowly begin to wiggle your fingers and toes. When you are ready, let go of the exercise and come back to the present.

This exercise builds an internal resource you can return to, a compassionate haven that we can come back to at any time. The more we practice, the stronger the association becomes. The compassionate haven is the place that enables you to restore a sense of balance and leaves you ready to take the next helpful *Wise Action* in response to overworking. This process is called resourcing, which is the ability to build and utilise an internal set of resources. Resourcing helps avoid reactive habits of working harder in response to stress and opens up new ways to respond in a more helpful way. Some of us find it hard to mentally picture images, and if you struggle with the exercise, then experiment with another empathy exercise from a different chapter.

Often, when we try to access the *Soothe* system, the inner critic will have something to say. Chapter 6 has more suggestions on how to compassionately embrace the inner critic, to allow access to the *Soothe* system and, where necessary, a compassionate correction.

∞

Wise Action

First, take a moment to reflect on what achievement means to you from a place of compassion, rather than from pressure or performance. Then, if it's helpful, explore the suggestions that follow, not as rules to stick to, but as ways to reconnect with what truly matters.

Wise Action

Reflective exercise for achievement and overworking

Given the awareness you have brought and the empathy that you have cultivated, what wise action would be helpful for yourself or others at this time as a response to overly focusing on achievement or working too hard?

Sometimes in challenging situations, we respond with habits that are helpful in the short term, but that may harm us in the long run. Can we also bring compassion to these responses, understand that it is a very common human experience to want to avoid suffering, and that we are managing the best we can? In these situations, it may be wise to remind ourselves that if the situation is objectively safe, we can try to act the opposite of what our threat system is telling us to do.

If we feel resistance to the action, we might like to ask ourselves, is the step too big? Are we slipping into rescuing, fixing, or avoidance? Is our action wise? Can we bring compassion to the acceptance that perhaps it can help to scale our action back or to take small steps for it to be wise, or remind ourselves of a longer timeline?

Sometimes we may not know what to do – the wise action may be unclear. We may need to tolerate this uncertainty. Sometimes the most helpful action is the action of non-action. This is an active non-action that includes continuing to observe ourselves and others, rather than practising avoidance. When our wise action is unclear or our capacity for compassion for ourselves or others is low, we may need to focus first on resourcing ourselves. We may like to consider how to call on both gentleness and fierceness to help guide our wise action.

We may make a mistake. With all our best intentions in heart, sometimes we take an action that doesn't work out as we hoped it would. After taking an action, we go back to Noticing and Empathise, to bring compassion for being human and making mistakes and learning as we go. It helps to generate compassion for ourselves that we are doing our best with what we know right now, and that our understanding may change in the future.

Considering the awareness you have generated, the understanding and empathy that you have connected with, what is the wise action that is helpful in this current situation?

Once you've engaged with empathy and the *Soothe* system, you are primed to then consider what *Wise Action* is helpful. I normally advise you to listen to your wisdom and experiment with curiosity – to explore what is most helpful. However, when there is a strong tendency to work harder, if your *Wise Action* is to work harder, you may wish to think again and detour back through *Notice* and *Empathise*. A tendency towards overwork requires large doses of *Soothe*, before *Wise Action* becomes apparent, otherwise you are likely to ping straight back into a *Drive* response. The trick to knowing how much rest and restoration is necessary is (spoiler alert)... You never know for sure!

Resistance to rest

Even when we have increased our awareness and cultivated empathy for ourselves, we may meet resistance when it comes to resting. It is common to worry that we will get stuck in a soothing response forever, becoming lazy or a failure. If you notice resistance to rest coming up, it can be helpful to change how we think about it. Rest is not doing nothing. It is an action to consciously choose. Once the emotional regulation system is closer to balance, then we can look forward to *Wise Action*. Karma shared that she had to rethink her assumptions about what her relatives would have thought about rest:

> My ancestors had to work from dawn to dusk to just keep food on the table. But am I honouring them by working myself to the bone? Am I better to honour them by saying – you survived so I can thrive, and to thrive, I have to rest. I mentioned that to someone in my family, and my relative said "Oh yeah, they would scold you for not using the tools you had at hand". I think that they would also say it is ok to rest, and when I think back, they always took time off to rest at lunch, and they would rest in the evenings, whereas I just go and go. So I wasn't honouring anybody by working 12-hour days.
>
> – Karma Metzler Fitzgerald, Collaborative Community Builder, Grant Writer, Consultant

You may be following an invisible rule, which acts like an internalised belief. Unless you bring awareness to your habits, you might not notice. This rule may have been passed down from your parents or grandparents; it may have previously served a function if they were in a survival state. But we may be acting out survival strategies rather than thriving. Remember, resting and reducing stress can increase our productivity. But more importantly it gives us the space to ask ourselves what it is that we are working so hard for.

If you are in a survival state right now due to objectively challenging conditions, then you may not be able to fully access a rest state. It may be a necessary and adaptive choice to overwork if you are struggling to keep a roof over your head or food on the table. However, even amidst the biggest difficulties, there are often still micro opportunities to find and connect with our *Soothe* system. Even the way you talk to yourself during the crisis can further stimulate the *Threat* or *Drive* systems. Self-compassionate talk that appropriately acknowledges the compounding causative factors (economic, political, social) rather than focusing on self-blame can be helpful. We are sold a story that rest can be expensive or a luxury, but this book has many suggestions that are free and which don't take long.

We can think that working hard was something from the past to do with survival that technological advances have liberated us from. At times, technology reproduces the demands to work hard. Engaging with social media can sometimes mean we are compelled to produce content to gain more likes, a higher profile, to satisfy the criteria of the algorithms powering the feeds. Social media can demand our constant attention. We are now living in an attention economy, where attracting your focus is commodified and gamified. The very forces that are used to keep you hooked are stimulating your *Threat* and *Drive* systems, getting you to pay attention. Even hobbies can become demanding if you have to produce and strive for excellence in order to meet the standards presented online.

Pause here for a moment to reflect...

- *When you think about resting, do you notice any resistance to doing so?*
- *What ideas about rest come from your ancestors or culture?*
- *How does technology impact your ability to rest?*

Beyond self-care

Once we are feeling overwhelmed, it can be hard to access an underdeveloped *Soothe* system. The best way to find out is to try. Be creative, curious and observant.

If we are wired and we try to come to a complete rest, we may find our body feels twitchy and our mind is jumping around. It can be helpful to think about shifting down through the gears. We may at first need a more active form of rest. Try going for a walk and start by walking as fast as your thoughts are going. Then begin to slow your walking pace down, but if your mind gets fast again, speed up your steps for a while. Experiment with trying to slow your steps without forcing it. We can apply that strategy to any activity. Start cleaning up the house, begin with a lot of energy and then begin to slow your movements down. Listen to energetic music, move your body and then choose progressively slower pieces of music. You might like to make a playlist that helps you to decelerate.

Practising and prioritising rest is not emphasised in modern society. We often assume that we will rest when we get to the weekend, or the holiday, or past the end of a project. We expect ourselves to be able to rest on command. It can be helpful to start practising the skill of rest when we are already feeling a fraction calmer, maybe early in the morning, or later in the evening. While it is true that when *Threat* and *Drive* are less active we may naturally find ourselves in a state of rest, often when on holiday we can bring another set of expectations, demands and goals with us. Our mind, which has been busy and worried, doesn't tend to let go of these thoughts because it is Saturday morning, or as we are getting in the car to drive to our holiday destination.

I am not a big fan of the term self-care. This is because it can become commodified – think expensive massages or holidays. While on the outside it can look like we are doing self-care, on the inside we may be having a very different experience. Imagine this example: I go to a yoga class at lunchtime. It sounds like a great self-care activity. But I get caught in traffic on the way there, and I end up running late. Then I can't find a park, and I rush into class, and my favourite place is already taken. I roll out my yoga mat, and as the class starts, I find myself noticing how much thinner and flexible all the other people in the class are, and I berate myself for not coming to yoga more regularly. What systems have I been in during this "self-care" activity? Instead of thinking about traditional ideas of "self-care" we may instead want to become curious about the cultivation of play and curiosity, aimless past-times, things that connect us with others and nature, that allow us to laugh and feel safe. Take a moment to get curious about what works for you...

- *What helps you feel really restful?*
- *What does rest feel like in your body?*

Starting to stop

If you find yourself struggling to find rest, then it may be helpful to aim for *"less frenetic"* rather than complete calm. It can be helpful to think about how to start stopping. What steps can be taken to at least not add more to your plate, or to reduce and slow down as much as possible? Sometimes it is hard to slow down when you work in a system that encourages the opposite. Yet we can look for small windows of opportunity. We may need to start small, and Karma describes what has helped her begin a new habit:

> Now, the reality is I wouldn't completely let it all go to hell, but I have been trying to set some boundaries. Saying no to things – it's really hard. I've done it all for free, because I have plenty. But at some point, it becomes a situation where they're gonna let you do it as long as you do it for free. But the minute you say, wait a minute...there's a boundary. Then suddenly, if they have to invest their own time and money into it, it's not that important.
>
> Well, I don't want to do that anymore. In the last couple of months, if I open up a project or get an email that doesn't bring me joy. Then I'm eliminating that thing. It might take me a while to close things up because I don't want to leave things hanging, but anything that I can get off my plate that does not give me energy – if it sucks more energy than it gives – it's going away.
>
> – Karma Metzler Fitzgerald, Collaborative Community Builder, Grant Writer, Consultant

You might like to pause and reflect on...

- *What do you need to do to support your Drive system to slow down?*
- *What boundaries do you need to draw with yourself and others?*
- *How would you know if you are adequately resourced to take Wise Action?*

We can begin to develop a relationship with soothing. It is a skill that can be learnt. There are benefits for our health, relationships and our planet from resting and resourcing ourselves. Rather than doing more, keep going and being more productive, rest is fuel for a richer, more meaningful and sustainable life.

Redefining success

Once we have stimulated our *Soothe* system, our next *Wise Action* may be to call on a balanced *Threat* and *Drive* response. We may need to say no, and to tolerate the distress (initially) of doing less, or worrying what others may think of us. When we step back from the tyranny of relentless striving, we may gain perspective. Have you ever had to take time off work for sickness, and when you go back, you realise that by and large things kept going just fine in your absence? Sometimes it is uncomfortable to know how replaceable we are. Rather than acknowledge this, we may throw ourselves into work twice as hard to make sure we are missed next time. But what if the knowledge that we are not as critical as we assume we are is, instead, freeing? As the old saying goes, no one on their deathbed regrets not staying later at work. Sometimes our ego wants to hold onto our own importance, whereas the *Soothe* system helps us gain a broader perspective and a healthy dose of humility.

Fierce Compassion invites us to consider a middle way – rather than care too much or not care at all, it might help us care and strive enough. There is a common worry that this approach will mean achieving less or falling behind. But remember the stress-performance curve, and if our over-effort is towards goals that don't actually satisfy us, then it leads to a hollow "success". Research shows that when we pursue extrinsic goals (such as fame, wealth and power), poorer mental health follows. When we focus on intrinsic goals (following our values and pursuing what matters to us), it is related to improved wellbeing.[41] The compassionate approach helps us to take a step back, to see the bigger picture and to realign our efforts so that we redefine success. Before moving on, give yourself a moment to consider…

- *What does a Fiercely Compassionate definition of success look like for you?*
- *How would you know if you were "successful"?*
- *How would you acknowledge and celebrate your successes?*

∞

This chapter is the first of two focusing on *Fierce Compassion* for ourselves. Working overly hard to achieve is a common issue for those in leadership positions, and while it may have brought success, overworking can also increase stress, making us less productive and negatively impacting our physical and mental health. If we are used to functioning well under moderate levels of stress, we can easily get stuck in the *Threat–Drive* feedback loop, trying harder to our own detriment. It takes awareness and practice to notice our tendencies towards overwork, and to cultivate an empathic response to ourselves. *Fierce Compassion* helps us to imagine how much hard work is "enough" and what success really means for us. But sometimes it is not just how much we work, but also how we work that impacts our sense of well-being. When only the very best is good enough, when we have high expectations, we can find ourselves under the tyranny of perfectionism. We explore how compassion can soften the grip of perfectionism in the next chapter.

∞

Chapter 5 Summary – redefining success

This chapter explored how *Fierce Compassion* can help us loosen the grip of achievement-driven overwork and redefine what success really means.

Notice

- Recognise the internal and external forces that drive overwork, perfectionism and constant striving
- Become aware of inherited definitions of success and the impact they have on wellbeing

Empathise

- Meet ambition with self-compassion instead of self-criticism
- Understand how early experiences shape our drive to prove our worth through achievement

Wise action

- Practice self-defined success based on values, not external validation
- Create space for rest, reflection and sustainable motivation

References

1. Yaribeygi, H., Panahi, Y., Sahraei, H., Johnston, T. P., & Sahebkar, A. (2017). The impact of stress on body function: A review. *EXCLI Journal*, *16*(1), 1057–1072. https://doi.org/10.17179/excli2017-480

2. Nemeroff, C. B., & Seligman, F. (2013). The pervasive and persistent neurobiological and clinical aftermath of child abuse and neglect. *The Journal of Clinical Psychiatry*, *74*(10), 999–1001. https://doi.org/10.4088/jcp.13com08633
3. Bradley, R. G., Binder, E. B., Epstein, M. P., Tang, Y., Nair, H. P., Liu, W., Gillespie, C. F., Berg, T., Evces, M., Newport, D. J., Stowe, Z. N., Heim, C. M., Nemeroff, C. B., Schwartz, A., Cubells, J. F., & Ressler, K. J. (2008). Influence of child abuse on adult depression. *Archives of General Psychiatry*, *65*(2), 190. https://doi.org/10.1001/archgenpsychiatry.2007.26
4. Heim, C., Newport, D. J., Mletzko, T., Miller, A. H., & Nemeroff, C. B. (2008). The link between childhood trauma and depression: Insights from HPA axis studies in humans. *Psychoneuroendocrinology*, *33*(6), 693–710. https://doi.org/10.1016/j.psyneuen.2008.03.008
5. Heim, C., & Nemeroff, C. B. (2001). The role of childhood trauma in the neurobiology of mood and anxiety disorders: Preclinical and clinical studies. *Biological Psychiatry*, *49*(12), 1023–1039. https://doi.org/10.1016/s0006-3223(01)01157-x
6. Safren, S. A., Gershuny, B. S., Marzol, P., Otto, M. W., & Pollack, M. H. (2002). History of childhood abuse in panic disorder, social phobia, and generalised anxiety disorder. *The Journal of Nervous and Mental Disease*, *190*(7), 453–456. https://doi.org/10.1097/00005053-200207000-00005
7. Bandelow, B., Späth, C., Tichauer, G. Á., Broocks, A., Hajak, G., & Rüther, E. (2002). Early traumatic life events, parental attitudes, family history, and birth risk factors in patients with panic disorder. *Comprehensive Psychiatry*, *43*(4), 269–278. https://doi.org/10.1053/comp.2002.33492
8. Nemeroff, C. B. (2004). Early-life adversity, CRF dysregulation, and vulnerability to mood and anxiety disorders. *PubMed*, *38*(1), 14–20.
9. Carpenter, L. L., Carvalho, J. P., Tyrka, A. R., Wier, L. M., Mello, A. F., Mello, M. F., Anderson, G. M., Wilkinson, C. W., & Price, L. H. (2007). Decreased adrenocorticotropic hormone and cortisol responses to stress in healthy adults reporting significant childhood maltreatment. *Biological Psychiatry*, *62*(10), 1080–1087. https://doi.org/10.1016/j.biopsych.2007.05.002
10. Copeland, W. E., Keeler, G., Angold, A., & Costello, E. J. (2007). Traumatic events and posttraumatic stress in childhood. *Archives of General Psychiatry*, *64*(5), 577. https://doi.org/10.1001/archpsyc.64.5.577
11. Zlotnick, C., Johnson, J., Kohn, R., Vicente, B., Rioseco, P., & Saldivia, S. (2008). Childhood trauma, trauma in adulthood, and psychiatric diagnoses: Results from a community sample. *Comprehensive Psychiatry*, *49*(2), 163–169. https://doi.org/10.1016/j.comppsych.2007.08.007
12. Shaver, J. L. F. (2002). Stress exposure, psychological distress, and physiological stress activation in midlife women with Insomnia. *Psychosomatic Medicine*, *64*(5), 793–802. https://doi.org/10.1097/01.psy.0000024235.11538.9a
13. Khan, S., & Khan, R. (2017). Annals of psychiatry and mental health cite this article. *Annals of Psychiatry Ment Health*, *5*(1), 1091. https://www.jscimedcentral.com/public/assets/articles/psychiatry-5-1091.pdf

14. Anisman, H., & Matheson, K. (2005). Stress, depression, and anhedonia: Caveats concerning animal models. *Neuroscience & Biobehavioral Reviews*, *29*(4–5), 525–546. https://doi.org/10.1016/j.neubiorev.2005.03.007
15. McEwen, B. S. (2008). Understanding the potency of stressful early life experiences on brain and body function. *Metabolism*, *57*(2), S11–S15. https://doi.org/10.1016/j.metabol.2008.07.006
16. Van der Molen, H. F., Nieuwenhuijsen, K., Frings-Dresen, M. H. W., & de Groene, G. (2020). Work-related psychosocial risk factors for stress-related mental disorders: An updated systematic review and meta-analysis. *BMJ Open*, *10*(7), e034849. https://doi.org/10.1136/bmjopen-2019-034849
17. Niedhammer, I., Bertrais, S., & Witt, K. (2021). Psychosocial work exposures and health outcomes: A meta-review of 72 literature reviews with meta-analysis. *Scandinavian Journal of Work, Environment & Health*, *47*(7), 489–508. https://doi.org/10.5271/sjweh.3968
18. Montgomery, R. M., & Gouvea, M. (2024). Impact of chronic stress on physical and mental health: A detailed analysis. *Journal of Genetic Engineering and Biotechnology Research*, *6*(2), 1–7. https://www.researchgate.net/publication/383531104_Impact_of_Chronic_Stress_on_Physical_and_Mental_Health_A_Detailed_Analysis
19. Yerkes, R. M., & Dodson, J. D. (1908). The relation of strength of stimulus to rapidity of habit-formation. *Journal of Comparative Neurology and Psychology*, *18*(5), 459–482. https://doi.org/10.1002/cne.920180503
20. Hebb, D. O. (1955). Drives and the C. N. S. (conceptual nervous system). *Psychological Review*, *62*(4), 243–254. https://doi.org/10.1037/h0041823
21. Bruggen, A. (2015). An empirical investigation of the relationship between workload and performance. *Management Decision*, *53*(10), 2377–2389. https://doi.org/10.1108/md-02-2015-0063
22. Bowling, N. A., & Hammond, G. D. (2008). A meta-analytic examination of the construct validity of the Michigan organizational assessment questionnaire job satisfaction subscale. *Journal of Vocational Behavior*, *73*(1), 63–77. https://doi.org/10.1016/j.jvb.2008.01.004
23. Gilboa, S., Shirom, A., & Fried, Y. (2005). A meta-analysis of stress and performance at work: Moderating effects of gender, age, and tenure. *Academy of Management Proceedings*, *2005*(1), A1–A6. https://doi.org/10.5465/ambpp.2005.18780289
24. Ford, M. T., Cerasoli, C. P., Higgins, J. A., & Decesare, A. L. (2011). Relationships between psychological, physical, and behavioural health and work performance: A review and meta-analysis. *Work & Stress*, *25*(3), 185–204. https://doi.org/10.1080/02678373.2011.609035
25. Kröll, C., Doebler, P., & Nüesch, S. (2017). Meta-analytic evidence of the effectiveness of stress management at work. *European Journal of Work and Organizational Psychology*, *26*(5), 677–693. https://doi.org/10.1080/1359432x.2017.1347157

26. Bosshard, M., & Gomez, P. (2024). Effectiveness of stress arousal reappraisal and stress-is-enhancing mindset interventions on task performance outcomes: A meta-analysis of randomized controlled trials. *Scientific Reports*, *14*(1), 7923. https://doi.org/10.1038/s41598-024-58408-w
27. Hancock, P. A., Ross, J. M., & Szalma, J. L. (2007). A meta-analysis of performance response under thermal stressors. *Human Factors: The Journal of the Human Factors and Ergonomics Society*, *49*(5), 851–877. https://doi.org/10.1518/001872007x230226
28. Pustovit, S., Miao, C., & Qian, S. (2024). Fear and work performance: A meta-analysis and future research directions. *Human Resource Management Review*, *34*(3), 101018–101018. https://doi.org/10.1016/j.hrmr.2024.101018
29. Byron, K., Khazanchi, S., & Nazarian, D. (2010). The relationship between stressors and creativity: A meta-analysis examining competing theoretical models. *Journal of Applied Psychology*, *95*(1), 201–212. https://doi.org/10.1037/a0017868
30. Lerman, M. P., Munyon, T. P., & Williams, D. W. (2020). The (not so) dark side of entrepreneurship: A meta-analysis of the well-being and performance consequences of entrepreneurial stress. *Strategic Entrepreneurship Journal*, *15*(3), 377–402. https://doi.org/10.1002/sej.1370
31. Golden, L. (2012). *The Effects of Working Time on Productivity and Firm Performance, Research Synthesis Paper*. Ssrn.com. https://papers.ssrn.com/sol3/papers.cfm?abstract_id=2149325
32. Anxo, D., & Karlsson, M. (2019, January 18). *Overtime Work: A Review of Literature and Initial Empirical Analysis*. https://www.researchgate.net/publication/330482933_Overtime_work_A_review_of_literature_and_initial_empirical_analysis
33. Kang, M.-Y. (2024). Working hours and labour productivity from the occupational medicine perspective. *Industrial Health*, *62*(4), 281–283. https://doi.org/10.2486/indhealth.2023-0191
34. Collewet, M., & Sauermann, J. (2017). Working hours and productivity. *Labour Economics*, *47*(10722), 96–106. https://doi.org/10.1016/j.labeco.2017.03.006.
35. Lee, D., & Lim, H. (2014). Nonlinearity in nexus between working hours and productivity. *SSRN Electronic Journal*, 1–33. https://doi.org/10.2139/ssrn.2580642.
36. Delmez, F., & Vandenberghe, V. (2018). Long working hours make us less productive but also less costly. *LABOUR*, *32*(4), 259–287. https://doi.org/10.1111/labr.12128
37. Lee, D., Lee, J., Kim, H., & Kang, M. (2020). Association of long working hours and health-related productivity loss, and its differential impact by income level: A cross-sectional study of the Korean workers. *Journal of Occupational Health*, *62*(1), e12190. https://doi.org/10.1002/1348-9585.12190
38. Chang, C.-K., & Woo, S. (2017). Critical review of previous studies on labor productivity loss due to overtime. *KSCE Journal of Civil Engineering*, *21*(7), 2551–2557. https://doi.org/10.1007/s12205-017-1652-0

39. Kuroda, S., & Yamamoto, I. (2013). Firms' demand for work hours: Evidence from matched firm-worker data in Japan. *Journal of the Japanese and International Economies*, *29*, 57–73. https://doi.org/10.1016/j.jjie.2013.06.005.
40. McKinsey & Company. (2022, October 19). *How Does Gen Z See Its Place in the Working World? With Trepidation*. Www.mckinsey.com. https://www.mckinsey.com/featured-insights/sustainable-inclusive-growth/future-of-america/how-does-gen-z-see-its-place-in-the-working-world-with-trepidation
41. Van den Broeck, A., Howard, J. L., Van Vaerenbergh, Y., Leroy, H., & Gagné, M. (2021). Beyond intrinsic and extrinsic motivation: A meta-analysis on self-determination theory's multidimensional conceptualization of work motivation. *Organizational Psychology Review*, *11*(3), 204138662110061. https://doi.org/10.1177/20413866211006173

6 Breaking free of tyranny

Fierce Compassion for perfectionism

Often, those in leadership positions are driven to excel. This can lead to great success, and yet it can mean focusing on the ability to perform perfectly. The previous chapter explored how achievement and working overly hard can reduce our performance. We now focus on a specific aspect of working overly hard that can be detrimental to leaders – perfectionism – which was a focus for many in the interviews. In my clinical experience, I see incredibly successful, intelligent and talented individuals holding leadership roles who are also incredibly hard on themselves. In this chapter, we explore the dark side of perfectionism and how compassion can help us escape its tyrannical grip.

∞

Notice

> I have a very deep habit of perfectionism and very high expectations of myself, and those high expectations of myself can sometimes get me into trouble. The inner critic can make it pretty tough to live up to those expectations of myself, and sometimes those expectations are not realistic.
>
> – Carolina, Vice President Innovation

We start by looking at the forces that drive perfectionism, and how this can affect wellbeing and relationships, before pausing to reflect on how these patterns may be playing out in our own lives.

DOI: 10.4324/9781003583080-6

The American Psychological Association defines perfectionism as "the tendency to demand of others or of oneself an extremely high or even flawless level of performance, in excess of what is required by the situation"[1] As a perfectionist, it is possible to read that sentence and wonder why that might be a bad thing! Perfectionism is often conflated with other more helpful traits – to strive, excel and hold lofty ideals can be helpful forces in our lives. There has been debate amongst academic researchers about whether perfectionism can be helpful, but this may be due to differences in how perfectionism is defined. Research supporting "helpful" perfectionism may conflate perfectionism with other traits such as conscientiousness, where we wish to do our duty well.[2] But there is a difference between the desire to excel and the desire to be perfect. Whereas desiring to excel can be motivational, desiring to be perfect triggers a cascade of cognitive biases,[3] for example:

- setting unrealistic and unrelenting standards
- selective attention to failures
- overgeneralisation of failures
- high levels of self-criticism
- all-or-nothing thinking

The construct of perfectionism can be thought of as having three dimensions: self-oriented, other-oriented and socially prescribed. Self-oriented perfectionism refers to the tendency to seek perfection in one's endeavours and to avoid failure.[3] Distress arises when a gap exists between the real self and the idealised self.[4] Other-oriented perfectionism is when these desires for perfectionism are turned outwards towards others, where there becomes an expectation of flawlessness and excessive criticism for failures from our loved ones and colleagues. This could look like expecting others to manage high workloads without complaint, or expecting our partners or children to be reasonable, nice and easy all the time, and this often leads to difficulties in social relationships. Socially prescribed perfectionism occurs when there is a belief that others expect us to be perfect and would be highly critical if we were not. This may be accurate (think of the child of a highly critical and demanding parent) or may be an assumption about the thoughts and expectations of others. The demands may come from (or be perceived to come from) a pressure to excel in the workplace, when studying or expectations from family and friends.

The impact of unrelenting standards in perfectionism and accompanying self-criticism has been well researched, with a large body of evidence showing associations with a range of mental health issues, including increased levels of anxiety,[5,6] social anxiety,[7] depression,[8] OCD,[5,6] eating disorders[9] and suicide.[10] Socially prescribed perfectionism is associated with burnout, job dissatisfaction and depression.[11] Self-oriented perfectionism is related to workplace depression.[11] A fear of failure or criticism can result in reduced risk-taking, creativity at work,[2] reduced productivity and lower efficiency,[4] lower tolerance for ambiguity leading to reduced workplace satisfaction,[11,12] an increased tendency to ruminate affecting the ability to relax outside of work[13] and burnout.[14]

But we tend not to talk about the pitfalls of perfectionism. The continual striving for excellence associated with perfectionism can come with outward successes such as praise and promotion. We tend to hold tightly to the belief that being perfect must be a good thing or we claim being a perfectionist as a "good flaw".

The perfectionist paradox

We may experience the pressure to excel in our working life, but expectations can show up in other areas too – perfection in our personal lives, and even in our work on self-improvement (including wanting to be more compassionate!). When our expectations of ourselves are a more ambiguous set of ideals, it can sometimes be hard to identify them. We want to be successful, admired, respected, funny, and likeable, and helpful, and loyal, and trustworthy, and caring and compassionate. All the time. We frequently hold ourselves to much higher standards than we do others. But the higher our expectations, the more likely it is that our *Threat* system will also be stimulated, as it responds to the perceived danger that we won't reach our goal.

We can think of high expectations as an over-expression of the *Threat* and *Drive* systems. *Drive* is there to help motivate us towards resources and is an essential part of our regulatory systems. But when *Drive* becomes overly dominant, it can mean striving for resources no matter what the cost. Under the pressure of these exacting standards, our *Threat* system becomes stimulated. Because our self-worth depends on reaching our goal, we perceive not reaching it as a danger. A host of perfectionistic responses are triggered – how we think, interpret our environment, compare ourselves to others and what we end up doing (or not doing).

All-or-nothing thinking occurs when we believe we can only either excel or fail, there is no in between. But remember, the higher the expectations, the more likely it is that we will fail. Charlotte, whose career is in the public service, became aware of the impact of high expectations on herself:

> I definitely think it's been coming from a high-performing organisation or being surrounded by high-performing people. I always have been very self-driven you know - I'm not ambitious, but I have very high standards of others and myself. And if I don't meet those high standards, I really give myself a hard time about it. So if I make a mistake as we inevitably do, because we're humans, I just won't let it go. I don't take criticism well, even the most constructive criticism in the world. I sit on it and just analyse it and criticise myself and all of that.
>
> – Charlotte Mason, New Zealand Public Service Manager

We may hold onto the unrealistic standard regardless of the circumstances, and when we inevitably make a small mistake, we catastrophise and blow it out of all proportion, deciding that there must be a deep flaw within ourselves. The key differentiator between striving to excel and perfectionism is that with perfectionism, the expectation is unreasonably high, and it is accompanied by rigorous self-criticism and rigidity.[4]

A clue that we are holding ourselves to high standards is the frequency with which the words SHOULD or MUST pop up. I SHOULD have done X. I MUST remember Y. When we notice our inner voice, it sounds demanding and relentless. We hold an ideal in mind, and when we are confronted with the reality of moving towards that goal, we are met with our frailties and faults that are part of being human and the inescapable reality of the conditions in which we exist.

Herein lies the perfectionist paradox. The higher we aim, the more likely we are to end up stuck in procrastination and paralysis as our *Threat* system causes us to freeze. Ironically, aiming so high reduces our performance, which then sends us into a blind panic. The most common responses when our *Threat* system engages like this are procrastination and avoidance, or excessively striving (behaviours), self-criticism (thoughts) and anxious feelings (emotions). While it is both necessary and helpful to have expectations and goals, they can tip towards becoming unreasonable and excessive. For leaders, this perfectionist loop can silently erode confidence, collaboration and adaptability.

If we do manage to push through and attain our goal (often whilst damaging our health and/or relationships), it is typical that we experience a fleeting (or non-existent) buzz followed by a sense of emptiness or even doom. The very thing that we rated as so important doesn't fulfil us after all. We may discount our success – *"I was just lucky, they were just being nice, they don't really think I am as good as they are saying"* which undermines our achievement and therefore diminishes our self-worth. As we feel deflated, and fraudulent – we don't FEEL all those things that people may be praising us for – we decide that the original goal obviously wasn't high enough. We go back to the beginning of the cycle, setting ourselves even higher standards to attain in order to feel good about ourselves. We are chasing a promise made, but it is false advertising – *"If I only achieve enough, I will feel good about myself"*. Just like the diet industry, long-term results are unattainable. If you disagree with me, consider this: if diets were successful, the multi-billion-dollar diet industry would not exist.

Mostly, because the standards are so unrealistic, we fail. Of course we do. We have set ourselves up for failure.

When we don't reach the standard that we set for ourselves, which is so important to our sense of self-worth, it feels terrible. Whether you failed at the promotion that hundreds of other applicants applied for or shouted at your toddler when you were trying so hard to be a "good" parent. It can feel awful to fail. As we fall further away from the expectation we set for ourselves, we then turn to the obvious explanation – ourselves. "*What is wrong with me?*" And self-criticism kicks in. When perfectionism is in charge, the seemingly obvious answer is that we didn't fail, but that WE are a failure. We personalise the problem. We launch into self-criticism. If you are a really great perfectionist, the chances are that you are excellent at self-criticism!

Pause here for a moment to reflect…

- *What high expectations are you holding onto?*
- *What are you not acknowledging about the challenges of meeting this expectation?*
- *What do you notice about the tone of voice that you are speaking to yourself with?*

Self-criticism is helpful! (Isn't it?)

Many people hold beliefs that self-criticism is helpful. People worry that if they aren't self-critical they will be arrogant, mediocre, or that they will let themselves off the hook, becoming lazy.[15] We may be so used to talking to ourselves critically or condescendingly that we barely notice we are doing it.

Our self-criticism may be our autopilot setting. But self-criticism has a dark edge. Like a sculptor working on a block of marble, we chip away at ourselves, imagining that we reveal our inner masterpiece. In reality, we chip away until we are left with a pile of rubble.

For some of us, when we were young, if we sought care and comfort for our suffering from a caregiver, we were met with criticism, indifference or threat. In the future, we may have a conditioned response to expect that we will receive threat and punishment rather than compassion when we are suffering. These conditioned responses can mean that we feel stuck or blocked when we try to access compassion for ourselves. These fears and concerns about compassion may mean that we avoid experiences of compassion. Research shows us that those who experienced little warmth or safety, and high levels of shame, in their caregiving relationships during childhood, had significantly higher fears of compassion, and higher levels of psychological distress, including self-criticism, shame, depression and anxiety.[16,17]

Compassion is first received from others (often our parents or caregivers). We may be socialised to extend compassion to others, but find it hard to give it to ourselves.[18] However, research shows that exploring these fears and expressing the grief that also comes from acknowledging the lack of received compassion can lead to a significant reduction in shame and self-criticism.[19] Becoming aware of self-critical moments and responding to them with self-compassion helps improve mood and increases the desire to repair difficulties and take responsibility for mistakes.[20] Conversely, self-criticism can increase despair, anxiety or depression.[21,22]

When we are under stress, struggling, unsure or uncertain, self-criticism is likely to show up. When our inner dialogue and self-view become overly harsh and negative, our confidence collapses, our anxiety increases, our productivity falls and we add additional suffering to ourselves. Evie, who works in broadcasting, describes how her struggles with eczema led to self-criticism:

> There was a time when I thought I could have shown myself compassion, but didn't – when I was overwhelmed with an allergic reaction.

> Everywhere on my body was covered and raging with a sore wet rash -- eczema – and that went on for months and months.
>
> I was so angry that my body could turn on itself, and that got in the way of being able to be compassionate to myself. At the time I was also caring for small children, so I was playing the carer role, yet I didn't do that for myself.
>
> It was obvious, I was having an allergic reaction, but I had some tests and nothing came up. So then it became a sense of hopelessness, I'm fighting the phantom, and it's the body doing it to itself. You know, it's an autoimmune condition, so you're fighting yourself.
>
> I think if I had chosen compassion and just sat with what was happening a bit more, I could have spared myself some of the pain associated with that condition. I think I could have advanced my healing much quicker if I'd had that realisation.
>
> – Evie Ashton, Broadcaster and Entrepreneur

Even self-improvement can become the target of our high expectations. We learn more skills, grow our empathy and insight, strive to develop ourselves and then find ourselves raging at the car in front of us when they cut us off. It's hard being human, with multiple, often competing, motivations driving our emotions and behaviours. Charlotte acknowledged the tension between professional development and self-criticism:

> Leadership training can focus on strengths and weaknesses, but there can be a lack of compassion in responding to our challenges; it can become just another problem to overcome.
>
> – Charlotte Mason, New Zealand Public Service Manager

Compassion offers a new possibility for change – compassionate correction. Self-reflection, honest appraisal and learning from our experiences are crucial skills for our growth and development. Part of that is acknowledging our habits of high expectations, perfectionism and self-criticism, and their true impact.

Pause here for a moment to reflect on your relationship with self-criticism…

- *What do you notice about your self-criticism (what does it say, and what is the tone of voice it uses)?*

- *If the self-critical voice were a person, what kind of person would they be?*
- *How do you believe self-criticism can help you?*
- *How does self-criticism affect you?*

Notice

Reflective exercise for perfectionism

Find a quiet space. Some people find it helpful to jot down notes or reflections as they go, or read the questions first and then close your eyes as you ask yourself them in your mind.

Begin by pressing pause. Using whatever practice suits you best, you may like to take a few slower breaths, or focus on your feet, or actions that you are doing. Imagine you are a scientist exploring the issue you are currently focusing on with curiosity and openness.

Describe the situation in which perfectionism is occurring, and try using a few short, factual sentences.

Notice what is happening in your body. Scan from your toes up your body to your head and notice any physical sensations. Name anything you notice without further comment or analysis. Just observe how you are right now.

Notice what is happening in your mind. When you think about this issue, notice where your mind goes. What thoughts do you have about this situation? Once you have noticed what you are thinking, bring your attention to how you are thinking. Notice the style or pattern of thinking. Perhaps your thoughts are critical, worrying or negative? Notice the tone of voice that these thoughts have. There is no need to change your thoughts or to get carried away by them, just notice them as they come and go.

Notice what is happening to your emotions. How do you feel regarding the situation? Can you name the emotion(s) that arise in response to this situation? If you are having difficulty naming the emotion, you may like to notice where you experience this feeling in the body instead. You are not trying to change how you feel, but rather to become curious and make space for whatever feelings arise.

Notice how you act. Tune into how this situation changes what you do. Perhaps you start acting differently, or maybe you stop or postpone doing something? Becoming aware, without judgement, of how this situation affects your behaviour.

Become aware of the bigger context in which this situation occurs – the work environment, your family environment, your society and culture. Notice what this broader perspective reveals.

Patterns might begin to emerge. Perhaps you are responding in a familiar way that may feel like a habit, or perhaps this response is new to you.

You have been finding the observer perspective, noticing and naming your experience. If you notice that the mind gets caught up in the story of what is happening or it begins to self-criticise, just come back to your breath. There is no right or wrong way, you are just observing what happens.

Take a few moments to write down what you have noticed about perfectionism. Practice using neutral language without judgement or comment.

∞

Empathise

If you are finding it hard to give compassion to yourself, you may find it helpful to know that you are not alone. Researchers at Stanford University worked to develop The Compassion Cultivation Training programme, which came out of a desire to turn the teachings of Buddhism and the Dalai Lama into a secular programme for Western people. The programme was developed by a team of Buddhist Scholars and researchers. Dr Jinpa, who was the Dalai Lama's English translator, was surprised to find that Western people often found it hard to be compassionate towards themselves – this wasn't expected, given that Western culture tends to focus on the individual rather than the collective.[23] As a result, the programme was adapted to focus on compassion for others first as an entry into compassionate experiences, before learning to slowly and carefully grow the ability to direct compassion back towards the self.

It can help to switch perspectives. Try to imagine an experience you're having happen to a friend or loved one. It can help us access the compassionate response, and, from here, we can practice turning that compassion towards ourselves. Maggie, a communication consultant, recalled a moment when finding a connection to her clients' experiences helped her find self-compassion:

> So it requires immense strength and discipline to be self-compassionate. It doesn't require all that energy for me to be compassionate to any of my clients or a family member. I do that with ease and love. That's easy for me. But when it comes to self-awareness, that's something I work on every day. Being self-aware - it requires massive work and looking at myself in the mirror and asking myself "Are you being authentic?"
>
> I've just been to a workshop. There was one exercise, and my brain just couldn't connect to it. I had to be really kind to myself to not judge myself. I saw everyone else in the classes got it except me. I said "This is really good, Maggie, because this is how your clients feel". Then I discovered at the break that three other people couldn't do it, and I said I thought it was just me. So, you know, in that exercise on that day, I had to keep on being kind to Maggie.
>
> – Maggie Eyre, Director of Fresh Eyre

If you want to test how helpful your self-criticism is, start by noticing how you are talking to yourself. Notice what you are saying and how you are saying it (what is the tone of voice?). Now imagine saying the same thing to a dear friend or young child.

Wow, right? What did you just notice then?

- *How would your comments, judgements and tone of voice affect them?*
- *What would the likely outcome be?*
- *What would be helpful about talking to them in this way?*

Empathise reflective practice

Help from our friends

If you find yourself caught in the trap of high expectations and self-criticism, try this exercise:

Close or lower your eyes. Bring to mind a loved one or friend – someone you care about. Imagine this loved one or friend is in a similar situation to yours. Imagine they are feeling just as you are feeling. Imagine listening to them criticise themselves. Bring awareness to how you feel towards them. What do you notice you would want to do for them? What would you tell them? Notice what tone of voice you would use, what your posture would be like.

Imagine yourself in your mind's eye, in the situation you find yourself in where you are criticising yourself. Now imagine speaking to yourself just as you would to a friend or a loved one. Hear the words and the tone of voice while you speak to yourself, as if you were a friend to yourself. Notice how this feels in your body.

Take a moment to think about this…

- *How will you feel about this high expectation in ten years when you look back on your life as it is now?*
- *What would you say to a friend who was criticising themselves in the same way?*
- *What helps you connect with your Soothe system when you are feeling self-critical?*

∞

Wise Action

Start by pausing to reflect on how perfectionism shows up for you, and what a gentler step forward might look like. Then, if you wish, explore the ideas that follow, not as tasks to complete, but as possibilities to support the freedom of being good enough.

Wise Action

Reflective exercise

Given the awareness you have brought and the empathy that you have cultivated, what wise action would be helpful for yourself or others at this time in response to perfectionism?

Sometimes in challenging situations, we respond with habits that are helpful in the short term, but that may harm us in the long run. Can we also bring compassion to these responses, understand that it is a very common human experience to want to avoid suffering, and that we are managing the best we can? In these situations, it may be wise to remind ourselves that if the situation is objectively safe, we can try to act the opposite of what our threat system is telling us to do.

If we feel resistance to the action, we might like to ask ourselves, is the step too big? Are we slipping into rescuing, fixing or avoidance? Is our action wise? Can we bring compassion to the acceptance that perhaps it can help to scale our action back or to take small steps for it to be wise, or remind ourselves of a longer timeline?

Sometimes we may not know what to do – the wise action may be unclear. We may need to tolerate this uncertainty. Sometimes the most helpful action is the action of non-action. This is an active non-action that includes continuing to observe ourselves and others, rather than practising avoidance. When our wise action is unclear or our capacity for compassion for ourselves or others is low, we may need to focus first on resourcing ourselves. We may like to consider how to call on both gentleness and fierceness to help guide our wise action.

We may make a mistake. With all our best intentions in heart, sometimes we take an action that doesn't work out as we hoped it would. After taking an action, we go back to Noticing and Empathise, to bring compassion for being human and making mistakes and learning as we go. It helps to generate compassion for ourselves that we are doing our best with what we know right now, and that our understanding may change in the future.

Considering the awareness you have generated, the understanding and empathy that you have connected with, what is the wise action that is helpful in this current situation?

Forgetting about the conditions

We may find ourselves resisting the idea that our expectations are too high, unrealistic or unhelpful. Sometimes a singular expectation on its own may be manageable, but we often forget two important things:

- The number of these expectations we are holding at any one time
- The conditions around us

To find *Wise Action*, it can be helpful to return to the *Notice* stage of the reflective cycle to increase your awareness of the conditions around you. If you take a moment to check in, you may notice there are expectations here, there and everywhere. Just how many are you holding onto? The volume of expectations we hold of ourselves, or that others hold of us, may just be too great. If you notice a traffic jam of expectations, ask yourself...

- *Where are these expectations taking you? (What is the consequence of holding onto them?)*
- *Is it possible to prioritise one thing?*

We may hold an expectation of ourselves but fail to notice the conditions in which we exist. We may want to pass the exam, but ignore that we are also working and caring for a sick relative. We want to finish the project, but we don't acknowledge that many components of the work rely on others to complete them, which are out of our control. We strive for the promotion and don't acknowledge the systemic biases that place hurdles in our way. This isn't to say that we should give up on challenges or feel hopeless in the face of systemic issues that are inherently unfair. Rather than that, it is helpful to adjust our expectations and assign responsibility for delays and setbacks where it is due. This helps avoid getting sucked into the labyrinth of self-criticism – when it isn't our fault and the outcome was never completely under our control. It can be useful to remember that mistakes are inevitable, and Charlotte explains how the compassionate reaction of her bosses to her mistakes helps her show that to others:

> I'm getting a bit better than I used to be, I'm trying to make some progress. I'm really fortunate, I've had wonderful bosses who have shown me compassion when I've made mistakes and this really helped me to do the same thing for others because I don't think it comes naturally to me. I think I can be quite harsh when other people make mistakes (in my head anyway) – I am judging you in my head, thinking you've done a really bad job. But I reminded myself

> that I must show compassion and people make mistakes and I've made mistakes. Now I am able to do that, because people allowed me to make mistakes.
>
> – Charlotte Mason, New Zealand Public Service Manager

Compassionate expectations

If high expectations are inherently tricky, then what do compassionate expectations look like? We can start to ask ourselves what a good enough expectation is, one that takes into account the broader perspective and comes from our compassionate selves. We can help ourselves and others by practising these more realistic expectations. There is a strength, a fierceness that is required to give yourself a break, to drop the incessant demands, to turn down the dial on where the standard SHOULD be. Refusing to be dominated by excessive expectations is an act of revolution. Carolina, who works in strategic leadership roles, emphasised the importance of "swimming against the tide" when we change a pattern that comes from our habitual responses:

> Compassion toward myself can look like giving myself a break – "it's okay, you're okay, it's okay to be". And so, one way that Fierce Compassion can show itself is by giving me permission to give myself a break and giving myself permission not to be perfect. I could equate giving myself a break in that instance to strength. Because you're fighting a habit, you're going against the tide. And that requires strength.
>
> – Carolina, Vice President Innovation

Take a moment here to explore…

- *What benefits would there be of letting go of the high expectations?*
- *What would happen if you compassionately amended your expectations?*

Compassionate correction

One of the most common concerns clients have about being more compassionate to themselves is that they will become soft, selfish, lazy and unmotivated (or something else along those lines). Usually, this is because it is easy to confuse being compassionate with being kind or nice. Yes, compassion may have elements of those things, but remember the sole aim is to try to alleviate suffering. If we switch from being overly self-critical – attacking and shaming ourselves – to being overly positive – a "delusional cheerleader" – it isn't necessarily helpful either. When we bypass our feelings to only dwell on the positive, we are not increasing our awareness, we are detaching ourselves from it. We risk developing a false confidence from this toxic positivity.

Instead, we can think about a continuum, with self-attack on one end, and positive delusion on the other. We are looking for a more compassionate way to give ourselves (or others) helpful critique and feedback, a compassionate correction. Charlotte observed that her approach with her team could be helpful in developing self-compassionate feedback:

> Often there are two categories of people in my organisation: those who really want to take the time to reflect and talk about what to do with it, and others who are just like, "no, no", you know, basically, "we've just got to move on. Let's just move on".
>
> I've tried to find ways. What do we want to celebrate and ensure that we're continuing to do, and then what are some things that didn't go well. And what are some things that were okay, but we might want to tinker with, as I always say? I genuinely believe they're equally important (what went well, and what didn't go well), but when I think about self-compassion – I don't ever do that to myself. I only ever focus on what went wrong.
>
> – Charlotte Mason, New Zealand Public Service Manager

- *What would a compassionate correction be?*

Compassionate boundaries

Remember how in Chapter 2 Jack Kornfield described:

> *"There is a yes in compassion, and there is also a no, said with the same courage of heart."*

Sometimes, to build fiercely compassionate expectations of ourselves and others, we need a compassionate "yes" and a compassionate "no". After engaging with empathy and connecting to our compassionate self, the yes and the no may be obvious. If they aren't, it can be helpful to hold in mind that the general orientation of compassion is to be helpful to ourselves and others. This may mean saying "no" to ourselves, "no" to our unrelenting standard that is paralysing us in procrastination, or "no" to our need to people-please and betray our boundaries. There may be a "yes" to things that then take us out of our comfort zone, and for this we need strength too, the fierceness to take a risk.

- *Where do you need to say "no" or draw a boundary (with others or yourself)?*
- *Where do you need to say "yes" (to yourself or others)?*

Courage and encouragement (small steps)

Have you ever noticed how the word "encouragement" contains the word "courage"? Encourage comes from an Old French word, "encouragier". The "en" is from the Latin "in" meaning "into",[24] "courage" is Old French for "heart, innermost feelings, temper", with the Latin root "cor" for heart.[10] So I always have a moment of delight, thinking that encouragement is actually going "into courage" – "into our heart". To find our courage, we may need some encouragement, to go into our heart and take the steps necessary to alleviate suffering.

If you have found yourself stuck in procrastination because of being under the self-oppression of excessively high standards, then you may need some courage to take *Wise Action*. It isn't any use getting out the big stick to beat yourself with after you realise where you are. Hopefully, having passed through empathy to access the compassionate self, it is already clear what is helpful. But the chances are that your *Threat* system is still on alert. This system is all about protection – it is doing its best to keep us safe from real and imagined fears. If objectively you can see the helpful path forward and there isn't any real danger to your safety (or danger that can be managed or mitigated), then to find courage, we can begin with small steps. Often, great decisions are waylaid when the initial step seems insurmountable. Choose a compassionate step. Something manageable, but also a fiercely compassionate step that calls on your courage. Take a moment to consider…

- *What would a fiercely compassionate next step be?*

∞

This chapter explored the second challenge regarding the self, identified by leaders: the unrelenting quest for perfection. Often overlooked as a minor personality trait, there is a dark side to perfectionism, which ironically impacts leaders' abilities to excel. Perfectionism triggers a cascade of unhelpful thinking styles and behaviours that can keep us stuck and reduce creativity. The self-criticism that accompanies perfectionism chips away at our confidence, undermining performance. *Fierce Compassion* can help us to explore how to escape the tyranny of perfectionism by readjusting our expectations and applying compassionate self-correction. The next chapter turns our attention to compassion for others who may be struggling, exploring the theme of how, as leaders, we can support them, without becoming overwhelmed.

Chapter 6 Summary – breaking free of tyranny

This chapter explored how *Fierce Compassion* can disrupt the rigid patterns of perfectionism and create space for growth, connection and humanity.

Notice

- Become aware of the inner critic and fear of failure that drive perfectionistic habits
- Notice how perfectionism narrows our perspective and disconnects us from others

Empathise

- Meet the perfectionist voice with understanding rather than judgement
- Recognise the protective origins of perfectionism, especially in early life experiences

Wise Action

- Take values-based risks that prioritise learning and authenticity over flawlessness
- Create internal and external conditions where mistakes are welcomed as part of growth

References

1. American Psychological Association. (2018, April 19). *APA Dictionary of Psychology*. Dictionary.apa.org. https://dictionary.apa.org/perfectionism
2. Sherry, S. B., Hewitt, P. L., Sherry, D. L., Flett, G. L., & Graham, A. R. (2010). Perfectionism dimensions and research productivity in psychology professors: Implications for understanding the (mal)adaptiveness of perfectionism. *Canadian Journal of Behavioural Science/Revue Canadienne Des Sciences Du Comportement*, *42*(4), 273–283. https://doi.org/10.1037/a0020466
3. Hewitt, P. L., & Flett, G. L. (1991). Perfectionism in the self and social contexts: Conceptualization, assessment, and association with psychopathology. *Journal of Personality and Social Psychology*, *60*(3), 456–470. https://doi.org/10.1037/0022-3514.60.3.456
4. Smith, M. M., Sherry, S. B., Ge, S. Y. J., Hewitt, P. L., Flett, G. L., & Baggley, D. L. (2021). Multidimensional perfectionism turns 30: A review of known knowns and known unknowns. *Canadian Psychology/Psychologie Canadienne*, *63*(1), 16–31. https://doi.org/10.1037/cap0000288
5. Callaghan, T., Greene, D., Shafran, R., Lunn, J., & Egan, S. J. (2023). The relationships between perfectionism and symptoms of depression, anxiety and obsessive-compulsive disorder in adults: a systematic review and meta-analysis. *Cognitive Behaviour Therapy*, *53*(2), 1–12. https://doi.org/10.1080/16506073.2023.2277121
6. Lunn, J., Greene, D., Callaghan, T., & Egan, S. J. (2023). Associations between perfectionism and symptoms of anxiety, obsessive-compulsive disorder and depression in young people: A meta-analysis. *Cognitive Behaviour Therapy*, *52*(5), 1–28. https://doi.org/10.1080/16506073.2023.2211736
7. Ferber, K. A., Chen, J., Tan, N., Sahib, A., Hannaford, T., & Zhang, B. (2024). Perfectionism and social anxiety: A systematic review and meta-analysis: Clinical psychology: Science and practice. *Clinical Psychology: Science and Practice*, *31*(3), 329–343. https://doi.org/10.1037/cps0000201
8. Smith, M. M., Sherry, S. B., Ray, C., Hewitt, P. L., & Flett, G. L. (2021). Is perfectionism a vulnerability factor for depressive symptoms, a complication of depressive symptoms, or both? A meta-analytic test of 67 longitudinal studies. *Clinical Psychology Review*, *84*, 101982. https://doi.org/10.1016/j.cpr.2021.101982
9. Stackpole, R., Greene, D., Bills, E., & Egan, S. J. (2023). The association between eating disorders and perfectionism in adults: A systematic review and meta-analysis. *Eating Behaviors*, *50*, 101769. https://doi.org/10.1016/j.eatbeh.2023.101769
10. Smith, M. M., Sherry, S. B., Chen, S., Saklofske, D. H., Mushquash, C., Flett, G. L., & Hewitt, P. L. (2017). The perniciousness of perfectionism: A meta-analytic review of the perfectionism-suicide relationship. *Journal of Personality*, *86*(3), 522–542. https://doi.org/10.1111/jopy.12333

11. Fairlie, P. (2003). Perfectionism at work: Impacts on burnout, job satisfaction and depression. *111th. Annual Convention of the American Psychological Association*. https://www.researchgate.net/publication/316249114_Perfectionism_at_work_Impacts_on_burnout_job_satisfaction_and_depression
12. Wittenberg, K. J., & Norcross, J. C. (2001). Practitioner perfectionism: Relationship to ambiguity tolerance and work satisfaction. *Journal of Clinical Psychology*, *57*(12), 1543–1550. https://doi.org/10.1002/jclp.1116
13. Flaxman, P. E., Ménard, J., Bond, F. W., & Kinman, G. (2012). Academics' experiences of a respite from work: Effects of self-critical perfectionism and perseverative cognition on postrespite well-being. *Journal of Applied Psychology*, *97*(4), 854–865. https://doi.org/10.1037/a0028055
14. Kinman, G., & Grant, L. (2022). Being "good enough": Perfectionism and well-being in social workers. *The British Journal of Social Work*, *52*(),4171–4188. https://doi.org/10.1093/bjsw/bcac010
15. Gilbert, P., McEwan, K., Matos, M., & Rivis, A. (2011). Fears of compassion: Development of three self-report measures. *Psychology and Psychotherapy: Theory, Research and Practice*, *84*(3), 239–255. https://doi.org/10.1348/147608310x526511
16. Matos, M., Duarte, J., & Pinto-Gouveia, J. (2017). The origins of fears of compassion: Shame and lack of safeness memories, fears of compassion and psychopathology. *The Journal of Psychology*, *151*(8), 804–819. https://doi.org/10.1080/00223980.2017.1393380
17. Kirby, J. N., Day, J., & Sagar, V. (2019). The "Flow" of compassion: A meta-analysis of the fears of compassion scales and psychological functioning. *Clinical Psychology Review*, *70*, 26–39. https://doi.org/10.1016/j.cpr.2019.03.001
18. López, A., Sanderman, R., Ranchor, A. V., & Schroevers, M. J. (2018). Compassion for others and self-compassion: Levels, correlates, and relationship with psychological well-being. *Mindfulness*, *9*(1), 325–331. https://doi.org/10.1007/s12671-017-0777-z
19. Gilbert, P., & Procter, S. (2006). Compassionate mind training for people with high shame and self-criticism: Overview and pilot study of a group therapy approach. *Clinical Psychology & Psychotherapy*, *13*(6), 353–379. https://doi.org/10.1002/cpp.507
20. Matos, M., Duarte, J., Duarte, C., Gilbert, P., & Pinto-Gouveia, J. (2018). How one experiences and embodies compassionate mind training influences its effectiveness. *Mindfulness*, *9*(4), 1224–1235. https://doi.org/10.1007/s12671-017-0864-1
21. Kim, J. J., Parker, S. L., Doty, J. R., Cunnington, R., Gilbert, P., & Kirby, J. N. (2020). Neurophysiological and behavioural markers of compassion. *Scientific Reports*, *10*(1), 1–9. https://doi.org/10.1038/s41598-020-63846-3

22. Werner, A. M., Tibubos, A. N., Rohrmann, S., & Reiss, N. (2019). The clinical trait self-criticism and its relation to psychopathology: A systematic review – Update. *Journal of Affective Disorders*, *246*, 530–547. https://doi.org/10.1016/j.jad.2018.12.069
23. Thupten, J. (2015). *A Fearless Heart: How the Courage to Be Compassionate Can Transform Our Lives*. Hudson Street Press.
24. *etymonline*. (2025). Etymonline. https://www.etymonline.com/word/encourage

7 The leadership balancing act

Fierce Compassion for supporting others

There is increasing awareness about the importance of leaders providing support to their team members.[1,2] We are seeing rising numbers of people experiencing mental health challenges and financial stress, impacting their ability to work.[3] Leaders play a key role in enabling them to function to their best ability.[4] However, leaders are people too. There can be a belief that leaders must take a heroic role – being amazing at supporting everyone else, limiting their ability to admit to their own challenges and stress.[5] In this chapter, we use the *Fierce Compassion* reflective cycle to explore ways leaders can support others effectively.

Challenges for leaders supporting others may come from several areas: a lack of skills, helping others in a way that unintentionally makes the situation worse, or limits on their capacity to help. Providing support to others in itself can be stressful.[6] Leaders may lack the necessary skills to provide support – it may not have been part of the training they have received, and depending on their life experiences, they may not be familiar with taking a supportive, caring role. Different leadership styles may also be more or less suited to extending care and support to others.[7,8] Being in a leadership position can be lonely and isolating.[5,9] Leaders can end up in a "CEO sandwich" between the staff and the board, unsupported from above and unable to connect socially below.[5] Taking on the stress of others increases their own stress load.[6] If they are struggling, it can be hard for leaders to be aware of how others are also struggling, which can limit their ability to respond.[10,11]

∞

DOI: 10.4324/9781003583080-7

Notice

> Being compassionate doesn't mean that you let somebody walk all over you, or accept that everything they do is okay. There is a self-care component for me that is really important. For me, being compassionate doesn't mean accepting that poor behaviour in the other person is acceptable. So I think being fierce might mean that you can respond in a way that is supportive, but that doesn't tear yourself down. Being compassionate shouldn't break me.
>
> – Carolina, Vice President Innovation

Let's begin by exploring the expectations placed on leaders to support others, and how this responsibility can impact them, before turning our attention inward to notice how we respond to these demands.

As a leader, we likely have others who work with us, for whom we are either directly responsible or who look to us for guidance or support. If those we provide support for are in distress, it can be stressful to manage. We may not know how to respond for the best, or we may react habitually or find ourselves overwhelmed by our own distress concerning their situation. We may have an urge to rush in to help or to run away. We may find ourselves wanting to problem-solve or fix the issue. Maybe we provide excessive reassurance. Perhaps we blame ourselves. "I should have anticipated this, prevented this, done more, or done something earlier. It's my fault, my responsibility". It can be hard to watch others suffer and doubly hard if we carry responsibility for them.

It's part of our evolution to care, to offer connection and support to one another. Depending on our culture and the conditioning around us, we may have absorbed ideas about the importance of caring for others from being the firstborn child, or the provider of the family, or from cultural ideas of the roles of genders.

Supporting others appears to be the very foundation of compassion, but what if our well-intentioned interventions actually increase the suffering of those we are trying to assist? If a child was distressed because they wanted to eat only treats for dinner, we wouldn't hand them a bag of sweets. When we respond by jumping in to fix issues, we may be reacting with short-term solutions that become long-term problems. Tolerating short-term periods of difficulty can lead to a long-term reduction in distress.

Karpman's triangle

When someone else is suffering, we may rush in to help support them. Our *Threat* system has likely registered their suffering as a danger. Karpman's triangle is a concept that gives us a way of understanding how we can take up different roles or positions in response to someone else.[12]

Karpman described three available positions on the triangle that we find ourselves drawn into – Victim, Persecutor and Rescuer. The victim role doesn't mean that the person is necessarily a victim, but it is more a description of helplessness, stuckness, and uncertainty in response to a challenging situation. If someone is in distress (the victim position), we may feel compelled to rush in to help them, taking the position of the rescuer. It is more likely that we will get drawn into the triangle if our *Threat* system has been stimulated by someone else's distress. While in some emergencies this can be a lifesaving response, mostly, those in distress are not actually in immediate danger.

The rescuer position can be characterised as rushing to solutions, advice-giving, problem-solving, or overly assisting and comforting the other to try to take away their distress. It can also be an unconscious attempt to reduce their own distress at the other's suffering. Charlotte became aware when responding to her staff how her own discomfort drove her behaviour:

> First I had to learn the fact that people expressing grief, fear or anxiety made me uncomfortable. And I didn't like it and I'd avoid it. So I had to learn that I couldn't avoid it. The next step was learning, like so many people I definitely get this from my mum, you want to fix people's problems. I was like that for a really long time. Someone would come to me upset or angry, and I'd want to fix their problem. In the last few years through studying leadership and watching others, I've learned not to be a fixer. Instead being able to sit with someone in their pain. To support them and hopefully support them in fixing what they can, but not trying to fix it yourself.
>
> – Charlotte Mason, New Zealand Public Service Manager

Sometimes, when we encounter another person in distress, we may react from the persecutor position, and we feel angry or cross with the victim. Perhaps we blame them for getting into the situation they are in, or are frustrated that they haven't taken our previously given (excellent) advice. When we disconnect from the suffering of others, it can lead to us "othering" them, seeing them as somehow different from ourselves. We may criticise or blame them. This may be an attempt to reassure ourselves that it wouldn't happen to us. We wouldn't have made the decisions that led them to that point.

When we take the rescuer or persecutor position, it encourages the person who's suffering to take up (or stay in) the position of victim. Inadvertently, our attempts to help sometimes keep the other person stuck in their victim position. While we may have noble intentions, when we try to solve the problem we're disempowering the person who's suffering from developing their own skills to cope with the situation. Of course, that doesn't mean we can't help and support them, but that's different from responding wisely to their distress. Perhaps you have been upset, and when you told someone, they immediately offered a solution, or you sensed that they were blaming you. It often feels disempowering and invalidating to be responded to in this way.

We may have a favourite position on the triangle that we find ourselves taking up when faced with someone in distress, but we can also move around the triangle, even in one conversation. Have you ever tried to give a friend in distress a "helpful" suggestion (rescuer) and then they snap at you that it's not helpful (persecutor)? You might find yourself moving from the rescuer to the victim position, saying something like "I was only trying to be helpful", and round and round the triangle we go.

Pause for a moment to reflect...

- *What sorts of situations would trigger you to take up a position on the triangle?*
- *What position do you most frequently take up on the triangle when someone else is suffering?*
- *What are the downsides of taking this position?*

We can escape these dynamics by taking up alternative positions. We can move from rescuing to coaching. The coach position offers support, but from the sidelines. We listen, and we may offer some well-timed suggestions, but it is clear that the other person is the one who is taking action. We can move from persecutor to challenger, where helpful feedback and reflection are given to support the other person to move forward from their victim role. We can move from the victim to surviving/thriving, where we search for new perspectives and skills that can be developed in response to a challenge.

It's all very well to be able to identify where we or others are on the triangle, but sometimes it isn't clear how to change positions. We can use the *NEW* reflective cycle to help us. When we engage our capacity for compassion, we help regulate this reactive response by stimulating our *Soothe* system. By coming from a regulated place, there is space to see the bigger picture and consider what might truly be helpful. Skills to support the coach and challenger positions are explored in the *Wise Action* section below.

Notice

Reflective exercise for supporting others

Find a quiet space. Some people find it helpful to jot down notes or reflections as they go, or read the questions first and then close your eyes as you ask yourself them in your mind.

Begin by pressing pause. Using whatever practice suits you best, you may like to take a few slower breaths, or focus on your feet, or actions that you are doing. Imagine you are a scientist exploring the issue you are currently focusing on with curiosity and openness.

Describe the situation in which the difficulty supporting others is occurring, and try using a few short, factual sentences.

Notice what is happening in your body. Scan from your toes up your body to your head and notice any physical sensations. Name anything you notice without further comment or analysis. Just observe how you are right now.

Notice what is happening in your mind. When you think about this issue, notice where your mind goes. What thoughts do you have about this situation? Once you have noticed what you are thinking, bring your attention to how you are thinking. Notice the style or pattern of thinking. Perhaps your thoughts are critical, worrying or negative? Notice the tone of voice that these thoughts have. There is no need to change your thoughts or to get carried away by them, just notice them as they come and go.

Notice what is happening to your emotions. How do you feel regarding the situation? Can you name the emotion(s) that arise in response to this situation? If you are having difficulty naming the emotion, you may like to notice where you experience this feeling in the body instead. You are not trying to change how you feel, but rather to become curious and make space for whatever feelings arise.

Notice how you act. Tune into how this situation changes what you do. Perhaps you start acting differently, or maybe you stop or postpone doing something? Becoming aware, without judgement, of how this situation affects your behaviour.

Become aware of the bigger context in which this situation occurs – the work environment, your family environment, your society and culture. Notice what this broader perspective reveals.

Patterns might begin to emerge. Perhaps you are responding in a familiar way, that may feel like a habit, or perhaps this response is new to you.

You have been finding the observer perspective, noticing, and naming your experience. If you notice that the mind gets caught up in the story of what is happening or it begins to self-criticise, just come back to your breath. There is no right or wrong way, you are just observing what happens.

Take a few moments to write down what you have noticed about supporting others. Practice using neutral language without judgement or comment.

∞

Empathise

Leaders often need to stay attuned to their team's wellbeing. However, some may be overly empathic and end up negatively affected by worry, anxiety, and overwhelm about the situation that another person is in. Some may be too busy themselves to notice how others are doing, or feel disconnected from their colleagues' difficulties. We can end up in a state of either over- or under-empathy for others.

Our ability to extend compassion to others is affected by our skill level, our capacity and the conditions we find ourselves in. To find a compassionate response, it can be helpful to explore our empathy for others AND self-empathy. It's not one or the other, but one AND the other. Empathy is understanding how another feels (or how we feel), but it doesn't tell us what to do with that feeling. We can end up in empathic distress if we are left stuck in the feeling component, whereas compassion moves us towards helpful action, and this sense of purpose is protective.[13] Here, there is a link between self-compassion and compassion for others. Generating self-compassion increases the chances of acting compassionately to others. For instance, an eight-week self-compassion training programme was shown to increase the likelihood by five times that people would give up their seat to someone using crutches in a crowded waiting room.[14] Conversely, when we are more compassionate to others, we can use this to grow compassion for ourselves. Charlotte noticed how her responses changed over time as her own experiences shaped her empathy:

> During Covid and with the isolation, for the first time in my life, I experienced an actual mental health condition; I got anxiety. The friends and colleagues who I told that I was experiencing this, it was really interesting to see how they responded to it. Those moments are really golden learning opportunities – you can see how people respond. I've always been a big ally for mental health and my organisation advocated hard for better mental health services. But having never experienced it myself, you know, in the last year, experiencing it first-hand – my level of empathy and compassion has just gone through the roof because I had no idea anxiety could be this bad. It has helped me support others going through it, and very much made me more empathetic and connected with it, I guess in a way that I wasn't before.
>
> – Charlotte Mason, New Zealand Public Service Manager

One practice that assists us in developing compassion for both the self and others is loving kindness meditation. This type of meditation is common in Buddhist traditions, and Dan Siegel, professor of psychiatry with a special focus on mindfulness techniques, adapted this technique for secular use in therapy. This technique focuses our awareness on warm feelings towards ourselves and others. Loving kindness meditation appears to help improve positive affect (feelings), while reducing stress and negative emotional states such as anxiety.[15] Loving kindness meditation helps foster a sense of connection to others, even with short practices of under ten minutes,[16] and has positive impacts on mental health.[17]

Sometimes people get distracted by the details in the meditation, thinking about whether you can wish health for someone who is currently ill or disabled. We can still convey a sense of wishing the best of health to them, given the circumstances they find themselves in. It is helpful in this practice to remember that we are not trying to manifest optimal conditions for ourselves or others, but rather the intention is to convey a sense of goodwill and generosity. Imagine that you are wishing someone well – notice the tone of voice that you would use and the sense of warmth that you would adopt. We can practice the meditation with a sense of kindness and generosity, rather than getting attached to whether the outcome of the wish is possible.

Empathise reflective practice

Loving kindness meditation

Find yourself a comfortable position, and repeat the following words in your mind:

May I be happy, May I be healthy, May I be safe, May I be completely at ease.

Repeat this phrase at least ten times.

Say the words at a pace that suits the sense of warmth and kindness. Focus on the feeling of care and wellbeing that you are sharing.

May they be happy, May they be healthy, May they be safe, May they be completely at ease.

Repeat this phrase at least ten times.

You may like to move between wishing yourself well and wishing others well, saying the sentences over as many times as you find useful.

Stay curious and notice what happens when you explore this practice...

- How does it feel to share this goodwill with yourself and others?
- Do you find one easier than the other?
- What might happen if you conveyed an equal level of empathy to both yourself and others?

We can practise switching into an empathic state with others. It is often our busyness and distraction that can interfere with our caring. To take a breath and be really present for another person is like changing gears.

Carolina became aware of how her ability to practice mindfulness led to growing understanding and empathy, rather than responding in an emotionally reactive way:

> Mindfulness supports me to be able to be more patient and understanding with that person's journey and where they're at. As opposed to where I would like them to be, or how I would like them to be. Mindfulness is absolutely core to my ability to respond in a healthy and helpful way because it supports my capacity to try to understand what that other person is going through. That can be really helpful as empathy is absolutely, I think, a critical component of Fierce Compassion. Because it's a tool to use in those types of situations where you want to be as supportive or as compassionate as you can. So empathy definitely is really critical. The impact on the other person when you can be fiercely compassionate, is that it allows the other person to really be themselves.
>
> – Carolina, Vice President Innovation

We may alternatively find that we leave ourselves out of the equation. We can become overwhelmed by their difficulties and find ourselves immersed in others' problems. Switching the focus to compassion for ourselves can help us see what is truly helpful, and remind us that we too are worthy of care, whilst we are caring for others.

- *What empathy can you extend to the other person AND yourself (not either/or, but both)?*

∞

Wise Action

Begin by taking a moment to reflect on what support means to you, and what your own limits and needs are. What follows is not a checklist, but a set of prompts to help you explore balance with clarity and compassion.

Wise Action

Reflective exercise for supporting others

Given the awareness you have brought and the empathy that you have cultivated, what wise action would be helpful for yourself or others at this time when you are supporting others?

Sometimes in challenging situations, we respond with habits that are helpful in the short term, but that may harm us in the long run. Can we also bring compassion to these responses, understand that it is a very common human experience to want to avoid suffering, and that we are managing the best we can? In these situations, it may be wise to remind ourselves that if the situation is objectively safe, we can try to act the opposite of what our threat system is telling us to do.

If we feel resistance to the action, we might like to ask ourselves, is the step too big? Are we slipping into rescuing, fixing, or avoidance? Is our action wise? Can we bring compassion to the acceptance that perhaps it can help to scale our action back or to take small steps for it to be wise, or remind ourselves of a longer timeline?

Sometimes we may not know what to do – the wise action may be unclear. We may need to tolerate this uncertainty. Sometimes the most helpful action is the action of non-action. This is an active non-action that includes continuing to observe ourselves and others, rather than practising avoidance. When our wise action is unclear or our capacity for compassion for ourselves or others is low, we may need to focus first on resourcing ourselves. We may like to consider how to call on both gentleness and fierceness to help guide our wise action.

We may make a mistake. With all our best intentions in heart, sometimes we take an action that doesn't work out as we hoped it would. After taking an action, we go back to Noticing and Empathise, to bring compassion for being human and making mistakes and learning as we go. It helps to generate compassion for ourselves that we are doing our best with what we know right now, and that our understanding may change in the future.

Considering the awareness you have generated, the understanding and empathy that you have connected with, what is the wise action that is helpful in this current situation?

Tolerating distress for ourselves and others

Our empathy can motivate us to ease another person's suffering in an altruistic manner. But our desire to extend compassion can also be motivated by alleviating our own distress when supporting someone who is suffering.[18] If we experience high personal distress in response to their suffering, our "helping" becomes driven by reducing our own distress. When the personal cost of giving support rises, we are more likely to move towards this self-serving motivation. As we increase our ability to be empathic to the suffering of others, we need to increase our ability to tolerate our own response to distress, so that we act more altruistically.

We can think of our ability to tolerate distress as having three components: reducing avoidance, acceptance and improvement. When we experience emotions that we perceive as unpleasant or negative, it is common to want to escape them. We may distract ourselves by keeping ourselves busy, drinking alcohol or scrolling on our phones. However, trying to avoid or push away the feelings often acts as an amplification.

The first step in building distress tolerance is to stop avoiding the distress. We need to be aware of the ways we distract ourselves and to have the courage to try a different approach. Next, we can practice acceptance of the emotion. It can be helpful to remember that challenging emotions are a normal part of life, which are helpful to our survival and wellbeing. Emotions are just information, and the information can be helpful to us. This doesn't mean that we want our emotions to be in charge of us – we experience emotions as waves of feelings that come and go all the time, so we wouldn't want to respond to every single one without some level of discernment. Acceptance and Commitment Therapy (ACT) uses a metaphor of seeing emotions like a passenger in the car or bus[19] – we can make space for them, and sometimes they might have some useful information, but the emotions aren't driving the vehicle. Because of their transient nature, it can be helpful to remember that emotions do come and go on their own; they don't all need a response from us.

Distress tolerance means making space for uncomfortable feelings and finding ways to support ourselves through them, rather than fighting against them. We don't have to like the feeling, yet we can practise accepting it and then try to improve our emotional state where possible. If we are suffering, we may like to try the opposite of our normal avoidance habit. For example, if we tend to isolate ourselves, meet a friend for coffee instead. We can also do something different: we can try distress improvement by being active in the moment, engaging in everyday tasks such as cleaning, gardening or walking. Alternatively, we can *Soothe* ourselves with calming activities such as having a shower or cuddling a pet, or doing breathing exercises. These improvement techniques are different to avoidance – we aren't trying to avoid the feeling, but are helping ourselves manage the wave of emotion, whilst acknowledging it is there. Distress tolerance is a dance between acceptance and improvement – doing all of one or the other wouldn't be helpful. We will likely need to experiment with what is helpful or unhelpful as we try acceptance and improvement strategies. This balance is echoed in the Serenity Prayer, attributed to Reinhold Neibuhr:[20]

> O God, give us the serenity to accept what cannot be changed, the courage to change what can be changed, and the wisdom to know the one from the other.

The form of the prayer has been quoted in many different ways, and if you are not religious, you may find it helpful to replace the word God with something that works for you. Evie emphasised the importance of making space for other people:

> To me, Fierce Compassion means you don't have to absorb everything that comes towards you. It can sit with you, but apart from you. I guess you might say it can tolerate joy and pain. So it makes a place to land for those things. Recognising what stuff is mine and having the strength to tolerate being wrong, or coming up against something uncomfortable. For me, it's also about being very honest about what motivates me, who I am, what I do, and why. Because, otherwise, growth is impossible. I think Fierce Compassion encourages you to sit with your real self. It encourages you because you can tolerate the reality of yourself. You can tolerate the reality of what's happening around you. You don't have to turn it into something else. You don't have to do anything. It's kind of like sitting with God, right? I imagine, and I'm not a religious person, but I imagine that when you die, if there is such a thing as God in heaven, you would go to heaven. There would be God, and nothing would need to be said,

because everybody knows. It's kind of like feeling very deeply known and understood.

– Evie Ashton, Broadcaster and Entrepreneur

Active listening

When we are anxious about the other person's distress or are under time pressure, we can find ourselves talking and fixing rather than listening. How often do we truly just listen to what the other person is saying, without forming our own ideas or opinions or commentary? One of my favourite exercises in group sessions is to take turns just listening to a partner talking about something that is concerning them. It is often enlightening to realise just how busy our mind is when we think we are listening. When we come up with ideas and suggestions, we aren't really with the other person, we are focused on ourselves. We can practise pausing and listening, not just to the words, but to the emotion and the intent behind the words. It's a great gift that we can give to those who are suffering when we listen.

One of the most destructive beliefs when we suffer is that we are alone in our suffering. It is a fundamental human desire to feel heard and understood, and this in itself is therapeutic. Perhaps you've had the experience where you share a difficulty with someone, and as you're talking, the situation becomes clearer in your mind, and sometimes a solution will form? This is what happens as our mind begins to regulate. Carl Rogers, founder of human-centred psychotherapy approaches, highlighted the benefits of being a non-judgemental listener to reduce the *Threat* response in the speaker.[21,22]

Listening is a form of co-regulation; when we regulate our own *Threat* response by slowing down and being present for the other person, it helps them to do the same. There is a sense of connection and trust that comes from being listened to well, and this fosters a deeper relationship.[23] Recent studies have shown that high-quality listening reduces both anxiety and defensive responses.[24] Indeed, functional magnetic resonance imaging (fMRI) shows that the area in the brain associated with reward is activated when a speaker perceives they are being actively listened to.[25] At work, leaders who listen skilfully are likely to help improve clarity within conversations, aid the development of novel ideas, and help the speaker feel connected to the listener.[26] A common complaint about listening is that we aren't *doing* anything to help. But anyone who has tried listening knows that it can be hard work. This type of listening is sometimes referred to as active listening, to emphasise that listening is not the same as doing nothing, but involves a specific set of skills, such as waiting for your turn to speak, maintaining eye contact, not getting distracted (by your phone or watch), and that your body posture and facial expression show interest and curiosity.[23] To maintain high-quality listening we need to keep three key aspects in mind – our undivided attention, a deep understanding of what is being said, and a positive intention towards the outcome of the conversation.[26] Bruce's own experiences helped him recognise the power of feeling heard by someone else:

> When I've had psychotherapy with a very, very warm therapist, I notice just how good it makes you feel when somebody's connecting with you. Yeah, the old seen, heard and understood thing is really huge. It's like Maya Angelou saying "It's not what you say or do, it's how you make people feel". I think if you're really in a compassionate mode, then I think you're making people feel seen, heard and understood.
>
> – Professor Bruce Arroll, Faculty of Medical and Health Sciences

It is important that behind these listening skills lies the motivation to be genuinely interested in the other person and their experience, and this is the key to being perceived as a good listener and to avoid conveying a sense that a tick box list of skills is being performed.[27] When we can step out of a "fixing" dynamic, it gives space for feelings – ours and the other person's. We give them the gift of support and great compassion without the burden and pressure of having to "resolve" it. Bruce comments on how this approach can be more effective than we might assume:

> They did this wonderful roleplay with a doctor acting as a patient and a doctor being the doctor. The first doctor was doing business as usual – "Yes, yes, yes, you've got this, you need to do that". He took longer to do the consultation than the doctor who listened and empathised with the patient, who finished in about 11 or 12 minutes. The other guy was still at it after 15 minutes, because things were coming up and not being dealt with, so then they came out in other ways. It was really interesting that it was actually quicker if the patient was seen, heard and understood. Really, the thing is to shut

up for the first three or four minutes, which is really hard as you're trying to keep the energy up and to get the show on the road. My whole thing had been learning to keep my mouth shut.

– Professor Bruce Arroll, Faculty of Medical and Health Sciences

Guided discovery

We may feel an urge to do more than just listen. It is really important to listen first before going into a more active role, to help ensure we aren't rushing into rescue mode. But sometimes we do need to offer a bit more. We can be alongside the other person, allowing them space to explore the issue, offering guided discovery. One way to help ourselves avoid getting caught in the rescuer or persecutor roles is to think about what a coaching response would sound like. Coaches are on the sideline; they might give encouragement and a few suggestions, but they aren't doing the actual task for their player.

We can move into a coaching role by focusing on core communication skills. There are many different ways to help us stay in the coaching role, but one that I find most useful with clients is OARS. This strategy comes from motivational interviewing techniques, which are counselling approaches aimed at helping clients create behavioural change.[28] OARS is an acronym for open-ended questions, Affirming, Reflecting and Summarising.[29] Asking *open-ended* questions helps the receiver to consider their experience and the options available to them. Whereas closed questions often only generate a yes/no response, and can make the receiver feel that there is a "right" answer, open-ended questions deepen the conversation. Typical *open-ended* questions start with

- What...
- How...
- Tell me...
- When...

Affirming others for their experience helps to validate that it is ok if they feel a certain way, it is understandable, and lets them know it's ok to talk about it. Affirming people improves their confidence and makes it more likely that they will take action. Here, it is helpful to focus on strengths and effort rather than outcomes. It is helpful to use "you" instead of "I"; for instance, "you worked really hard on the report", rather than "I am proud of your report".

We can use *reflective* skills to mirror back what we have heard (not adding in our own judgements, thoughts and opinions), which is helpful in two ways – firstly, it checks that we have understood the other correctly and gives them a chance to correct any misunderstandings; but it also is helpful for them to hear back what has been shared. Simple reflective listening involves repeating back or paraphrasing what you have heard, being careful not to add your own interpretations. I am sure you have had the experience of not being able to see the wood for the trees, and having our experience reflected to us helps bring clarity. After a period of listening and enquiring, we might want to offer a *summary* of what we have heard, which is a form of reflective listening that captures the whole conversation – again, good for checking that we have understood correctly.

A concern people have when using these skills is that we can end up condoning behaviour that we think is unhelpful or unacceptable. But we can acknowledge the other person's perspective by holding a non-judgemental attitude without agreeing with the content of what they are saying.[30] Validation is the ability to say that, from where we stand, we can understand their experience. As Nick, who works with criminal psychopaths, puts it:

> Validation doesn't mean that you are encouraging a loss of responsibility.
> – Dr Nick Wilson, Principal Advisor, Psychology, Department of Corrections

People are much more likely to engage in a compassionate and helpful conversation if they feel that their experience is understood and validated. It helps others to reflect on their behaviours, consequences and desired outcomes, as they aren't caught in a defensive response.

We give people a wonderful gift by witnessing them and being alongside them without trying to fix them. It sends the implicit message that we think they are capable – they have the inner wisdom to know how to move forward. Occasionally, we may feel that it is helpful to offer some suggestions or guidance (often, we probably find ourselves jumping to this immediately when we see someone in distress). So we must remain in the coach or challenger role when making our observations, feedback or suggestions. We can do this by taking a "wise guide" role, where we make our suggestions tentative, inviting the other person to engage with the idea (rather than stating our idea as a fact or superior to their own judgement). Helpful sentence starters for suggestions or feedback are "I notice…", or "I wonder…".

Compassionate boundaries

> For things I care about, like charities or something specific that I want to help move forward, I'll take action or raise money, or contribute in those specific areas – those are the priority areas. But I've learned that compassion for myself comes first. When I flip it like that, I get the best results in my life. Because I'm being taken care of. I am taking care of myself. Then I'm there for others because I'm more likely to be at my best. When I don't do that, I feel depleted. Because anything is fair game. So any news story or any type of emotional plea can become something that is a priority that I need to talk about or care about right now. It feels draining. It does feel like a burden.
>
> – Victoria Lucia Castillo, Storyteller for Thought Leaders

We've been exploring how rescuing behaviour may, in the long run, prove harmful; it may keep that person stuck in their victim position. As we explored in previous chapters, chronic overwork and perfectionism can also reduce our capacity to offer genuine care. It is not that our ability to be compassionate runs out, but rather when we are unsupported ourselves and experiencing burnout, it is harder to then access compassion for others. Carolina described her experience of supporting others:

> Breaks are one way to replenish compassion, literally. Recognising people can be very needy, and people can expect something of you. You know, if they're leaning on you, if you're an understanding person, you're a kind person, you're a nice person, you care about them. So, if they are asking too much, one of the best ways to replenish is to take a break. And, that's okay. That is actually compassion toward ourselves.
>
> – Carolina, Vice President Innovation

Sometimes, for the person who is suffering, and also for ourselves, it is most helpful to draw a compassionate boundary. This healthy boundary gives space for those who are suffering to begin to explore their coping capacity. For the boundary to be compassionate, the intention is to reduce suffering (for ourselves or them). It also gives us space to manage our emotional response and needs so we can be there for our colleague or friend in a genuine, wholehearted way, rather than from a place of resentment or over-responsibility. Here we are focusing on our individual capacity to offer compassion and what a helpful, compassionate response looks like. But it is an important point that the systems, the environments we exist in – whether in our work or home lives – may aid or hinder our compassion, and this is explored further in Chapter 10. We may be able to find empathy for the other person more easily than we can for ourselves. However, it does not need to be compassion for the other OR oneself, but instead compassion for the self AND the other. Sometimes, when we want to help, it's necessary to put our oxygen mask on first. Katerina who works with human-centred design processes in the public service, notices that this approach may not come naturally, and that focusing on how it is helpful can support us to practice.

> I think naturally, I'm very compassionate and understanding towards others. I do think for a long time I was more compassionate to other people than I ever was to myself. That put me in a situation where I'd often deplete myself in relationships. I wouldn't attend to my emotional or physical needs. I've only started shifting that in the last few years, to also make space for that same compassion to take root for myself. I just have to be sure that I'm balancing the natural compassion I have for other people with a little bit more of the effort that I need to put into being compassionate for myself.
>
> The benefit is that even if it takes a little longer for me to get to whatever the next stage is in a relationship, I feel safe taking risks again. I feel whole again. It's just a better part of me going to others rather than maybe the touchy, oversensitive, you know, tapped-out, depleted version. That happens to me when I give, give, give, give and care, care, care. But then there's not much left of me, and, at some point, it does catch up with me.
>
> I wasn't socialised to be aware of my personal needs that way, I just wasn't raised that way. So it took some years of practice to understand what the positive outcomes of doing that for myself were. I was

> not raised to be attentive to my needs above others, ever. That was just not a thing. And I think a lot of my female friends were raised to like that – to think about raising kids and all these other things where we're both giving and nurturing. But we never saw it – other women turning it toward themselves.
>
> – Katerina Daniel, Canadian Public Service Executive

Pause here for a moment to reflect…

- *What would a compassionate boundary look like?*
- *What supports you to draw a compassionate boundary?*
- *How does a compassionate boundary help both you and the other?*

∞

In this chapter, we discussed the challenges leaders may find when giving support to others, slipping into rescuer roles, or under-giving support and becoming critical or unavailable. Acknowledging the relationship between the self and the other person, and extending compassion to all, can help find a more balanced way to provide support. Skills in active listening and the wise-guide approach can assist leaders to stay in the coach or challenger roles, and encourage others to develop their coping skills. When we can tolerate our own distress, we free up capacity to support others. The *NEW* framework helps develop skills so that leaders can successfully support others without breaking themselves in the process. As well as a supporting role, leaders need to give feedback to others. Challenging conversations can be hard to handle, and we explore the need for courageous conversations in the next chapter.

∞

Chapter 7 Summary – the leadership balancing act

This chapter explored how *Fierce Compassion* supports leaders to care for others without losing themselves in the process.

Notice

- Recognise when care for others is tipping into over-responsibility or burnout
- Become aware of the subtle shift from supportive to self-sacrificing behaviour

Empathise

- Acknowledge the emotional toll of leadership and the limits of what one person can hold
- Meet yourself and others with understanding when support feels complex or messy

Wise action

- Set boundaries that protect both relationships and wellbeing
- Respond with courage and care, even when it means saying no or holding others accountable

References

1. Badura, B., Ducki, A., Schröder, H., Klose, J., & Meyer, M. (Eds.). (2020). *Fehlzeiten-Report 2020*. Springer Berlin Heidelberg. https://doi.org/10.1007/978-3-662-61524-9
2. Harms, P. D., Credé, M., Tynan, M., Leon, M., & Jeung, W. (2017). Leadership and stress: A meta-analytic review. *The Leadership Quarterly*, *28*(1), 178–194. https://doi.org/10.1016/j.leaqua.2016.10.006
3. Murray, C. J. L., Vos, T., Lozano, R., Naghavi, M., Flaxman, A. D., Michaud, C., Ezzati, M., Shibuya, K., Salomon, J. A., Abdalla, S., Aboyans, V., Abraham, J., Ackerman, I., Aggarwal, R., Ahn, S. Y., Ali, M. K., AlMazroa, M. A., Alvarado, M., Anderson, H. R., & Anderson, L. M. (2012). Disability-Adjusted Life Years (DALYs) for 291 diseases and injuries in 21 regions, 1990–2010: A systematic analysis for the Global Burden of Disease Study 2010. *The Lancet*, *380*(9859), 2197–2223. https://doi.org/10.1016/s0140-6736(12)61689-4
4. Skakon, J., Nielsen, K., Borg, V. & Guzman, J. (2010, April). *Are Leaders' Well-Being Behaviours and Style Associated with the Affective Well-Being of Employees? A Systematic Review of Three Decades of Research*. Taylor & Francis (Routledge). https://www.researchgate.net/publication/247511100_Are_leaders

5. Zumaeta, J. (2018). Lonely at the top: How do senior leaders navigate the need to belong? *Journal of Leadership & Organizational Studies*, *26*(1), 111–135. https://doi.org/10.1177/1548051818774548
6. Shapiro, J. (2023). Burning bright or burning out: A qualitative investigation of leader vitality. *Frontiers in Psychology*, *14*, 1–17. https://doi.org/10.3389/fpsyg.2023.1244089
7. Zopiatis, A., & Constanti, P. (2010). Leadership styles and burnout: Is there an association? *International Journal of Contemporary Hospitality Management*, *22*(3), 300–320. https://doi.org/10.1108/09596111011035927
8. Hubbart, J. A. (2024). Understanding and mitigating leadership fear-based behaviors on employee and organizational success. *Administrative Sciences*, *14*(9), 225. https://doi.org/10.3390/admsci14090225
9. Silard, A., & Wright, S. (2020). The price of wearing (or not wearing) the crown: The effects of loneliness on leaders and followers. *Leadership*, *16*(4), 174271501989382. https://doi.org/10.1177/1742715019893828
10. Dimoff, J. K., & Kelloway, E. K. (2018). Signs of Struggle (SOS): The development and validation of a behavioural mental health checklist for the workplace. *Work & Stress*, *33*(3), 295–313. https://doi.org/10.1080/02678373.2018.1503359
11. Pischel, S., Felfe, J., & Krick, A. (2022). Health-oriented leadership: Antecedents of leaders' awareness regarding warning signals of emerging depression and burnout. *German Journal of Human Resource Management: Zeitschrift Für Personalforschung*, *37*(3), 239700222211307. https://doi.org/10.1177/23970022221130754
12. Karpman S. B. (1968). Fairy tales and script drama analysis. *Transactional Analysis Bulletin*, *7*(26), 39–43.
13. Dowling, T. (2018). Compassion does not fatigue! *The Canadian Veterinary Journal*, *59*(7), 749. https://pmc.ncbi.nlm.nih.gov/articles/PMC6005077/
14. Condon, P., Desbordes, G., Miller, W. B., & DeSteno, D. (2013). Meditation increases compassionate responses to suffering. *Psychological Science*, *24*(10), 2125–2127. https://doi.org/10.1177/0956797613485603
15. Hofmann, S. G., Grossman, P., & Hinton, D. E. (2011). Loving-kindness and compassion meditation: Potential for psychological interventions. *Clinical Psychology Review*, *31*(7), 1126–1132. https://doi.org/10.1016/j.cpr.2011.07.003
16. Seppala, E. M., Hutcherson, C. A., Nguyen, D. T., Doty, J. R., & Gross, J. J. (2014). Loving-kindness meditation: A tool to improve healthcare provider compassion, resilience, and patient care. *Journal of Compassionate Health Care*, *1*(1), 1–9. https://doi.org/10.1186/s40639-014-0005-9
17. Petrovic, J., Mettler, J., Cho, S., & Heath, N. L. (2024). The effects of loving-kindness interventions on positive and negative mental health outcomes: A systematic review and meta-analysis. *Clinical Psychology Review*, *110*, 102433–102433. https://doi.org/10.1016/j.cpr.2024.102433
18. Batson, C. D., & et al. (1983). Influence of self-reported distress and empathy on egoistic versus altruistic motivation to help. *Journal of Personality and Social Psychology*, *45*(3), 706–718. https://doi.org/10.1037/0022-3514.45.3.706
19. Harris, R. (2008). *The Happiness Trap*. Robinson.

20. Wygal, W. (1940). *We Plan Our Own Worship Services: Business Girls Practice the Act and the Art of Group Worship*. Womans Press.
21. Rogers, C. R. (1959). *A Theory of Therapy, Personality, and Interpersonal Relationships*. McGraw-Hill.
22. Rogers, C. (1980). *A Way of Being*. Houghton Mifflin Co.
23. Weinstein, N., Itzchakov, G., & Legate, N. (2022). The motivational value of listening during intimate and difficult conversations. *Social and Personality Psychology Compass*, *16*(2), e12651. https://doi.org/10.1111/spc3.12651
24. Itzchakov, G., Kluger, A. N., & Castro, D. R. (2016). I am aware of my inconsistencies but can tolerate them. *Personality and Social Psychology Bulletin*, *43*(1), 105–120. https://doi.org/10.1177/0146167216675339
25. Kawamichi, H., Yoshihara, K., Sasaki, A. T., Sugawara, S. K., Tanabe, H. C., Shinohara, R., Sugisawa, Y., Tokutake, K., Mochizuki, Y., Anme, T., & Sadato, N. (2015). Perceiving active listening activates the reward system and improves the impression of relevant experiences. *Social Neuroscience*, *10*(1), 16–26. https://doi.org/10.1080/17470919.2014.954732
26. Kluger, A. N., & Itzchakov, G. (2022). The power of listening at work. *Annual Review of Organizational Psychology and Organizational Behavior*, *9*(1), 121–146. https://dx.doi.org/10.1146/annurev-orgpsych-012420-091013
27. Tyler, J. A. (2011). Reclaiming rare listening as a means of organizational re-enchantment. *Journal of Organizational Change Management*, *24*(1), 143–157. https://doi.org/10.1108/09534811111102328
28. Miller, W. R., & Rollnick, S. (2012). *Motivational Interviewing: Helping People Change* (3rd ed.). The Guilford Press.
29. Substance Abuse and Mental Health Services Administration. (2019). Motivational interviewing as a counseling style. In *www.ncbi.nlm.nih.gov*. Substance Abuse and Mental Health Services Administration (US). https://www.ncbi.nlm.nih.gov/books/NBK571068/
30. Rogers, C. R. (1961). The process equation of psychotherapy. *American Journal of Psychotherapy*, *15*(1), 27–45. https://doi.org/10.1176/appi.psychotherapy.1961.15.1.27

8 Courageous conversations Fierce Compassion for navigating conflict

In this chapter we explore the challenges, benefits and costs of conflict, disagreement and feedback. We explore how we can develop skills to respond more compassionately to others, and that interactions also call for us to understand ourselves with compassion. Leaders might notice a tendency to become reactive, rushing into tricky conversations, or find themselves avoiding them entirely. When we notice our own patterns and tendencies it helps us to shift to a curious, clear and helpful orientation that can guide us during these high-stake communications.

∞

Notice

> So, I will never forget this – I was giving a performance assessment with one of my staff and she was very high performing, had done an exceptional job and was to be given a high performance rating, which comes with the tiniest amount of additional money and things like that. But anyway, we spent an hour and a half or something with me telling her all the things that she had done well through the course of the year and talking about her capabilities and attributes and things like that. We spent 90 minutes telling her all these great things she did. But because, in our head, we always say we've got to give people things to work on and so you need to say there's a couple of things to work on and whether it would be helpful to discuss them. And she said yes, yes, that would be helpful. So I gave those points to her…

DOI: 10.4324/9781003583080-8

> And she just sat there and cried. Then all she wanted to talk about was that I was raising these things. Because in her mind, clearly, she had done something really bad.
>
> – Charlotte Mason, New Zealand Public Service Manager

To begin, we consider how conflict shows up in leadership and life, and why these conversations can feel so difficult, before reflecting on our personal reactions when tension or disagreement arises.

Part of the role of a leader is the requirement to have challenging conversations. As professional responsibility grows, so does the intensity and frequency of difficult conversations.[1] Performance reviews, complaints, grievances, disciplinary action, change management, redundancy and addressing employee requests can have enormous impacts on people's lives, and, when the stakes are high, the emotions tend to follow. Even day-to-day conversations can be fraught with misunderstandings, unspoken expectations and the impacts of power imbalances. Leaders can also be on the receiving end of challenging conversations from governance and other senior leadership, where stakeholder expectations have to be managed. In this chapter, we explore how *Fierce Compassion* can help us find the courage to have these conversations skilfully.

Of course, challenging conversations don't just happen at work – our private lives are littered with conversations that didn't go well or that were avoided entirely. The speaking style we adopt at work can also prove challenging when we bring it home; finding that you are not the CEO of your family can be confronting.

When it comes to difficult conversations, we likely feel uncomfortable. Even if we take our time and try hard to be nice, we may find others react badly when we try to raise issues. When we are on the receiving end of feedback we may become defensive. On the other hand, we can adopt a "rip the band-aid off" approach and rush through conversations to get our discomfort over with as soon as possible but may cause upset to those around us in the process. We are social beings, primed to care about how others view us. Going back to our evolutionary roots, we needed to stay connected to the group for our survival and so we react to information that suggests we may be rejected. These signals can stimulate our *Threat* response.

Pause for a moment to reflect...

- *When faced with a challenging conversation, what is your instinctual urge?*
- *What are the factors from your upbringing and culture that may influence how you respond?*
- *What do you notice about the situation and the conditions around you that make it harder or easier to have this conversation?*

The cost of conflict

Conflict comes at a cost both emotionally and economically. A study of nine countries showed that workplace conflict took an average of 0.9–3.3 hours per week per employee.[2] The average time lost in the United States was 2.8 hours which equated to losses of $359 billion in 2008, based on average hourly earnings.[2] Conflict can include workplace incivility and bullying, with a worldwide prevalence of workplace bullying estimated at 15% globally.[3] The impacts of bullying include mental and physical health problems, increased sick leave, complaints and litigation, as well as decreased productivity.[4] In high-conflict workplaces rates of employee turnover and absenteeism are higher.

Being able to handle challenging conversations and difficult interpersonal interactions well pays off. When we have conversations that feel constructive and helpful, they can lead to feelings of closeness, shared effort and increased productivity.[5] Even when we disagree or have to discuss something controversial, conversations can still strengthen connections, especially if they occur in a supportive atmosphere.[6–9] It is empathy that helps us to balance the task at hand with the relationships.[10]

Feeling heard and understood is a fundamental human desire, and the way that we engage in conversations as leaders presents an opportunity to bring out the best in those around us. Autonomy, connection and a sense of capability are key to wellbeing.[11] Self-Determination Theory shows that when these basic needs are met we are more likely to engage with others in an open and non-defensive manner,[11] helping us to pursue actions with energy and perseverance.[12] Adopting an autonomy-supporting leadership style has tangible benefits. When people feel deeply heard and less judged, they're more likely to share openly.[13] This kind of open, respectful dialogue reduces social anxiety and defensiveness and improves relationships and emotional wellbeing.[14–20] Paul, a leader in

Financial Services, emphasised the importance of training to avoid more problems:

> We're not really trained in those difficult conversations where they're still also connected. What I see a lot is that people want to avoid them one way or another, which sometimes looks like being a steamroller. You just kind of roll over somebody and then you don't have to feel the feels. Or they avoid it, and this perpetuates the problem, which actually isn't compassionate. If someone isn't in the right role, if they're not thriving. If you think about compassion being the amelioration of suffering… actually, it's perpetuating suffering by avoiding the conversation.
>
> – Paul, Senior Leader in the Financial Services Sector

Conflict avoidance

If we are raising an issue that has caused some difficulty for us, or hearing challenging feedback, we may find that our *Threat* system has been stimulated. Helpful behaviours for managing conflict can become conflict-avoidant behaviours depending on whether we are acting from a *Threat* system reaction or an emotionally regulated response. Consider how strategies such as avoiding, accommodating, yielding or collaborating are unhelpful and may add to conflict avoidance[21] if they are in reaction to our internal flight or freeze state. Compare this to an emotionally regulated *Wise Action* response that may include these as strategies. We may respond differently depending on the intensity of the conflict, which ranges from differences, misunderstandings, disagreements and discord to polarisation.[22] However, common to all these varying levels of conflict is that the first step towards resolving them is to communicate skilfully[22] Evie reflects on how developing communication skills as a leader can positively impact those around us.

> When there's that honesty with yourself, you'll know if it's your stuff or someone else's stuff. With that insight, you can then inform how you respond. You can go easy on someone if it's not your stuff, it's theirs. You go easy on them because you can understand actually there's something very personal going on for them at the moment. You can actually treat somebody who's having an issue more respectfully because you

> recognize it's not to do with me, and they're struggling with something here. Something has upset them. Because that's real for that person.
>
> It's the biggest gift that you can give somebody else – to be strong in yourself. Because then people know where they stand. Those sorts of people are dependable, they're reliable. They're the sort of people you're going to tell when you've got an issue or a big problem. Because they don't make it about them. That's just such a gift for the other person.
>
> – Evie Ashton, Broadcaster and entrepreneur

First, we have to come back to ourselves and *Notice* our own system responses, *Soothe* ourselves, and then take *Wise Action.*

You may like to reflect on...

- *What types of conversations do you find particularly challenging?*
- *What do you notice goes through your mind when you think about having a potentially challenging conversation?*
- *What happens in your body when you think about giving feedback?*

It can be helpful to reflect on these questions frequently, as the answers to these questions will likely change depending on the context of the conversation, the amount of support around you, and the person you are engaging with.

It is more likely that you will be able to deliver difficult news with professionalism and empathy if you have prepared and planned for difficult conversations.[23] There are many models for conflict management, but common principles include engagement and learning skills including emotional skills that require self-awareness.[24] *Fierce Compassion* goes a step further than awareness to include priming oneself towards empathy and helpfulness before considering the best course of action. The first step towards compassionate communication is to bring our attention to our reactive habits.

Notice

Reflective exercise for courageous conversations

Find a quiet space. Some people find it helpful to jot down notes or reflections as they go, or read the questions first and then close your eyes as you ask yourself them in your mind.

Begin by pressing pause. Using whatever practice suits you best, you may like to take a few slower breaths, or focus on your feet, or actions that you are doing. Imagine you are a scientist exploring the issue you are currently focusing on with curiosity and openness.

Describe the situation in which the challenging conversation is occurring, and try using a few short, factual sentences.

Notice what is happening in your body. Scan from your toes up your body to your head and notice any physical sensations. Name anything you notice without further comment or analysis. Just observe how you are right now.

Notice what is happening in your mind. When you think about this issue, notice where your mind goes. What thoughts do you have about this situation? Once you have noticed what you are thinking, bring your attention to how you are thinking. Notice the style or pattern of thinking. Perhaps your thoughts are critical, worrying or negative? Notice the tone of voice that these thoughts have. There is no need to change your thoughts or to get carried away by them, just notice them as they come and go.

Notice what is happening to your emotions. How do you feel regarding the situation? Can you name the emotion(s) that arise in response to this situation? If you are having difficulty naming the emotion, you may like to notice where you experience this feeling in the body instead. You are not trying to change how you feel, but rather to become curious and make space for whatever feelings arise.

Notice how you act. Tune into how this situation changes what you do. Perhaps you start acting differently, or maybe you stop or postpone doing something? Becoming aware, without judgement, of how this situation affects your behaviour.

Become aware of the bigger context in which this situation occurs – the work environment, your family environment, your society and culture. Notice what this broader perspective reveals.

Patterns might begin to emerge. Perhaps you are responding in a familiar way that may feel like a habit, or perhaps this response is new to you.

You have been finding the observer perspective, noticing, and naming your experience. If you notice that the mind gets caught up in the story of what is happening or it begins to self-criticise, just come back to your breath. There is no right or wrong way, you are just observing what happens.

Take a few moments to write down what you have noticed about challenging conversations. Practice using neutral language without judgement or comment.

∞

Empathise

Initiating the conversation from a compassionate perspective may require us to first attend to our own discomfort. A helpful way to navigate conflict is preparation for the interaction, and managing our own reactivity. Once we are in a high-intensity conflict, it is unlikely to be resolved until there is emotional regulation. Once we have soothed ourselves, we can then provide a regulated response, with a compassionate orientation. A regulated, compassionate orientation doesn't guarantee a "perfect" response from the other person, but it does make a better outcome more likely. We can't be sure how the other person involved will react. What can help, as we find the courage to converse, is to keep coming back to our compassionate self – the safe haven we can cultivate within ourselves. If we, despite our best intentions, get a difficult response, then we need to return to noticing and finding empathy once more.

Validate our feelings

It can be confronting as we become aware of our not-so-enlightened tendencies when facing challenging conversations. We may feel many ways, including being scared, angry or jealous. We are complicated beings formed by layers of evolution, childhood development, culture and experience. When we find parts of ourselves that we deem unacceptable, we can default to criticising ourselves for our response or shutting down.

Can we instead make space for these feelings, the "unexpected visitors", as Rumi calls them?[25] We don't have to like the fact that we get angry or that we would rather eat our arm off than have an awkward conversation with a coworker. But whatever feelings do show up, can we allow them to be there? Can we make space for them and get curious about them?

Our emotions are essentially a message system bringing us information. But they can also be fickle and impulsive, so we don't necessarily want to act on all of them. You might recall from earlier that we can have our emotions in the passenger seat of the car, rather than handing them the steering wheel. As we build this capacity, let's explore how we can stay with our feelings for a little while, rather than reacting right away.

Empathise reflection practice

Making space for feelings

Find a quiet place to sit or lie down. Bring to mind the feeling that you notice is arising in response to the challenging conversation ahead. We are going to explore this feeling with curiosity. There is no need to change it or get rid of it; we will instead make space for it.

When you bring this feeling to mind, what do you notice in your body? Imagine being able to scan the body slowly from your feet up your legs through your torso and arms, to your neck and head. Become aware of any sensations that you notice in your body when you hold this emotion in mind.

Whatever you experience, can you allow your attention to focus on one sensation in the body? Describe to yourself this sensation – how does it feel – is it sharp, or dull, hot or cold, fuzzy or clear?

If you had to draw an edge around this feeling, how big would it be? What shape would it be? What colour would this sensation be?

Notice if the feeling stays the same or if it moves and changes – the aim is not to change the feeling, but if it does change just allow it to.

Imagine now that you are making space for this feeling to be there. When you breathe in, imagine that you can send your breath into and around this feeling, acknowledging its presence. Practice this a few times, noticing the sensation, and breathing into and around it. There is no need to change the sensation, just allow it to be there as it is.

You may feel an urge to push the feeling away or to avoid noticing the feeling. Instead, just allow your focus to come back to your breath and gently imagine that breath wrapping around the sensation.

We have been making space for this one feeling in your body, shining a spotlight on it. Now start becoming aware of the rest of yourself, slowly wiggling your fingers and toes. Imagine broadening your awareness to include your whole body. You may like to give yourself a luxurious stretch with a deep inhale and exhale, and let go of the exercise.

Often, our suffering is increased by trying to resist or avoid feelings that we have deemed unacceptable. We can help reduce our distress by making space for these feelings, to allow them to be there instead of suppressing them. It doesn't mean that we need to respond to the feelings – feelings tend to come and go like waves, and the acknowledgement of the feelings may be all that is needed. At other times, the feelings may give us useful information and we may decide to act on them wisely. This is different to a reactive response to an impulsive emotional urge.

We are developing the capacity to create this compassionate self – a place inside ourselves where we experience understanding and acceptance. When we are exploring the emotion present we are doing so from our compassionate self. The compassionate self provides a safe haven that is non-judgemental and warm and with our best intentions at heart, full of care and helpfulness. We can use any of the empathy exercises from other chapters to help develop this compassionate self.

When we are working on accepting our emotions, we may find some are easier to work with than others. Because the habits and associations we form around emotions are often developed at a young age and are influenced by our genetics, our culture and our life experiences, sometimes we need some help to understand them. If you find the empathy exercises challenging or if they bring up questions that you would like to explore, it is a fiercely compassionate and wise act to seek additional support from a therapist who works with compassion-based approaches.

Making space for others

Once we have emotionally regulated ourselves, we can then explore our empathy for the others involved in the current challenge. As we have noticed our own habit patterns, we can use our awareness of reactive or avoidant tendencies to then check in using the *Fierce-Gentle* continuum. If we habitually avoid conflict, it may be helpful to call on the *Fierce* side of compassion. If we habitually become reactive in response to conflict we may benefit from drawing on the *Gentle* side of compassion. To increase our empathy for others it may be helpful to practice skills, including loving kindness meditation (Chapter 7) or orientation to helpfulness (Chapter 10).

When we are approaching a challenging conversation and we wish to engage our empathy for others, it can be helpful to try to put ourselves in their position. Once we are more emotionally regulated ourselves, we may find this comes easily to us. At other times we may struggle with traits we dislike, exclaiming "I would never act the way they are", or "I can't understand why they are being so x or y". In these cases, we can use a reflective exercise to identify similar traits in ourselves.

Empathy reflective practice

Making space for others

Take the emotion or behaviour of the other person that you are struggling to empathise with.

Now cast your mind back in time to find an example where you have also felt or acted this way.

For instance, if you find the other person to be unreasonable, can you find a time when you were acting unreasonably?

It can help to recall what it was like for you at that time, and to extend curiosity to how the other person may be experiencing the current situation.

We can also ask ourselves reflective questions

- How can you understand the other person's experience?
- Consider if what you want to say is necessary?
- Consider if what you want to say is helpful?

We can waste a lot of time and energy in the struggle of wishing that the other person was acting differently than they are. Instead, we can practice the radical acceptance of the other person, that for whatever reason, unknown to us, they are acting in a particular way. It doesn't mean that we have to like it, or want it to be that way, but can we accept that that is the reality of the situation right now? We can't control how another person thinks, feels or behaves, but we can bring our focus back to what we can influence – our own responses.

Aligning our intention to compassion doesn't guarantee the outcome we would like or ensure that the conversation goes perfectly, but it does help to activate the system required to make these helpful outcomes more likely. The invitation is for you to experiment with these approaches to see if they are helpful in your relationships.

∞

Wise Action

First, pause and reflect on what feels important or unresolved for you when it comes to conflict and communication. Then, you might explore a few practices that follow, not necessarily as the right way to proceed, but as possible tools for clarity and connection.

Wise Action

Reflective exercise for courageous conversations

Given the awareness you have brought and the empathy that you have cultivated, what wise action would be helpful for yourself or others at this time when navigating a challenging conversation?

Sometimes in challenging situations, we respond with habits that are helpful in the short term, but that may harm us in the long run. Can we also bring compassion to these responses, understand that it is a very common human experience to want to avoid suffering, and that we are managing the best we can? In these situations, it may be wise to remind ourselves that if the situation is objectively safe, we can try to act the opposite of what our threat system is telling us to do.

If we feel resistance to the action, we might like to ask ourselves, is the step too big? Are we slipping into rescuing, fixing, or avoidance? Is our action wise? Can we bring compassion to the acceptance that perhaps it can help to scale our action back or to take small steps for it to be wise, or remind ourselves of a longer timeline?

Sometimes we may not know what to do – the wise action may be unclear. We may need to tolerate this uncertainty. Sometimes the most helpful action is the action of non-action. This is an active non-action that includes continuing to observe ourselves and others, rather than practising avoidance. When our wise action is unclear or our capacity for compassion for ourselves or others is low, we may need to focus first on resourcing ourselves. We may like to consider how to call on both gentleness and fierceness to help guide our wise action.

We may make a mistake. With all our best intentions in heart, sometimes we take an action that doesn't work out as we hoped it would. After taking an action, we go back to Noticing and Empathise, to bring compassion for being human and making mistakes and learning as we go. It helps to generate compassion for ourselves that we are doing our best with what we know right now, and that our understanding may change in the future.

Considering the awareness you have generated, the understanding and empathy that you have connected with, what is the wise action that is helpful in this current situation?

Difficult conversations are a core part of leadership, yet many shy away from them. Whether giving or receiving feedback, the words we choose, tone of voice and non-verbal signals like posture, affect how the conversation is received.[26,27] The best way to manage conflict is to practice helpful skills as soon as we notice a difficulty arising, because once both parties are emotionally dysregulated a successful outcome is less likely. We may want to avoid discomfort, soften the message, or even skirt around the issue entirely. But true compassion isn't about being nice – it's about being clear, direct and constructive while maintaining a sense of connection and care. At other times we may find ourselves responding in a reactive manner, and reviewing the reflections in Chapter 7 may also be helpful when we are. Depending on our previous experiences with giving and receiving feedback, or how much practice we have had can influence how confident we feel, and there are specific skills that can help us to navigate the challenge.

Curiosity

Courageous conversations can involve giving feedback. It can be helpful to maintain a state of curiosity and openness. This is the opposite of judgement. Mindfulness emphasises the importance of curiosity and non-judgement and how this can help us to be more compassionate. Buddhist monk Thich Nhat Hanh suggests that the reflective question "Are you sure?", can help us to remember that it is likely that there are things we don't know.[28] When others feel our judgement it typically triggers them to shut down and become defensive. To keep the relationship intact and to encourage a sense of connection, essential to a compassionate stance, we can approach the discussion as a "team".

- How do we understand this?
- This is what is happening for me – what is happening for you?

Taking time to explore the issue we can both validate our own and the other person's experiences and move towards a consensus decision. Even when things haven't gone so well, Charlotte explains the importance of understanding why:

> We've talked about that performance review since and she said it was, basically, that what she couldn't say was that she was so uncomfortable with me telling her what she was doing well, that all she wanted to focus on was where she wasn't and then when I told her things she was doing badly all of a sudden she catastrophised. And I watched her do it and it was like a disastrous performance assessment. We both learned a lot from it.
>
> – Charlotte Mason, New Zealand Public Service Manager

Clarity

If we feel uncomfortable about communicating, we may end up trying to soften the blow with positives or avoid the issue, we hint or imply, we may go broad, or intellectualise the issue. Our discomfort leads to a lack of clarity.

Charlotte explains how clear feedback was helpful to her in the early stages of her career:

> When I was relatively new in my role, I had a boss who just did a superb job of pointing out some of my weaknesses. A performance issue that I had, which is still really around to this day is that when I'm unconscious if I have self-doubt, or I feel intimidated or something like that in the situation I'm in, I tend to overcompensate by being aggressive or putting a point forward too stringently.
>
> And so this wonderful boss and I were working on a project, which was full of all senior, very senior executives, and I was very junior, and I felt very intimidated. And the way I dealt with that was by being overly assertive. And she had obviously heard through her colleagues about this, and came along to one of these meetings with me just to observe and then afterwards took me aside. In a very compassionate way she gave me feedback and basically explained that I was doing a great job and my work was excellent. But the way that I was approaching people was hindering my effectiveness and ability to implement it. In my memory, she does this with huge compassion, but also being very clear and very direct about what I was getting wrong.
>
> – Charlotte Mason, New Zealand Public Service Manager

When we pussy-foot around trying to be "nice", our ambiguity is likely to cause uncertainty in the other. A quirk of our mind is that when we are uncertain we assume the worst. Being vague is not compassionate. Compassion is focused on the alleviation of suffering, not trying to be nice or liked. For example, poor performance may mean there is an area for improvement; if we are not discussing this it can cause future harm. We may like to set the scene, starting the conversation by clarifying that the aim is to be helpful, not harmful. Reminding ourselves that this orientation to helpfulness can give us the courage to start the conversation. In her work with senior leaders, Kemi finds that emphasising the importance of clear feedback is essential.

> One thing that is so embedded in me through my training as a Dare To Lead™ Facilitator, is "clear is kind, unclear, is unkind". I've worked with so many leaders who think that kindness is not

saying the difficult thing, which actually creates confusion, miscommunication, disconnection, lack of priorities and lack of respect. It is harder for someone to have to try and work out what it is that you are saying to them than you just saying it to them. Compassion is actually saying "You did great on this bit of the project, this is where we need you to step up", or "This is where we're not quite hitting what it is that we need". For me, Fierce Compassion is giving feedback. We all want to do our best work, and we cannot do it if people don't give us feedback. How we give feedback can be unkind, there's no doubt about that. And we don't want that, but we do want it to be clear.

– Kemi Nekvapil, Executive and Personal Coach, Author, Speaker

The greater good

Sometimes what can hold us back is the fear that we are going to hurt the other person's feelings. This can be so unpleasant that we would rather avoid the situation altogether. What helps relieve distress in the long term may indeed mean some short-term upset (for both the other person and ourselves). It may help to hold in mind our compassionate intent and to acknowledge that, afterwards, we may need to come back to soothing ourselves so that we can cope and tolerate any uncomfortable feelings that have arisen.

We may notice our vulnerability when we share our true thoughts and feelings or are expressing a need. It can be helpful to have a framework to use to practise this kind of compassionate and authentic feedback. There are many different models that you can use, but one that I like to use myself and that I share with my clients is DESC,[29] which has four parts:

1. Describe the situation as accurately as possible (just the facts)
2. Express your thoughts and feelings about the situation (stick to "I" statements)
3. Specify what behaviour or change you would like to see happen
4. Consequences – share the outcome if the new behaviour happens (positive or negative)

Imagine you are the leader of a team, where one senior member is being dismissive to the junior members in meetings, creating a negative team dynamic. A DESC strategy might sound like:

Describe

In recent meetings, I've noticed that when the junior team members contribute you sometimes interrupt them or are quick to dismiss their ideas. For example, in yesterday's meeting, when Sam made a suggestion you cut her off mid-sentence with a different idea.

Express

I'm concerned because this might discourage new members from contributing, which means we lose their input.

Specify

Next meeting I would like you to give others space to share their ideas fully. If you disagree with them, I'd like you to acknowledge their suggestion first or ask for more clarification before sharing your ideas.

Consequences

If everyone gets a chance to share their ideas in the meetings we end up with a richer and more valuable discussion. However, if this pattern continues then I will need to step in more actively to make sure that we have constructive meetings.

The feedback given in this way is clear and direct but focuses on changing behaviour rather than personal criticism. This approach can help reduce defensiveness and keep the conversation professional. We can also use this approach to deliver positive feedback and praise, which can sometimes be as uncomfortable as delivering critique. Many leaders find it hard to give direct feedback or struggle with some types of feedback or specific topics. It can be useful to practice empathy skills and then say the words out loud or find someone willing to role-play the conversation. Charlotte offered this explanation of how seemingly difficult feedback is a great example of compassionate leadership:

> But we think of compassion as just being constant kindness. So there are people who are not pulling their weight, or haven't turned up for weeks, or not really doing their job well, but I have to keep being nice. But when we talk about compassion, it's not actually about just being nice because if someone is consistently underperforming then compassion can be helping someone to either see that and move through it or to build a capability. That's compassion.
>
> – Charlotte Mason, New Zealand Public Service Manager

Receiving feedback

It is not just what is said that matters, or how it's said, but also the way we listen that matters. We reflected on listening to others in Chapter 7; here we look at the benefits of receiving feedback. Johari's Window[30] is a way of conceptualising different parts of our awareness and illustrates why being open to feedback is helpful. In Johari's Window, there are four quadrants. The first quadrant is the "open" space where we are aware of our values, behaviours and ways of being in the world, and of which others are also aware. The second quadrant, "hidden", represents parts of ourselves that we know, but that others are unaware of. Perhaps these parts are attitudes that we don't feel so proud of or are worried about being judged by, but they can also be ways we perceive ourselves that others don't. The third quadrant, "blind spot", is an area where others observe things about us that we are not aware of – habits and patterns that are not in our consciousness but that others witness. The fourth quadrant, "unknown", is for motivations or behaviours that we don't notice in ourselves and that others don't either. We can use the four panes of this window to think about the benefit of courageous conversations. As we both disclose more information about ourselves and receive more feedback from others about ourselves, the size of the open quadrant increases, while the hidden, blind spot and unknown quadrants decrease. Within the open quadrant, we feel free to be ourselves, confident in knowing both who we are and how others see us.

When we receive feedback from others, it can be helpful to clarify it and let it sit with us for a little while. We are looking to see which parts may be true and helpful, and whether any other parts may be about the other person and not to do with us. Of course, there is no rule about where this distinction lies – we can only do our best and proceed with awareness, openness and our compassionate selves.

We've been thinking about challenging conversations and giving clear feedback, and it is helpful to remember that the feedback can also be sharing a positive experience. Sometimes people find this just as uncomfortable as sharing a problem. Charlotte recognised a shift in herself when she became a leader:

> I'd like to think about compassion in both directions. In terms of leaders we've talked a lot about showing compassion to our staff. What I notice now I am a leader, is showing compassion to our leaders as well. We have an organisation where we tend to always look up and blame. There is a problem and you are the leader, therefore it is your fault, you need to fix this. Now I see leadership is difficult, so have compassion for your leaders. They will make mistakes and as leaders sometimes you just see it differently. I would like to see as we develop our organisation and elsewhere, that compassion is a two-way situation.
>
> – Charlotte Mason, New Zealand Public Service Manager

Rupture and repair

We are human. Of course, along the way, we make mistakes. We make assumptions and rush to judgements. We can be so sure that the negative look they gave us during our presentation meant (insert your own example), but now we hear they had stomach aches and were grimacing in pain.

We made an assumption and jumped to a conclusion. Now, suddenly we can see the broader picture, and the unseen part becomes clear. We made a mistake. We don't need to over-explain. Our apology can also be clear and kind. We are sorry, we made a mistake or an incorrect assumption. We can thank them for clarifying. We may like to add that next time we will enquire first rather than thinking the worst.

Courageous communication requires us to sit with our discomfort, that no matter how hard we try we will inevitably get it wrong sometimes, make mistakes and upset people. Katerina found strength in the ability to accept mistakes:

> It is courage, because trying something means that you're risking failure, or making a mistake. At first, I was so afraid to make a mistake that I wasn't part of the conversation and today I see it in others. It's the fear of 'I don't want to offend, I don't want to hurt', but if we can rise and push a little bit past that. Like labour you push through the pain and something new awaits at the end. I do think that's the fierceness, the bravery to believe that there's something more, something better on the other side, rather than hanging on to fear that brings us into a sort of comfort but stuck in inaction.
>
> – Katerina Daniel, Canadian Public Service Executive

Thinking again about our tendencies to avoid our discomfort or those of the other person when faced with a challenging situation, it can be helpful to remember that we are doing this in the service of being genuinely helpful. At the heart of that helpfulness is a connection to the other person. The relationship is not just important during the conversation, but also in an ongoing way. Paul explains that it is much easier to have difficult conversations if we already have a foundation of trust built on open and honest communication:

> Having a human connection allowed the challenging conversations to not feel so challenging. I liked meeting with people regularly and in a semi-formal setting as it helped me to understand who they are as well as where they were at and what they were doing work-wise. So any sort of challenges would become fairly obvious. But also it meant that I built a relationship with them and that's the key word – relationship. To be able to say "This isn't looking so great", or "This isn't good", or "Hey, why did you do that?", and for it to come from a position of support, rather than oversight and reprimand.
>
> – Paul, Senior Leader in the Financial Services Sector

While we may focus on the risks of having the difficult conversation we likely end up ignoring the risks of NOT having the difficult conversation. It can be helpful to reflect on the dangers of not giving difficult feedback:

> Two things happen – one is that other people see that person's performance or issues, and more damaging than that is they see the

> lack of action from those who should take action. So what ends up happening is you go from one challenge to two or more. My feeling above all is that regular, authentic conversations that are equitable are what is so vital – you know, in business, in your life, in your relationships.
>
> – Paul, Senior Leader in the Financial Services Sector

- *What might happen if we don't give feedback?*
- *What might **not** happen if we don't give feedback?*
- *How will we feel in the long term if we don't give this feedback?*

∞

Courageous conversations are compassion in action. It takes courage to step into the uncomfortable space of doing something differently. We live in a busy world and may find ourselves rushing into tricky conversations with little self-preparation or avoiding the issue completely. *Fierce Compassion* offers practical steps so we can navigate conversations skilfully. We can lean into the *NEW* reflective learning cycle as we face different relational challenges. Who knows where your courageous conversations will take you? Each one is a chance to grow connections with others, and with yourself. In this chapter, we've been focusing on compassion for our conversations with others, in the next two chapters we explore the systems we live in and how *Fierce Compassion* can help us navigate the challenges.

∞

Chapter 8 Summary – courageous conversations

This chapter explored how *Fierce Compassion* can help us approach conflict and feedback with clarity, courage and care.

Notice

- Become aware of your physiological and emotional responses to conflict
- Notice habitual patterns like avoidance, defensiveness or domination

Empathise

- Stay curious about what might be happening beneath the surface – for yourself and others
- Understand how power dynamics, identity and past experiences shape reactions

Wise Action

- Practice honest, values-aligned communication even when it feels uncomfortable
- Choose when to engage, pause or walk away with discernment and mutual respect

References

1. Prober, C. G., Grousbeck, H. I., & Meehan, W. F. (2022). Managing difficult conversations: An essential communication skill for all professionals and leaders. *Academic Medicine, Publish Ahead of Print, 97*(7), 973–976. https://doi.org/10.1097/acm.0000000000004692
2. Hayes, J. (2008). *Workplace Conflict and How Businesses Can Harness it to Thrive*. CCP Global Human Capital Report, Maximizing People Performance. https://www.themyersbriggs.com/-/media/f39a8b7fb4fe4daface552d9f485c825.ashx
3. Nielsen, M. B., Matthiesen, S. B., & Einarsen, S. (2010). The impact of methodological moderators on prevalence rates of workplace bullying. A meta-analysis. *Journal of Occupational and organizational Psychology, 83*(4), 955–979.
4. Nielsen, M. B., Einarsen, S. V., Parveen, S., & Rosander, M. (2024). Witnessing workplace bullying — A systematic review and meta-analysis of individual health and well-being outcomes. *Aggression and Violent Behavior, 75*, 101908. https://doi.org/10.1016/j.avb.2023.101908
5. Reis, H. T. (2017). The interpersonal process model of intimacy: Maintaining intimacy through self-disclosure and responsiveness. In J. Fitzgerald (Ed.), *Foundations for couples' therapy: Research for the real world* (pp. 216–225). Routledge/Taylor & Francis Group. https://doi.org/10.4324/9781315678610-22
6. Katriel, T. (1992). Allen Grimshaw (ed.), Conflict talk: Sociolinguistic investigations of arguments in conversations. Cambridge: Cambridge University Press, 1990. Pp. x + 356. *Language in Society, 21*(2), 312–316. https://doi.org/10.1017/s0047404500015347

7. Zhang, J., Chang, J. P., Cristian Danescu-Niculescu-Mizil, Dixon, L., Hua, Y., Taraborelli, D., & Thain, N. (2018). Conversations gone awry: Detecting early signs of conversational failure. *ArXiv (Cornell University)*. https://doi.org/10.18653/v1/p18-1125
8. Stone, D., Patton, B., & Heen, S. (2010). *Difficult Conversations: How to Discuss What Matters Most*. Portfolio Penguin.
9. Tjosvold, D., Wong, A. S. H., & Feng Chen, N. Y. (2014). Constructively managing conflicts in organizations. *Annual Review of Organizational Psychology and Organizational Behavior*, *1*(1), 545–568. https://doi.org/10.1146/annurev-orgpsych-031413-091306
10. Bradley, G. L., & Campbell, A. C. (2016). Managing difficult workplace conversations. *International Journal of Business Communication*, *53*(4), 443–464. https://doi.org/10.1177/2329488414525468
11. Weinstein, N., Przybylski, A. K., & Ryan, R. M. (2013). The integrative process. *Current Directions in Psychological Science*, *22*(1), 69–74. https://doi.org/10.1177/0963721412468001
12. Van den Broeck, A., Vansteenkiste, M., De Witte, H., & Lens, W. (2008). Explaining the relationships between job characteristics, burnout, and engagement: The role of basic psychological need satisfaction. *Work & Stress*, *22*(3), 277–294. https://doi.org/10.1080/02678370802393672
13. Deci, E. L., & Ryan, R. M. (2014). Autonomy and need satisfaction in close relationships: Relationships motivation theory. *Human Motivation and Interpersonal Relationships*, 53–73. https://doi.org/10.1007/978-94-017-8542-6_3
14. Legate, N., Ngyuen, T., Weinstein, N., Moller, A., Legault, L., Vally, Z., Tajchman, Z., Zsido, A. N., Zrimsek, M., Chen, Z., Ziano, I., Gialitaki, Z., Ceary, C. D., Jang, Y., Lin, Y., Kunisato, Y., Yamada, Y., Xiao, Q., Jiang, X., & Du, X. (2022). A global experiment on motivating social distancing during the COVID-19 pandemic. *Proceedings of the National Academy of Sciences*, *119*(22), e2111091119. https://doi.org/10.1073/pnas.2111091119
15. Castro, D. R., Kluger, A. N., & Itzchakov, G. (2016). Does avoidance-attachment style attenuate the benefits of being listened to? *European Journal of Social Psychology*, *46*(6), 762–775. https://doi.org/10.1002/ejsp.2185
16. Rogers, C. R. (1959). *A Theory of Therapy, Personality, and Interpersonal Relationships*. McGraw-Hill.
17. Rogers, C. (1980). *A Way of Being*. Houghton Mifflin Co.
18. Itzchakov, G., & Kluger, A. N. (2017). The listening circle: A simple tool to enhance listening and reduce extremism among employees. *Organizational Dynamics*, *46*(4), 220–226. https://doi.org/10.1016/j.orgdyn.2017.05.005
19. Itzchakov, G. (2020). Can listening training empower service employees? The mediating roles of anxiety and perspective-taking. *European Journal of Work and Organizational Psychology*, *29*(6), 1–15. https://doi.org/10.1080/1359432x.2020.1776701

20. Broockman, D., & Kalla, J. (2016). Durably Reducing transphobia: A field experiment on door-to-door canvassing. *Science*, *352*(6282), 220–224. https://doi.org/10.1126/science.aad9713
21. Weinstein, N., Itzchakov, G., & Legate, N. (2022). The motivational value of listening during intimate and difficult conversations. *Social and Personality Psychology Compass*, *16*(2), 1–14. https://doi.org/10.1111/spc3.12651
22. Ryan, R. M., Deci, E. L., Vansteenkiste, M., & Soenens, B. (2021). Building a science of motivated persons: Self-determination theory's empirical approach to human experience and the regulation of behavior. *Motivation Science*, *7*(2), 97–110. https://doi.org/10.1037/mot0000194
23. Quinn, R. (2021). *Becoming a Master Manager: A Competing Values Approach*. John Wiley.
24. Runde, C. E., & Flanagan, T. A. (2010). *Developing Your Conflict Competence: A Hands-On Guide for Leaders, Managers, Facilitators and Teams*. Jossey-Bass; Center for Creative Leadership.
25. Jalāl Al-Dīn Rūmī, Maulana. (2004). *Selected Poems* (C. Barks & J. Moyne, Eds.). Penguin.
26. Holtgraves, T. (2010). Social psychology and language: Words, utterances, and conversations. In S. T. Fiske, D. T. Gilbert, & G. Lindzey (Eds.), *Handbook of Social Psychology* (pp. 1386–1422). John Wiley.
27. Monaghan, L. (2012). *Conversations: The Link between Words and the World* (pp. 152–156). Blackwell.
28. Hanh, T. N. (2006). *True Love*. Shambhala Publications.
29. Bower, G. H., & Bower, S. A. (2004). *Asserting Yourself: A Practical Guide for Positive Change*. Da Capo Life Long.
30. Luft, J., & Ingham, H. (1955). The Johari window: A graphic model of interpersonal awareness. *Proceedings of the Western Training Laboratory in Group Development*. University of California.

9 Bridging the divide

Fierce Compassion for embracing diversity

We've explored how to lead with compassion for ourselves and others. But compassion doesn't exist in a vacuum, it's shaped by the systems we're part of. In this chapter, we turn our attention to diversity, and in the next, to the wider organisational systems that can either support or suppress compassion. Embracing diversity is a value many leaders endorse – but when it comes to turning that value into action, the path can feel unclear, fraught or even unsafe.

Over the previous decades, trends in increasing economic globalisation and technological development have driven increased diversity in the workplace.[1–5] Discrimination and inequality.[6–9] have come with these changes, requiring leaders to practice inclusivity,[10] and, while there have been improvements, challenges remain. There are many benefits to inclusivity, including improved individual and organisational performance,[11–15] increased innovation,[1,16,17] higher productivity[4] and creativity, and enhanced marketing and recruitment opportunities.[18] Inclusivity can also be protective against events such as loss of personnel and discrimination complaints.[19] Many factors can help improve inclusive practices,[20–24] but leaders themselves can make the biggest difference.[25–28] In this chapter, we explore how *Fierce Compassion* can help leaders embrace inclusivity in practical steps.

∞

DOI: 10.4324/9781003583080-9

Notice

> It's more allowing dignity for yourself, and allowing respect and dignity for the other. So allowing people to remain intact. You don't have to dismantle people to hold yourself.
>
> I think that compassion is something that will allow us to tolerate diversity. Because you're making room for something else. You don't have to fill the space. You can tolerate others.
>
> – Evie Ashton, Broadcaster and entrepreneur

We begin by looking at the systems and cultural contexts we live in, and how they influence our understanding of difference and belonging, before reflecting on our own experience within those systems.

In current usage, the word diversity most likely brings to mind the important work of breaking down harmful prejudicial processes and systems that disadvantage groups of people often based on their ethnicity, culture or religion. Because of the strong opinions surrounding this issue, the word diversity itself can become misconstrued. The *Cambridge Dictionary* defines diversity as[29]

- The fact of many different types of things or people being included in something; a range of different things or people
- The fact that there are many different ideas or opinions about something

While current usage often focuses on group-based inequities, this definition reminds us that diversity at its core is about difference and variety. How we relate to difference is central to our capacity for compassion. In the workplace, Diversity, Equity and Inclusion (DEI) programmes have both increased awareness and also faced backlash. One approach, through a compassionate lens, is to try to understand part of the problem as a lack of understanding of our inherent biases (*Noticing* and *Empathise*) and underdeveloped skills (*Wise Action*) for managing them.

Before we can think about what skills are useful, first we need to notice our responses to variety and difference. We can be different from each other in so many ways – race, gender, ethnicity, age, personality, cognitive style, education, spiritual practice, sexual orientation, our background[4] and even what sports team we support. Some of these differences have been used to justify acts of great harm, but they also add to the rich variety of what it means to be human.

As leaders, it is helpful to reflect on what differences we find easier to accept and what factors have influenced our views. How we view differences can impact our ability to show compassion. We mostly find it easier to be compassionate to those who are similar to us in some way.[30] It is like we keep a moral circle – those within our circle are worthy of help and support, compared to those outside our circle who are not.[31] We tend to place greater value on those close to us in terms of relationship or physical distance.

To better understand our tendencies to include or exclude others, we are going to take a deeper look into what affects our ability to be compassionate. Empathy can be influenced by our intuitive feelings as well as cognitive and regulative systems.[32]

We vicariously experience the emotional states of others and have related sensory responses ourselves. Feeling responses – where we can understand the emotional states of others – seem to be influenced by the brain's mirror system. Mirror neurons reflect other peoples' experiences onto our mind state.[33–36] This is a useful ability, otherwise we wouldn't feel scared when we watch horror movies! When we look at how mirror neurons react to stimuli, we can get information on how we are generating empathy. When we relate to people we consider to be "in" our group, there is greater activity in the area of the brain where mirror neurons are found than when we don't know people as well.[37,38] We more easily understand the actions of those who we deem similar in some way.[39,40] On the other hand, when we look at the brains of people who express higher levels of prejudice, lower mirror neuron activity is seen.[41] We may literally feel less empathy for those who we think we are dissimilar to.

There are many ways in which we end up defining our "in-group", and we may be more aware of some of these biases than others. When other people are ethnically similar to ourselves, we appear to experience more empathy for them than for other people.[42–48] We can also include people in our "in-group" because they share certain characteristics or alliances with us, like a sports team, which makes us more empathic towards them than rival members.[49,50] While we might assume that these "in-group" biases are fairly fixed, in fact, when we regroup people it can overcome biases. For instance, when a player who is ethically different to us joins our sports team, it reduces racial bias.[51]

The mirroring of emotional states is not the only component of the ability to empathise; cognitive appraisal also plays a role. Cognitive empathy depends on the theory of mind, which involves different areas of the brain than the areas accommodating mirror neurons. As described previously, the Theory of Mind allows us to think about and imagine what others might be thinking or feeling. This area of the brain appears to be important in how we understand others.[45–56] with higher activation when we categorise others as belonging to our group.[57–61] Studies with Japanese Americans, White Americans and Korean participants all showed that they judged members of their own ethnicity more accurately than those from other groups.[52,62]

The area of the brain associated with the Theory of Mind also has a role in how we appraise others. We make snap judgements about others as either threatening or nurturing, and this influences how we feel towards them.[32] When we dislike or disrespect others it changes our neural patterns to ones associated with disgust. These patterns are more similar to how we judge objects rather than other humans.[63] It appears that when we judge others harshly, we dehumanise them.

We can experience empathy as both an emotional and cognitive response, and so it makes sense that we need some kind of system to help regulate these alternatives.[51] A regulative system helps stop us from being overwhelmed by our emotional response when there is a greater goal in mind. Think of a surgeon who needs to operate on a child – the ability to take a scalpel to young skin is a confusing act of both great violence and great compassion. This cognitive appraisal can help to reduce emotional empathy responses so that we can function adaptively to any given situation.[51]

Kemi acknowledged the importance of being honest about our own judgements and appraisals:

> We've had to be judgmental from when we lived in the Savannah. You just have to judge – is that person a danger? Are they not? We know that we have an inherent bias, but the power comes in, or the self-compassion comes in when we don't pretend we're non-judgemental. Self-compassion is to acknowledge that I was raised in a family where we were told that people like that are scary or can't be trusted or whatever. Then we can ask ourselves – okay, that's interesting. I'll get curious about that. What is my experience? How do I create other narratives around that kind of person? How can I educate myself about finding out where that belief comes from? And then what do I need to change

about that? That's what I love about stories, that we get immersed in other people's realities that maybe otherwise we wouldn't have access to.
– Kemi Nekvapil. Executive and Personal Coach, Author, Speaker

Consider how you respond to differences and variety...

- *What differences do you find easy to understand, accept or tolerate in others?*
- *What differences do you find challenging to understand, accept or tolerate in others?*

Complexity, uncertainty

Let's turn next to how our brains respond to complexity and uncertainty, two forces that can amplify bias and reduce empathy. The plethora of ways in which we can be different brings complexity to the way we see the world. To make sense of the world around us we draw on references from our experiences, often shaped in childhood, of how we understand ourselves, others and our environment. We are influenced by the culture we are born into, and the messages and modelling we received from our families and communities. The sense of "self" we cling to is co-created with our environment. If you are struggling to believe this about yourself, imagine for a moment that you were born on a different continent, into a different culture, with a different language and expectations – how might this have shaped your view of the world? Our internal framework of experiences, from which we understand the world around us, is vulnerable to the limits of our perspective and the assumptions and biases we may have developed.

Pause here for a moment to reflect...

- *How did the culture and time you were born into influence your view of yourself?*
- *What impact did your family have on the way you see others?*
- *What messages from society have you picked up about those who are different from you?*

When we are met with complexity or uncertainty, our brains can register the situation we're in as a potential threat. When we have to make decisions our brain relies on inaccurate mental shortcuts.[64–66] While some of these unconscious biases may have innocuous effects, when they are discriminatory they cause harmful outcomes in the workplace.[67–74]

As we explored in Chapter 4, when viewed through an evolutionary lens it made sense to be cautious in the face of novel situations. When we are uncertain our brain tends to generate a list of "worst-case-scenario" outcomes. The aim is to keep us safe; however, the unintended consequence is that we may feel very confident that we are headed for disaster, whereas, in reality, the outcome is merely uncertain. We could have a positive or at the very least neutral outcome, but our consciousness may overlook these possibilities entirely. Consider when you have faced a situation with a degree of uncertainty – a job interview, a negotiation or a public speech – how often do you predict that the outcome will be terrible? Yet after the fact we are surprised at how well it went, or that it was at least "ok".

When overwhelmed our brain tends to oversimplify. It's a way to reduce overload – a mental shortcut that simplifies our world. We move to see things as all one way or all the other: "dichotomous thinking" and in all-or-nothing terms. We return to the comfort and simplicity of a younger age when we understood people and the world as "good or bad", "right or wrong".

When our brain has flagged a danger, an additional thinking bias occurs – we start to notice everything that supports this negative view, and discount or overlook entirely any contrary information. We become more convinced of our perspective, more sure, and more rigid in our thinking. We simplify the complexity around us by drawing on our biases.[75] Nick discusses wanting to make complex things simple:

> Why do we oversimplify things? Well, we don't want people to be complex. We want things to be predictable. We want to be able to make decisions and not have to revisit them. So we're brought up on simplistic heuristics to make sense of the world. I got caught up in this too for many years and I used to try and simplify things. Now I've realised that the danger was that it encouraged people to make simple judgments and simple solutions. So now I tell people, no, it's complex. You need to embrace the complexity and yet people don't want complexity – they want the certainty of getting it right.
>
> – Dr Nick Wilson, Principal Advisor Psychology,
> Department of Corrections

Take a moment to notice when you are responding to someone with different views to yourself…

- *When do you end up anticipating the worst?*
- *When do you notice you engage in all-or-nothing thinking?*
- *When do you focus on information that only supports your opinion?*

We have a brain that responds in a negative, simplistic and biased way when it comes across something different. It's not our fault – it is our inheritance. Some of us may find that we have flexibility with these responses, whereas others may default into reaction but are unaware of the source, and this capacity can vary depending on time and circumstance. At the same time, our environment – the culture we live in – is getting increasingly complicated. The speed of change is accelerating through the forces of globalisation, technological innovation and climate change. It is easy to conceive that the meeting of this overly reactive and negative brain, with increasing diversity and uncertainty, may mean that we are heading for stormy waters.

Volatility, polarisation

While we may have an evolutionary disposition to be wary of differences, we can magnify these effects by our current actions. When we focus on differences and binaries it increases the likelihood of a *Threat* response and decreases our ability to access compassion. Nick shared an example of how societal changes may impact our ability to understand those who are different from ourselves:

> American politics is very toxic at the moment, with an almost inability of either side to accept not just the other person's view, but the other person even being able to exist. Now, you know, there's always been disagreement in politics, but that total separation, which goes beyond politics, to even just acceptance of the other person having the value to be alive or being part of your community, that's another whole level. I was listening to somebody who's talked about how it's never been worse in America, probably since the Civil War. But there was a time when the sides were a lot closer. That was a time after the war and particularly the Second World War. The American army was volunteers and at the start of the Second World War America had this incredibly

> small army of 100,000 people, but they had to rapidly grow. So that means that people from all walks of life suddenly went off to war together. They were eating, drinking, being scared together – fighting for each other. So when they came back from the war, they continued to have contact with each other, whether it was through bowling leagues, Lions Clubs or whatever. For quite a period, you might vote for a different political party, but you were still part of each other's lives. But, over time there's been increased separation so they won't go into the same bowling team. They won't belong to the same clubs. Even down to the Republicans who now have set up their own dating sites, because they don't want to be on sites where they might find themselves dating a Democrat *and vice versa*. When you get such separation, you can't understand and you then move to these very black-and-white understandings. I know integration gets a bad name, but in fact, there's a need for integration of certain communities, otherwise there is a lack of understanding and conspiracies about other groups.
>
> – Dr Nick Wilson Principal Advisor Psychology, Department of Corrections

At a societal level, it appears that our tolerance for difference is decreasing. Research shows that acceptance of others with different political views has decreased over the past 50 years.[76] There are risks associated with societies that become increasingly polarised, from a rise in "us and them" rhetoric, unwillingness to date or marry those with opposing views, and rises in political violence.[76] In the 1960s in the United States, 5% of parents would be unhappy if their child married someone from a different political party, but this figure had risen to 33–45% by 2010.[77] Researchers Jennifer McCoy and Benjamin Press, talk about the dangers of "pernicious polarisation", with their study of nations across the world showing that severe polarisation correlates with serious democratic decline.[76] Their research points to how differences in society have been reduced to simplistic binaries to politicise issues and exacerbate pre-existing insecurities and grievances, often to suit the agenda of the rich and powerful. When one side takes an extreme position it often prompts others to take the opposite stance, and can inadvertently lock in two extreme positions.[78] Once societal level polarisation begins it can be challenging to reverse, but Dame Anne Salmond, Distinguished Professor of Māori Studies and Anthropology, suggests there are ways to reduce polarisation, including upholding the rule of law and processes that support centrist positions.[78]

As a leader, it can be helpful to reflect at the individual level. We can become aware of our tendency to take extreme positions or our reactions to others who do. We can use a compassionate lens to orient ourselves towards helpfulness, and this may guide us in finding a middle ground and consensus building. But it is also important to remember the *Fierce* side of compassion that speaks out against harm.

Pause here to reflect...

- *When do you "other" another group, culture or person?*
- *How do you feel when faced with a group that believes something you disagree with?*

It may be easier to agree that it is beneficial to increase diversity and decrease discrimination, but sometimes HOW to do this helpfully is complex. It can be like we are trying to complete a marathon when we haven't practised a shorter run. Thinking of it in this way, it makes sense to start with a manageable step and build up our skill base so that we can cope with increasingly complex and challenging issues. Starting to run short distances doesn't mean that the marathon isn't important; it highlights our commitment to it. It takes humility to acknowledge that we may need to train ourselves to understand and shift tendencies that evolved through evolutionary pressures, cultural, historical and social factors.

Notice

Reflective exercise for embracing differences

Find a quiet space. Some people find it helpful to jot down notes or reflections as they go, or read the questions first and then close your eyes as you ask yourself them in your mind.

Begin by pressing pause. Using whatever practice suits you best, you may like to take a few slower breaths, or focus on your feet, or actions that you are doing. Imagine you are a scientist exploring the issue you are currently focusing on with curiosity and openness.

Describe the situation in which difference is occurring, and try using a few short, factual sentences.

Notice what is happening in your body. Scan from your toes up your body to your head and notice any physical sensations. Name anything you notice without further comment or analysis. Just observe how you are right now.

Notice what is happening in your mind. When you think about this issue, notice where your mind goes. What thoughts do you have about this situation? Once you have noticed what you are thinking, bring your attention to how you are thinking. Notice the style or pattern of thinking. Perhaps your thoughts are critical, or worrying, or negative? Notice the tone of voice that these thoughts have. There is no need to change your thoughts or to get carried away by them, just notice them as they come and go.

Notice what is happening to your emotions. How do you feel regarding the situation? Can you name the emotion(s) that arise in response to this situation? If you are having difficulty naming the emotion, you may like to notice where you experience this feeling in the body instead. You are not trying to change how you feel, but rather to become curious and make space for whatever feelings arise.

Notice how you act. Tune into how this situation changes what you do. Perhaps you start acting differently, or maybe you stop or postpone doing something? Becoming aware, without judgement, of how this situation affects your behaviour.

Become aware of the bigger context in which this situation occurs – the work environment, your family environment, your society and culture. Notice what this broader perspective reveals.

Patterns might begin to emerge. Perhaps you are responding in a familiar way, that may feel like a habit, or perhaps this response is new to you.

You have been finding the observer perspective, noticing and naming your experience. If you notice that the mind gets caught up in the story of what is happening or it begins to self-criticise, just come back to your breath. There is no right or wrong way, you are just observing what happens.

Take a few moments to write down what you have noticed about differences. Practice using neutral language without judgement or comment.

∞

Empathise

We can think of empathy as having three directions: to yourself, from others and to others. For yourself, it can be helpful to acknowledge and understand where bias has come from, that we are all hijacked by our brains from time to time, that we make errors of judgement, that we don't and can't know it all – we are all limited by our own perspective – and that we also have the capacity for causing harm. We may need both tenderness for ourselves as we navigate tricky situations and a healthy dose of humility – that we too have flaws and make mistakes. When we have made an error or stumbled in some way, it can be helpful to open ourselves to the grace and compassion of others, who are often more tolerant of us than we are of ourselves.

To support ourselves, we can return to the intention of compassion. The fundamental orientation of compassion is to be helpful rather than harmful. This helps stimulate the *Soothe* system in both ourselves and others. We can do this by priming the idea of a helpful orientation with the following exercise from CFT.

Empathise reflective practice

Helpful orientation

Take a moment to breathe slowly and more deeply.

Say to yourself – I am here to work on ways to be helpful to myself, to learn to support others as best I can on their journey and to learn to be open to the helpfulness of others.

You may like to make a gentle smile to yourself as you say this.

Slowly repeat this sentence a few times as you breathe slowly.

Notice how this feels in your body, notice any changes in your posture or facial expression.

Before offering empathy and warmth to others, we first need to pause and ask ourselves, is it safe, helpful and wise? Here we need to use our judgement – perhaps we have noticed in ourselves a tendency to rush to judgement, criticism or distancing from the "other" and it would be helpful to concentrate on our capacity for connection. However, there are circumstances where we may cause ourselves harm. For instance, if someone has abused us physically or emotionally, then we may need to tread carefully. We will likely need to set a boundary, to acknowledge that their actions caused us harm. This is highly skilled work and may well require professional support from a mental health therapist to guide the process. Be wise and choose your exercise and focus carefully.

A second category for caution when trying to practice compassion is for figures who have been known to cause great suffering, like Adolf Hitler. Here there are three points to consider: firstly, is it helpful to focus on a figure like this? For most of us, we suffer enough with our colleagues, friends and loved ones, and increasing our compassion capacity in these areas is likely to have the most significant impact in our lives (and for those of others). Secondly, are we setting ourselves up for compassion failure or further suffering? Picking a hugely challenging target for compassion is like trying to complete a marathon when you have never even run before. Thirdly, it may be useful to think of increasing our understanding rather than feeling the warmth of empathy. Understanding is a cognitive form of empathy. If we can understand the conditions in which harmful deeds arose then we are more likely to take action in the future to prevent the same conditions from occurring.

Whether we are turning our attention to ourselves or others, a helpful starting point is curiosity. From non-judgemental curiosity comes understanding, and when we understand we are more likely to be able to empathise as the walls of division are eroded. We can start with small steps, building up compassion capacity, and having patience – this is a lifetime of work.

∞

Wise Action

Start by taking time to reflect on your own experiences and responses to difference, identity and belonging. The ideas that follow aren't meant to provide answers but are perspectives to explore as you continue learning and exploring.

Wise Action

Reflective exercise for embracing differences

Given the awareness you have brought and the empathy that you have cultivated, what wise action would be helpful for yourself or others at this time regarding embracing differences?

Sometimes in challenging situations, we respond with habits that are helpful in the short term, but that may harm us in the long run. Can we also bring compassion to these responses, understand that it is a very common human experience to want to avoid suffering, and that we are managing the best we can? In these situations, it may be wise to remind ourselves that if the situation is objectively safe, we can try to act the opposite of what our threat system is telling us to do.

If we feel resistance to the action, we might like to ask ourselves, is the step too big? Are we slipping into rescuing, fixing, or avoidance? Is our action wise? Can we bring compassion to the acceptance that perhaps it can help to scale our action back or to take small steps for it to be wise, or remind ourselves of a longer timeline?

Sometimes we may not know what to do – the wise action may be unclear. We may need to tolerate this uncertainty. Sometimes the most helpful action is the action of non-action. This is an active non-action that includes continuing to observe ourselves and others, rather than practising avoidance. When our wise action is unclear or our capacity for compassion for ourselves or others is low, we may need to focus first on resourcing ourselves. We may like to consider how to call on both gentleness and fierceness to help guide our wise action.

We may make a mistake. With all our best intentions in heart, sometimes we take an action that doesn't work out as we hoped it would. After taking an action, we go back to Noticing and Empathise, to bring compassion for being human and making mistakes and learning as we go. It helps to generate compassion for ourselves that we are doing our best with what we know right now, and that our understanding may change in the future.

Considering the awareness you have generated, the understanding and empathy that you have connected with, what is the wise action that is helpful in this current situation?

Leading in an inclusive way requires an increase in knowledge and awareness of processes and how these can enact discrimination and prejudice, as well as skills to enact goals and relational behaviours.[79] *Fierce Compassion* argues that as well as the capacities of *Noticing* and action, the outcome is better realised when empathetic skills lead to a compassionate *Wise Action*. Once we have primed ourselves towards an empathic and helpful response we can turn our attention to areas where we may want to build our skills.

Shared humanity

Leaders set the tone for inclusive practices. Staff respond to inclusive behaviours modelled by the leader and the values they demonstrate.[80] The most effective way to reduce bias is still unclear,[81] but this lack of clarity doesn't negate the importance of striving to do so. Using a compassionate framework, leaders can shift the focus from differences to our shared humanity – finding commonalities and building understanding of those who are different to us. Positive strategies are those that include high involvement from participants,[81] exploration of how to bring awareness to in-group and out-group biases, and exposure to examples that counter typical stereotypes.[82] The *Fierce Compassion* framework helps support us to notice our tendencies and challenge them with empathy-building strategies to help us find similarities. To create space to find our shared humanity, we can lean into core listening skills explored in Chapters 7 and 8. When prejudices are discussed with someone who is a good listener it leads to increased insight and lowers prejudice.[83] Controversial topics stimulate the *Threat* response, and so high-quality listening, which lowers the *Threat* response, helps others to express their true attitudes.[84] As we listen we increase our awareness of others and we can help expand the range of people we deem worthy of compassion: our moral circle. There is evidence that the size of our moral circle has expanded over time,[85] most likely due to our increased awareness (with the aid of technology and travel) of others who may lead different lives to ourselves. However, a fear of being compassionate – that somehow you or those close to you will be disadvantaged by being compassionate, through losing resources as an example – predicts a smaller moral circle.

Another way to increase understanding is to know the story of the other person, which is linked to having an emotionally compassionate response and makes it more likely that we will help an individual. Thinking statistically or analytically, on the other hand, makes it less likely that we will help as much.[86] Commonly, those teaching DEI emphasise rationale and strategy in an attempt to change behaviour, but it is likely that creating space for open conversations where challenges, fears and hopes can be discussed will be more effective.[87] Tactics that include lecturing or using guilt and shame are shown to be ineffective strategies to create change.[88,89] They may reduce people's sense of autonomy, which can increase prejudicial attitudes.[90] Conversely, inclusive leadership styles are positively associated with increased psychological safety of both the individual and the team, supporting individual and team performance.[1] Kemi shares how leaders can make a difference by making space to listen to the experiences of others:

> I think one of the most powerful things we can do for each other is to listen. So then, when I have shared over the years, my experiences of racism, the people that I have trusted are the people that have been able to hold my story without trying to diminish the story, change the story, make light of the story, to just listen and to maybe say "that is shit", or "I'm sorry that you have to go through that", or "I'm sorry that this is the world". That is one of the most compassionate things we can do – listen.
>
> I've now spoken my truth out into the world in my book, POWER. I still know it's not safe for me as a Black woman in the world. It's just that I trust the people I have in my life. If I'm unsafe, I will be heard and I will be held. I'm willing to go out into the world in a way that I wasn't before.
>
> Anyone who doesn't sit within the dominant narrative culture, knows it can take courage (and fierce self-compassion) for some of us to even get out of bed in the morning, and I feel very blessed that has never hit me so hard that I've wanted to stay in bed for months and months on end.
>
> – Kemi Nekvapil, Executive and Personal Coach, Author, Speaker

Consider for yourself...

- *How do you create the space for listening to others' experiences and stories?*
- *Who do you quote, praise or promote at work?*
- *How do you find commonalities with people who you perceive as different from you?*

Compassion isn't condoning

We are spending this chapter considering how to embrace diversity, with skills in understanding and tolerance. Yet, there is an important area to mention: when we become aware of a difference that is causing objective harm. We are looking to grow our understanding and tolerance towards others who are different from ourselves. However, there is a difference between understanding and agreeing or condoning. There are times when we want to call on the *Fierce* side of compassion. When others are causing objective suffering or using violence, for example, it wouldn't be compassionate to them or others if we just stood by. Yes, we need to grow our understanding to truly reduce suffering in the long term, but we will also need to draw boundaries, state that behaviour is not ok, and follow through with consequences. Nick offered this example to highlight that validation doesn't mean avoiding helpful feedback:

> There is a difference between validation and agreement. It is a really important point – we can be compassionate and validate someone else's experience, but we can't allow that to take us away from perhaps another role, which might highlight responsibility. Johnny's really upset with the way the custodial staff are treating him. However, he's also engaging in unhelpful behaviour so I can't refrain from pointing that out. The consequential behaviour needs to be pointed out.
>
> – Dr Nick Wilson, Principal Advisor Psychology, Department of Corrections

A criticism of compassionate approaches is that they aren't effective against those causing great harm. Here we can turn to Martin Luther King, who sought to change generations of racial oppression in the United States, for some words of guidance:

> The ultimate weakness of violence is that it is a descending spiral begetting the very thing it seeks to destroy, instead of diminishing evil, it multiplies it. Through violence, you may murder the liar, but you cannot murder the lie, nor establish the truth. Through violence, you may murder the hater, but you do not murder hate. In fact, violence merely increases hate. Returning violence for violence multiplies violence, adding deeper darkness to a night already devoid of

> stars. Darkness cannot drive out darkness; only light can do that. Hate cannot drive out hate; only love can do that.[91]

A piece of interesting research shows that even for those with some of the worst kinds of traits we can imagine, compassion can be helpful. For teenagers who are already in youth detention and have psychopathic traits – impulsivity, lack of remorse, grandiosity, manipulation and lack of emotion – if compassion training is offered these antisocial traits can be reduced.[92] Nick described his experience working with violent offenders:

> Even though I specialise in the assessment and treatment of criminal psychopaths. I've never lost the ability to see them as people. People would get all "Oh but they are psychopaths" – but they're still people, they are not aliens. They're not a different species.
>
> – Dr Nick Wilson, Principal Advisor Psychology, Department of Corrections

When we hear or see others act violently or do something we find objectionable we may wish to respond in kind, which can perpetuate the harm. As leaders, we create space for listening, but we also need to create space to resource ourselves and others for hearing about difficult differences that may challenge us. We can use the *Fierce Compassion* framework to come back to ourselves before we react and use our skills in noticing and empathy building to resource ourselves towards *Wise Action*.

- *When do you notice hate or violence arising in yourself towards others?*
- *How can you recognise the person's humanity, and name harmful behaviours?*

Respect

> There but for the grace of God go I? In a nutshell, I think about so many situations in my life where I hurt other people and compassion feels like an antidote. If I'm able to be compassionate towards myself in a situation where I've hurt someone else or if I'm able to interrupt that cycle of beating myself up, then I'm not destroying my future. It's also a product of having had so many different experiences with

> people in different places and having a case of fundamental compassion for what it means to be human.
>
> – Morna MacGillivray, Founder Revolutionary Woman Global

When we are faced with a strong opinion or view that we disagree with it is easy for our *Threat* system to get triggered – to perceive the difference as a danger. But if we can emotionally regulate, we can hold space for our feelings and opinions and acknowledge that other people are different in a way that we may not like or approve of. At times our *Threat* system may let us know when it is helpful to draw a boundary or exert a consequence for serious behaviour that causes harm. But if our internal "smoke detector" goes off every time there is a small disagreement then we have a problem. Both over-reacting and under-reacting can be problematic. When we see others being intolerant, it won't be helpful if we are intolerant of their intolerance. Taking time to come back to our compassion, for ourselves and others, can help us navigate the middle way. Remember that we can call on our cognitive empathy skills to help regulate our felt emotional response of dislike and disapproval and this can prevent us from dehumanising those with whom we disagree. Otherwise, we drown in the noise of reaction and counter-reaction. You only have to take a few minutes going down a toxic thread of people disagreeing on social media to see the suffering that is caused. Perhaps at work you have a colleague who you find antagonistic. Nick shows that we can use compassion to find a space where we don't have to like the other person or agree with them, but where we can hold respect for them as a human being:

> I am always aware of my own frailty. I'm always aware of my own pathology. So one of the reasons that I don't begin to be preachy with other people is I recognise within myself that under certain circumstances, or if life had treated me differently, I could have easily been sitting on the other side of the table.
>
> I think part of it is you have to have a strong sense of self. If you can admit to frailty or deviancy in yourself, you have to have a reasonably strong sense of self to realise that that doesn't mean you are that person. A deviant thought doesn't equal a deviant action, but also that you're not a totally good person.

> You know, that you may not like what they do or their lives, but they're still human beings and they still have people that love them, and people that they love.
>
> – Dr Nick Wilson, Principal Advisor Psychology, Department of Corrections

Amicable disagreement

There is a robustness in being able to sit alongside those with whom we disagree, but from whom we are willing to listen and learn. Diversity of thought comes from having a diverse range of people involved in the conversation.[93] As a leader, it can be tempting to stay in the comfort zone of being in rooms with people who will agree with us. We risk missing vital information. Making space for amicable disagreement creates room to learn from others' perspectives. It holds humility that we may not have it "right", even when we really, really think we are. To reclaim the middle ground – the space in the grey, the complexity of human experience – is where *Fierce Compassion* helps us to reside. This is the rich compost where life grows:

> Compassion is not pity. Compassion, to me, implies a value on both sides of the emotional equation – there is dignity in me and there is dignity in you. I will endeavour to keep both of those intact and if somebody is in an argument or somebody is hurting or somebody is different, compassion can be a bridge because you are seeing the dignity in them and you are holding the dignity of yourself. I think compassion positively bestows power on the other person because you are saying, you deserve to be your whole self just as I deserve to be my whole self.
>
> – Evie Ashton, Broadcaster and entrepreneur

∞

Seeing diversity as variety can help us understand the systems within us that create biases in our brains. These biases may trip us up when we are met with complexity and uncertainty. As change around us accelerates, we are finding views becoming increasingly polarised – as though we are living in an age of division. Systemic stereotypes impact how we see ourselves and others. The goal isn't to resolve or eradicate differences. By developing our awareness we can slow down to unhook from our habitual responses, develop our understanding, focus on people's stories and set our guiding intention to be helpful. We can use compassion to help us embrace our differences, so we can appreciate the diversity and richness of the range of human experience while also setting boundaries, and naming harm when we see it. With compassion, we make an unwavering commitment to helpfulness to ourselves and others to transform hurtful and limiting bias. This chapter has focused on opportunities for leaders to bridge the divide and embrace diversity. But when we only focus on the individual behaviours that support inclusivity, we risk losing the historical, social and political contexts that embed prejudice and maintain inequality.[94] While it is important to explore unconscious biases at an individual level, it can leave the responsibility for discrimination with individuals and no attention is given to systems-level issues.[95] We explore how to navigate challenging systems issues with compassion in Chapter 10.

∞

Chapter 9 Summary – bridging the divide

This chapter explored how *Fierce Compassion* supports the work of inclusion, equity and bridging differences with integrity and care.

Notice

- Become aware of our own social conditioning, bias and cultural norms
- Notice when defensiveness or discomfort arise in conversations about identity or power

Empathise

- Listen with humility to experiences different from our own
- Prime ourselves towards helpfulness

Wise Action

- Take responsibility for learning, repair and inclusive leadership
- Stay engaged in the discomfort of growth, rather than opting out or shutting down

References

1. Li, T., & Tang, N. (2022). Inclusive leadership and innovative performance: A multi-level mediation model of psychological safety. *Frontiers in Psychology*, *13*(1), 1–13. https://doi.org/10.3389/fpsyg.2022.934831
2. Rahman, U. H. F. B. (2019). Diversity management and the role of leader. *Open Economics*, 2(1), 30–39. researchgate.
3. Chua, S. W. Y., Sun, P. Y., & Sinha, P. (2023). Making sense of cultural diversity's complexity: Addressing an emerging challenge for leadership. *International Journal of Cross Cultural Management*, *23*(3), 635–659. https://doi.org/10.1177/14705958231214623
4. Farnsworth, D., Clark, J., Green, K., Lopez, M., Wysocki, A., & Kepner, K. (2020, October 8). *Diversity in the Workplace: Benefits, Challenges, and the Required Managerial Tools*. Edis.ifas.ufl.edu; University of Florida. https://edis.ifas.ufl.edu/publication/HR022
5. Pelled, L. H., Ledford, Jr, G. E., & Mohrman, S. A. (1999). Demographic dissimilarity and workplace inclusion. *Journal of Management Studies*, *36*(7), 1013–1031. https://doi.org/10.1111/1467-6486.00168
6. Kelly, E., & Dobbin, F. (1998). How affirmative action became diversity management. *American Behavioral Scientist*, *41*(7), 960–984. https://doi.org/10.1177/0002764298041007008
7. Mor Barak, M. E., Findler, L., & Wind, L. H. (2003). Cross-cultural aspects of diversity and well-being in the workplace: An international perspective. *Journal of Social Work Research and Evaluation*, *4*(2), 145–169.
8. Mor-Barak, M. E. (2014). *Managing Diversity: Toward a Globally Inclusive Workplace*. Sage Publications.
9. Smith, A. N., Morgan, W. B., King, E. B., Hebl, M. R., & Peddie, C. I. (2012). The ins and outs of diversity management: The effect of authenticity on outsider perceptions and insider behaviors. *Journal of Applied Social Psychology*, *42*, E21–E55. https://doi.org/10.1111/j.1559-1816.2012.01021.x
10. Nishii, L. H., & Rich, R. E. (2014). Creating inclusive climates in diverse organizations. In B. M. Ferdman & B. R. Deane (Eds.), *Diversity at Work: The Practice of Inclusion* (pp. 205–228). Jossey-Bass.

11. Pless, N., & Maak, T. (2004). Building an inclusive diversity culture: Principles, processes and practice. *Journal of Business Ethics*, *54*(2), 129–147. https://doi.org/10.1007/s10551-004-9465-8
12. Echols, S. (2009). *Transformational/Servant Leadership: A Potential Synergism for an Inclusive Leadership Style*. https://arl-jrl.org/wp-content/uploads/2016/02/Echols-Transformational-Servant-Leadership-2009-Fall.pdf
13. Shore, L. M., Randel, A. E., Chung, B. G., Dean, M. A., Holcombe Ehrhart, K., & Singh, G. (2011). Inclusion and diversity in work groups: A review and model for future research. *Journal of Management*, *37*(4), 1262–1289. https://doi.org/10.1177/0149206310385943
14. Bowers, K. W., Robertson, M., & Parchman, M. L. (2024). How inclusive leadership can help your practice adapt to change: The most effective leaders realize that everyone's input is valuable. *Family Practice Management*, *19*(1), 8. https://pmc.ncbi.nlm.nih.gov/articles/PMC3796957/
15. Amabile, T. M. (2019). *A Model of Creativity and Innovation in Organizations*. Hbs.edu. https://www.hbs.edu/faculty/Pages/item.aspx?num=7441
16. Govendo, J. A. (2005). Workforce, diversity and corporate creativity. *Handbook of Business Strategy*, *6*(1), 213–218. https://doi.org/10.1108/08944310510557495
17. Mohammadi, A., Broström, A., & Franzoni, C. (2017). Workforce composition and innovation: How diversity in employees' ethnic and educational backgrounds facilitates firm-level innovativeness. *Journal of Product Innovation Management*, *34*(4), 406–426.
18. Esty, K. C., Griffin, R., & Hirsch, M.S. (1995). *Workplace Diversity*. Adams Publ.
19. Devoe, D. (1999). *Managing a Diverse Workforce*. InfoWorld Media Group.
20. Richard, O. C., Kirby, S. L., & Chadwick, K. (2013). The impact of racial and gender diversity in management on financial performance: how participative strategy making features can unleash a diversity advantage. *The International Journal of Human Resource Management*, *24*(13), 2571–2582. https://doi.org/10.1080/09585192.2012.744335
21. Kossek, E. E., Lobel, S. A., & Brown, J. (2006). Human resource strategies to manage workforce diversity: Examining "The Business Case." In A. M. Konrad, P. Prasad, J. K. Pringle (Eds.), *Handbook of Workplace Diversity*, (pp. 54–75). SAGE Publications Ltd. https://doi.org/10.4135/9781848608092.n3
22. Ahonen, P., Tienari, J., Meriläinen, S., & Pullen, A. (2013). Hidden contexts and invisible power relations: A Foucauldian reading of diversity research. *Human Relations*, *67*(3), 263–286. https://doi.org/10.1177/0018726713491772
23. Zanoni, P., & Janssens, M. (2015). The power of diversity discourses at work: On the interlocking nature of diversities and occupations. *Organization Studies*, *36*(11), 1463–1483. https://doi.org/10.1177/0170840615593584
24. Özbilgin, M. F., Beauregard, T. A., Tatli, A., & Bell, M. P. (2010). Work-life, diversity and intersectionality: A critical review and research agenda. *International Journal of Management Reviews*, *13*(2), 177–198. https://doi.org/10.1111/j.1468-2370.2010.00291.x

25. Boekhorst, J. A. (2014). The role of authentic leadership in fostering workplace inclusion: A social information processing perspective. *Human Resource Management*, *54*(2), 241–264. https://doi.org/10.1002/hrm.21669
26. Curtis, E. F., & Dreachslin, J. L. (2008). Diversity management interventions and organizational performance: A synthesis of current literature. *Human Resource Development Review*, *7*(1), 107–134. https://doi.org/10.1177/1534484307311700. https://www.researchgate.net/publication/234588443_Diversity_Management_Interventions_and_Organizational_Performance_A_Synthesis_of_Current_Literature
27. Ng, E. S. W. (2008). Why organizations choose to manage diversity? Toward a leadership-based theoretical framework. *Human Resource Development Review*, *7*(1), 58–78. https://doi.org/10.1177/1534484307311592
28. Ng, E. S. W., & Wyrick, C. R. (2011). Motivational bases for managing diversity: A model of leadership commitment. *Human Resource Management Review*, *21*(4), 368–376. https://doi.org/10.1016/j.hrmr.2011.05.002
29. Cambridge Dictionary. (2023, September 27). *Diversity*. @CambridgeWords. https://dictionary.cambridge.org/dictionary/english/diversity#google_vignette
30. Bloom, P. (2017). Empathy and its discontents. *Trends in Cognitive Sciences*, *21*(1), 24–31. https://doi.org/10.1016/j.tics.2016.11.004
31. Singer, P. (2011). *The Expanding Circle*. Princeton University Press.
32. Decety, J. (2011). Dissecting the neural mechanisms mediating empathy. *Emotion Review*, *3*(1), 92–108. https://doi.org/10.1177/1754073910374662
33. Preston, S. D., & de Waal, F. B. M. (2002). Empathy: Its ultimate and proximate bases. *Behavioral and Brain Sciences*, *25*(1), 1–20. https://doi.org/10.1017/s0140525x02000018
34. Rizzolatti, G., & Fabbri-Destro, M. (2008). The mirror system and its role in social cognition. *Current Opinion in Neurobiology*, *18*(2), 179–184. https://doi.org/10.1016/j.conb.2008.08.001
35. Keysers, C., Kaas, J. H., & Gazzola, V. (2010). Somatosensation in social perception. *Nature Reviews Neuroscience*, *11*(6), 417–428. https://doi.org/10.1038/nrn2833
36. Rizzolatti, G., & Sinigaglia, C. (2010). The functional role of the parieto-frontal mirror circuit: Interpretations and misinterpretations. *Nature Reviews Neuroscience*, *11*(4), 264–274. https://doi.org/10.1038/nrn2805
37. Iacoboni, M. (1999). Cortical mechanisms of human imitation. *Science*, *286*(5449), 2526–2528. https://doi.org/10.1126/science.286.5449.2526
38. Rizzolatti, G., Fogassi, L., & Gallese, V. (2001). Neurophysiological mechanisms underlying the understanding and imitation of action. *Nature Reviews Neuroscience*, *2*(9), 661–670. https://doi.org/10.1038/35090060
39. Molenberghs, P., Hayward, L., Mattingley, J. B., & Cunnington, R. (2012). Activation patterns during action observation are modulated by context in mirror system areas. *NeuroImage*, *59*(1), 608–615. https://doi.org/10.1016/j.neuroimage.2011.07.080

40. Molenberghs, P., Halász, V., Mattingley, J. B., Vanman, E. J., & Cunnington, R. (2012). Seeing is believing: Neural mechanisms of action-perception are biased by team membership. *Human Brain Mapping*, *34*(9), 2055–2068. https://doi.org/10.1002/hbm.22044
41. Gutsell, J. N., & Inzlicht, M. (2010). Empathy constrained: Prejudice predicts reduced mental simulation of actions during observation of outgroups. *Journal of Experimental Social Psychology*, *46*(5), 841–845. https://doi.org/10.1016/j.jesp.2010.03.011
42. Avenanti, A., Paluello, I. M., Bufalari, I., & Aglioti, S. M. (2006). Stimulus-driven modulation of motor-evoked potentials during observation of others' pain. *NeuroImage*, *32*(1), 316–324. https://doi.org/10.1016/j.neuroimage.2006.03.010
43. Ito, T. A., & Bartholow, B. D. (2009). The neural correlates of race. *Trends in Cognitive Sciences*, *13*(12), 524–531. https://doi.org/10.1016/j.tics.2009.10.002
44. Xu, X., Zuo, X., Wang, X., & Han, S. (2009). Do you feel my pain? Racial group membership modulates empathic neural responses. *Journal of Neuroscience*, *29*(26), 8525–8529. https://doi.org/10.1523/jneurosci.2418-09.2009
45. Chiao, J. Y., & Mathur, V. A. (2010). Intergroup empathy: How does race affect empathic neural responses? *Current Biology*, *20*(11), R478–R480. https://doi.org/10.1016/j.cub.2010.04.001
46. Azevedo, R. T., Macaluso, E., Avenanti, A., Santangelo, V., Cazzato, V., & Aglioti, S. M. (2012). Their pain is not our pain: Brain and autonomic correlates of empathic resonance with the pain of same and different race individuals. *Human Brain Mapping*, *34*(12), 3168–3181. https://doi.org/10.1002/hbm.22133
47. Gutsell, J. N., & Inzlicht, M. (2011). Intergroup differences in the sharing of emotive states: Neural evidence of an empathy gap. *Social Cognitive and Affective Neuroscience*, *7*(5), 596–603. https://doi.org/10.1093/scan/nsr035
48. Sessa, P., Meconi, F., Castelli, L., & Dell'Acqua, R. (2013). Taking one's time in feeling other-race pain: An event-related potential investigation on the time-course of cross-racial empathy. *Social Cognitive and Affective Neuroscience*, *9*(4), 454–463. https://doi.org/10.1093/scan/nst003
49. Hein, G., Silani, G., Preuschoff, K., Batson, C. D., & Singer, T. (2010). Neural responses to ingroup and outgroup members' suffering predict individual differences in costly helping. *Neuron*, *68*(1), 149–160. https://doi.org/10.1016/j.neuron.2010.09.003
50. Cikara, M., Botvinick, M. M., & Fiske, S. T. (2011). Us versus them: Social identity shapes neural responses to intergroup competition and harm. *Psychological Science*, *22*(3), 306–313. https://doi.org/10.1177/0956797610397667
51. Eres, R., & Molenberghs, P. (2013). The influence of group membership on the neural correlates involved in empathy. *Frontiers in Human Neuroscience*, *7*, 1–6. https://doi.org/10.3389/fnhum.2013.00176
52. Adams, R. B., Rule, N. O., Franklin, R. G., Wang, E., Stevenson, M. T., Yoshikawa, S., Nomura, M., Sato, W., Kveraga, K., & Ambady, N. (2010). Cross-cultural

Reading the Mind in the Eyes: An fMRI Investigation. *Journal of Cognitive Neuroscience*, *22*(1), 97–108. https://doi.org/10.1162/jocn.2009.21187
53. Fletcher, P. (1995). Other minds in the brain: A functional imaging study of "theory of mind" in story comprehension. *Cognition*, *57*(2), 109–128. https://doi.org/10.1016/0010-0277(95)00692-r
54. Allison, T., Puce, A., & McCarthy, G. (2000). Social perception from visual cues: Role of the STS region. *Trends in Cognitive Sciences*, *4*(7), 267–278. https://doi.org/10.1016/s1364-6613(00)01501-1
55. Gallagher, H. L., & Frith, C. D. (2003). Functional imaging of "theory of mind." *Trends in Cognitive Sciences*, *7*(2), 77–83. https://doi.org/10.1016/s1364-6613(02)00025-6
56. Amodio, D. M., & Frith, C. D. (2006). Meeting of minds: The medial frontal cortex and social cognition. *Nature Reviews Neuroscience*, *7*(4), 268–277. https://doi.org/10.1038/nrn1884
57. Morrison, S., Decety, J., & Molenberghs, P. (2012). The neuroscience of group membership. *Neuropsychologia*, *50*(8), 2114–2120. https://doi.org/10.1016/j.neuropsychologia.2012.05.014
58. Molenberghs, P., & Morrison, S. (2012). The role of the medial prefrontal cortex in social categorization. *Social Cognitive and Affective Neuroscience*, *9*(3), 292–296. https://doi.org/10.1093/scan/nss135
59. Volz, K. G., Kessler, T., & von Cramon, D. Y. (2009). In-group as part of the self: In-group favoritism is mediated by medial prefrontal cortex activation. *Social Neuroscience*, *4*(3), 244–260. https://doi.org/10.1080/17470910802553565
60. Tajfel, H., Billig, M. G., Bundy, R. P., & Flament, C. (1971). Social categorization and intergroup behaviour. *European Journal of Social Psychology*, *1*(2), 149–178. https://doi.org/10.1002/ejsp.2420010202
61. Mathur, V. A., Harada, T., Lipke, T., & Chiao, J. Y. (2010). Neural basis of extraordinary empathy and altruistic motivation. *NeuroImage*, *51*(4), 1468–1475. https://doi.org/10.1016/j.neuroimage.2010.03.025
62. Cheon, B. K., Im, D., Harada, T., Kim, J.-S., Mathur, V. A., Scimeca, J. M., Parrish, T. B., Park, H. W., & Chiao, J. Y. (2011). Cultural influences on neural basis of intergroup empathy. *NeuroImage*, *57*(2), 642–650. https://doi.org/10.1016/j.neuroimage.2011.04.031
63. Harris, L. T., & Fiske, S. T. (2006). Dehumanizing the lowest of the low. *Psychological Science*, *17*(10), 847–853. https://doi.org/10.1111/j.1467-9280.2006.01793.x
64. Kahneman, D., Knetsch, J. L., & Thaler, R. H. (1991). Anomalies: The endowment effect, loss aversion, and status quo bias. *Journal of Economic Perspectives*, *5*(1), 193–206. https://doi.org/10.1257/jep.5.1.193
65. Kahneman, D., Lovallo, D., & Sibony, O. (2019, March 4). *A Structured Approach to Strategic Decisions*. MIT Sloan Management Review. https://sloanreview.mit.edu/article/a-structured-approach-to-strategic-decisions/
66. Thaler, R. H. (2016). *Misbehaving: The Making of Behavioral Economics*. W.W. Norton & Company.

67. Bano, A., & Nadeem, S. (2017). Exploring discrimination on the basis of international experience: The colonial mindset bias in the context of Pakistan. *Human Resource Management*, *57*(1), 211–233. https://doi.org/10.1002/hrm.21824
68. Shih, J. (2006). Circumventing discrimination. *Gender & Society*, *20*(2), 177–206. https://doi.org/10.1177/0891243205285474
69. Tetlock, P. E., & Mitchell, G. (2009). Implicit bias and accountability systems: What must organizations do to prevent discrimination? *Research in Organizational Behavior*, *29*(29), 3–38. https://doi.org/10.1016/j.riob.2009.10.002
70. Trentham, S., & Larwood, L. (1998). Gender discrimination and the workplace: An examination of rational bias theory. *Sex Roles*, *38*(1), 1–28. https://doi.org/10.1023/A:1018782226876
71. Colella, A., DeNisi, A. S., & Varma, A. (1997). Appraising the performance of employees with disabilities: A review and model. *Human Resource Management Review*, *7*(1), 27–53. https://doi.org/10.1016/s1053-4822(97)90004-8
72. Derous, E., Buijsrogge, A., Roulin, N., & Duyck, W. (2016). Why your stigma isn't hired: A dual-process framework of interview bias. *Human Resource Management Review*, *26*(2), 90–111. https://doi.org/10.1016/j.hrmr.2015.09.006
73. Weiner, N. J. (1991). Job evaluation systems: A critique. *Human Resource Management Review*, *1*(2), 119–132. https://doi.org/10.1016/s1053-4822(05)80004-x
74. Jordan, S. L., Ferris, G. R., & Lamont, B. T. (2019). A framework for understanding the effects of past experiences on justice expectations and perceptions of human resource inclusion practices. *Human Resource Management Review*, *29*(3), 386–399. https://doi.org/10.1016/j.hrmr.2018.07.003
75. Jost, J. T., Rudman, L. A., Blair, I. V., Carney, D. R., Dasgupta, N., Glaser, J., & Hardin, C. D. (2009). The existence of implicit bias is beyond reasonable doubt: A refutation of ideological and methodological objections and executive summary of ten studies that no manager should ignore. *Research in Organizational Behavior*, *29*(29), 39–69. https://doi.org/10.1016/j.riob.2009.10.001
76. McCoy, J., & Press, B. (2022, January 18). *What Happens When Democracies Become Perniciously Polarized?* Carnegieendowment.org. https://carnegieendowment.org/research/2022/01/what-happens-when-democracies-become-perniciously-polarized?lang=en
77. Zaki, J. (2019). *The War for Kindness: Building Empathy in a Fractured World.* Crown Publishing Group.
78. Salmond, D. A. (2024, January 12). *Dame Anne Salmond: How to Split a Society*. Newsroom. https://newsroom.co.nz/2024/01/13/dame-anne-salmond-how-to-split-a-societ/
79. Homan, A. C., Gündemir, S., Buengeler, C., & van Kleef, G. A. (2020). Leading diversity: Towards a theory of functional leadership in diverse teams. *Journal of Applied Psychology*, *105*(10), 1101–1128. https://dx. doi.org/10.1037/apl0000482

80. Downey, S. N., van der Werff, L., Thomas, K. M., & Plaut, V. C. (2015). The role of diversity practices and inclusion in promoting trust and employee engagement. *Journal of Applied Social Psychology*, *45*(1), 35–44.
81. Lai, C. K., Marini, M., Lehr, S. A., Cerruti, C., Shin, J.-E. L., Joy-Gaba, J. A., Ho, A. K., Teachman, B. A., Wojcik, S. P., Koleva, S. P., Frazier, R. S., Heiphetz, L., Chen, E. E., Turner, R. N., Haidt, J., Kesebir, S., Hawkins, C. B., Schaefer, H. S., Rubichi, S., & Sartori, G. (2014). Reducing implicit racial preferences: I. A comparative investigation of 17 interventions. *Journal of Experimental Psychology: General*, *143*(4), 1765–1785. https://doi.org/10.1037/a0036260
82. FitzGerald, C., Martin, A., Berner, D., & Hurst, S. (2019). Interventions designed to reduce implicit prejudices and implicit stereotypes in real world contexts: A systematic review. *BMC Psychology*, *7*(29), 1–12. https://doi.org/10.1186/s40359-019-0299-7
83. Itzchakov, G., Reis, H. T., & Weinstein, N. (2021). How to foster perceived partner responsiveness: High-quality listening is key. *Social and Personality Psychology Compass*, *16*(1), 1–64. https://doi.org/10.1111/spc3.12648
84. Itzchakov, G., & Weinstein, N. (2021). High-quality listening supports speakers' autonomy and self-esteem when discussing prejudice. *Human Communication Research*, *47*(3), 248–283. https://doi.org/10.1093/hcr/hqab003
85. Laham, S. M. (2009). Expanding the moral circle: Inclusion and exclusion mindsets and the circle of moral regard. *Journal of Experimental Social Psychology*, *45*(1), 250–253. https://doi.org/10.1016/j.jesp.2008.08.012
86. Slovic, P. (2007). "If I look at the mass I will never act": Psychic numbing and genocide. *Judgment and Decision Making*, *2*(2), 79–95. https://doi.org/10.1017/s1930297500000061
87. Weinstein, N., Itzchakov, G., & Legate, N. (2022). The motivational value of listening during intimate and difficult conversations. *Social and Personality Psychology Compass*, *16*(2), e12651. https://doi.org/10.1111/spc3.12651
88. Legate, N., Ryan, R. M., & Weinstein, N. (2011). Is coming out always a "Good Thing"? Exploring the relations of autonomy support, outness, and wellness for lesbian, gay, and bisexual individuals. *Social Psychological and Personality Science*, *3*(2), 145–152. https://doi.org/10.1177/1948550611411929
89. Ryan, R. M., & Deci, E. L. (2017). *Self-Determination Theory: Basic Psychological Needs in Motivation, Development, and Wellness*. Guilford Press.
90. Legault, L., Gutsell, J. N., & Inzlicht, M. (2011). Ironic effects of antiprejudice messages. *Psychological Science*, *22*(12), 1472–1477. https://doi.org/10.1177/0956797611427918
91. King, M. L., & King, C. S. K. (2010). *Where Do We Go from Here: Chaos or Community?* Beacon Press.
92. Ribeiro da Silva, D., Rijo, D., Brazão, N., Paulo, M., Miguel, R., Castilho, P., Vagos, P., Gilbert, P., & Salekin, R. T. (2021). The efficacy of the PSYCHOPATHY.COMP program in reducing psychopathic traits: A controlled trial with

male detained youth. *Journal of Consulting and Clinical Psychology, 89*(6), 499–513. https://doi.org/10.1037/ccp0000659

93. Sharma, A. (2016). Managing diversity and equality in the workplace. *Cogent Business & Management*, *3*(1), 1–14. Tandfonline. https://doi.org/10.1080/23311975.2016.1212682
94. Pritlove, C., Juando-Prats, C., Ala-leppilampi, K., & Parsons, J. A. (2019). The good, the bad, and the ugly of implicit bias. *The Lancet*, *393*(10171), 502–504. https://doi.org/10.1016/s0140-6736(18)32267-0
95. Storm, K. I. L., Reiss, L. K., Guenther, E. A., Clar-Novak, M., & Muhr, S. L. (2023). Unconscious Bias in the HRM literature: Towards a critical-reflexive Approach. *Human Resource Management Review*, *33*(3), 1–32. https://doi.org/10.1016/j.hrmr.2023.100969

10 Navigating complex systems

Fierce Compassion for the future of leadership

In this chapter, we focus on how the systems we work and live in impact our compassion capacity. It makes sense that when we are in supportive systems, it may be easier to take a compassionate stance. Yet we often overlook the impact of what is happening around us on our ability to enact compassion. It is part of our human experience to meet stresses and challenges in our daily lives. But sometimes the challenge is too great, our resources are stretched and we can find ourselves overwhelmed or burnt out. We may first look to ourselves to increase our resilience, to solve the problem or to find a way forward. However, there is a ceiling effect for how much we can increase our individual coping capacity. If our *Threat* and *Drive* systems are overstimulated, it becomes hard to find space for a *Soothe* response at all. We can be left feeling wired, flustered or on high alert.

∞

Notice

Let's start by acknowledging the structures and cultures of the wider systems we operate within. We'll then reflect on how these systems affect our thoughts, feelings and capacity to act.

There are many reasons why our *Threat* and *Drive* systems may swing into action; some of these may lie in our own genetic and psychological make-up. However, reasons also come from the conditions around

DOI: 10.4324/9781003583080-10

us – cultural, social, political, economic, environmental and competitive influences. Here are just a few examples:

- The culture at work is highly competitive, pitting people against each other
- The physical work environment is dangerous
- There are (hidden or explicit) biases in the system that prejudice against certain people
- Those in a position of power act in a controlling or aggressive way to those who work under them

The impacts of these challenges vary – from causing serious harm, physically or psychologically, to the grind of everyday frustrations. Systems act like microcosms, creating their own mini cultural climates. The attempt to manage the conditions to survive or succeed shapes the behaviour of those who work within them. Paul became aware of how competing forces can work against creativity and change:

> One of the main reasons I wanted to take a break from corporate was this need from certain people to just put their mark on things. I had an idea and I don't even remember what the idea was, but I remember the path when I took it to my boss, who put their stamp on it and went to their boss who put their stamp on it and then it went to the CEO who put their stamp on it and went to Head Office... they put their stamp on it, it came back to the CEO who put another stamp on it. And back down the line it came to me. Now the idea was so unrecognisable, convoluted and complicated, that it wasn't worth doing anymore, because it was so far removed from the coalface. But I like to think it must've been quite a good idea and that's why people wanted to be part of it. But then it came to be a bad idea because everybody was trying to be noticed.
>
> – Paul, Senior Leader in the Financial Services Sector

We may find ourselves thinking that people around us are being selfish, stupid or mean, but many times their behaviour can be understood as rational given the conditions that surround them. For instance, the system that demands the success of the individual or a team may lead to them protecting their IP, which can stifle creativity and progress. But if you are the one experiencing your ideas being hijacked and rendered useless by others, it can be hard to find compassion for yourself or those around you. Systems can also mean that those working in them face contradictory pressures, leading to processes that can cause harm. Kim, an HR manager, highlighted the emotional toll when an organisation acts in ways contradictory to the values it espouses.

> I felt like we were part of something special and bigger than ourselves, and it was a wonderful place to work. I was also part of that indoctrination for others, being part of the HR team, programmes, recruiting and training, because I truly believed it.
>
> Then to have the light switch flipped – the company is changing, and these positions are changing, the position I am in is considered redundant. How they communicated that was completely counter to all of the messaging over years and years of being fed the organisation's story of being like family.
>
> So it hit hard. There was a mismatch between those values and the way it was done. It took me out emotionally. It felt like being kicked out of a community. It was so heartbreaking. It was like a death. It was all a lie. I got sucked in. I felt stupid. I felt like I had been conned, and it was really hard to come to terms with the fact that I was part of selling that to others too.
>
> – Kim, former Programme Manager, HR Team Services

Challenging systems impact our ability to be compassionate

Let's take healthcare, one industry where compassion is an inherently desirable component. Here, system processes may impact whether people can show compassion. For example, medical systems often end up emphasising clinical categorisation and triage processes, which may decrease compassion,[1] as does the emphasis on efficiency and clinical urgency.[2–7] And it's not just the structure of the system per se, but its impact on people who interact with it. The patients who may be suffering, but who are perceived as "difficult" can trigger a *Threat* response from clinicians, impeding a compassionate response.[8]

A lack of compassion in a caring profession such as health is a problem, and compassion fatigue has been suggested as a way of understanding it. But compassion fatigue is poorly defined and not well understood.[9] It may be better represented as a form of burnout. Research with nurses shows that they want additional staff so that they can spend more time with patients – even though that means increasing the time spent with the suffering of others. This is the opposite of what you would expect if they were experiencing a lack of compassion. They aren't trying to avoid helping with the suffering, they are just feeling unsupported to do so. It is often a reflection of the time and cost pressures on medical professionals, detrimental to care, rather than reflecting a lack of desire to be compassionate.[10] There is no evidence that compassion is a finite resource that can be drained or run out, and this conceptualisation of compassion can be used to blame the individual for not being compassionate.[11] The concept of compassion fatigue tends to place the responsibility back on the individual, whereas seeing the system pressures as an impediment to health professionals giving compassion switches the focus to where intervention may be most effective.

Some ways in which we generate compassion are more easily impacted by the system than others. For example, suffering requiring urgent care may trigger a reflexive response where compassion seems to come more quickly.[12] Less urgent situations may require the employment of habitual or goal-directed strategies to generate compassion. Habitual or goal-oriented strategies seem to be more easily influenced by external conditions that exist in the systems in which we work.[13]

While these studies focus on healthcare systems, the findings have wider relevance. Compassion can be impacted by processes in the system, how urgent the issue is perceived to be, whether the compassion comes from a reactive response or a habit/goal-driven response, the personal interactions with others in the system, and whether there is support with resources necessary to allow compassion.

Pause for a moment to reflect...

- *How does the system you work in impact your ability to be compassionate?*

We experience systems differently

The level to which system issues impact us will vary depending on our experiences in the world. Depending on the disadvantages, prejudices or privileges we have experienced, the way we can exist in certain spaces will be different from others. The stress load we carry from navigating bias may be invisible to others. As people's seniority at work increases there is a risk they help others less.[14]

Some workplace systems may include actions aimed at reducing stressors, but these actions may only be partly successful if there is no careful integration into the system. Many organisations delegate wellbeing to the individual, with an underlying premise that if we can all work on our resilience we will be healthier and more productive. Organisations may offer individual counselling sessions for support to manage their symptoms, and wellbeing supports that can be helpful. However, there is a risk that when wellbeing concepts are co-opted, hyper-individualised, and geared towards productivity the implicit message is that the problem resides with the individual rather than the system. Paul acknowledges the tension between talk and action:

> Many businesses talk about compassion, and diversity and inclusion. But these are just words because they aren't built into the system.
>
> – Paul, Senior Leader in the Financial Services Sector

Systems that affect us are not just in the workplace, they are also in the environments we live in – for example, the geographic and economic conditions. When we look at compassion around the world, often people in wealthier cities are less likely to help others. Around 80% of people would spontaneously stop and help others in a non-emergency situation in Rio, San Jose (Costa Rica) and Lilongwe (Malawi), whereas only 40% would help in the richer countries of Singapore, New York and Kuala Lumpur.[15] Cultures that value simpatia – spontaneous friendliness and helpfulness to strangers (typically Spanish and Latin American cultures) – are more likely to express compassion than those without these traditions.[15] Raising our awareness of our own and others' experiences of systems is helpful when we come to think about what is a *Wise Action.*

Reasons for staying

We may stay in systems that overwhelm us for several reasons. It is easy to move through life on an autopilot setting – reacting habitually to the environment around us. Our habitual responses may keep us from noticing or questioning the conditions we work in, and we can absorb cultural and social assumptions about different work systems that seem inevitable. For instance, Law, Medicine and Finance are known for being highly competitive environments. We may have economic reasons to stay – whether we are fighting to keep food on the table, are saddled with debt or chasing external representations of our "success". We may be holding a greater sense of purpose – working in medicine because we want to help others or for an NGO because we care about the organisation's mission. We can also end up staying in challenging systems because we experience shame at the thought of leaving. We look around us and see other people "coping" and take our difficulty to mean that there is something wrong with us. Whether we remain in or leave a system that causes us difficulty, it can be helpful to reflect on the system and its effects.

- *What cultural, social, political, economic, environmental and competitive influences exist in your work system?*
- *What challenging conditions have you experienced due to your work environment?*
- *What was the impact of these conditions on you and others?*

It is unlikely that there is one "answer" on how to create change in systems so they are healthier for us; rather, a multilayered approach emerges. Instead of reaching for reactive solutions, *Fierce Compassion* proposes a process, a reflective state to lean into and the helpfulness of *Wise Action* to create change in systems. This is not the "Ten Steps to Success" version of change, but a model, a way of being, where we learn iteratively and work collectively towards the changes we want to see. When we share our stories of walking this path of compassion, we share the hope that the future can be a brighter place that works better for everyone.

Notice

Reflective exercise for complex systems

Find a quiet space. Some people find it helpful to jot down notes or reflections as they go, or read the questions first and then close your eyes as you ask yourself them in your mind.

Begin by pressing pause. Using whatever practice suits you best, you may like to take a few slower breaths, or focus on your feet, or actions that you are doing. Imagine you are a scientist exploring the issue you are currently focusing on with curiosity and openness.

Describe the situation in which the difficulty caused by complex systems is occurring, and try using a few short, factual sentences.

Notice what is happening in your body. Scan from your toes up your body to your head and notice any physical sensations. Name anything you notice without further comment or analysis. Just observe how you are right now.

Notice what is happening in your mind. When you think about this issue, notice where your mind goes. What thoughts do you have about this situation? Once you have noticed what you are thinking, bring your attention to how you are thinking. Notice the style or pattern of thinking. Perhaps your thoughts are critical, or worrying, or negative? Notice the tone of voice that these thoughts have. There is no need to change your thoughts or to get carried away by them, just notice them as they come and go.

Notice what is happening to your emotions. How do you feel regarding the situation? Can you name the emotion(s) that arise in response to this situation? If you are having difficulty naming the emotion, you may like to notice where you experience this feeling in the body instead. You are not trying to change how you feel, but rather to become curious and make space for whatever feelings arise.

Notice how you act. Tune into how this situation changes what you do. Perhaps you start acting differently, or maybe you stop or postpone doing something? Becoming aware, without judgement, of how this situation affects your behaviour.

Become aware of the bigger context in which this situation occurs – the work environment, your family environment, your society and culture. Notice what this broader perspective reveals.

Patterns might begin to emerge. Perhaps you are responding in a familiar way, that may feel like a habit, or perhaps this response is new to you.

You have been finding the observer perspective, noticing, and naming your experience. If you notice that the mind gets caught up in the story of what is happening or it begins to self-criticise, just come back to your breath. There is no right or wrong way, you are just observing what happens.

Take a few moments to write down what you have noticed about working in complex systems. Practice using neutral language without judgement or comment.

∞

Empathise

When we consider the factors in systems that can be overwhelming, our *Threat* or *Drive* systems, it can be tempting to immediately reach for a solution to fix the problem. But if we don't attend to our own *Soothe* system first, our ideas are likely to be governed by the *Threat* system and may be more reactive or avoidant than is helpful in the long run. So if you notice your mind jumping ahead to solution thinking first come back to building the *feelings* of compassion, warmth and empathy.

The connection with a sense of something greater than our individual experience, a state of self-transcendence, is thought to be related to cultivating self-compassion and compassion for others.[16] The scale of the problems that exist with systems can feel overwhelming, and to access the warmth of empathy it can be helpful to lean into something bigger than ourselves. Nature, for example.

Accessing nature can help support our parasympathetic nervous system to reduce our experience of stress. When we are in a threat-based state it can impede our ability to empathise with ourselves and others. Recent systematic reviews and meta-analyses of the data have found that nature-based recreation can improve mental health, cognition and wellbeing,[17] while "forest bathing" can improve physical and psychological health.[18] Nature walks can decrease anxiety and depression.[19] If you can't get out into nature, even urban green spaces help reduce brain activity and stress.[20–22] Exposure to real plants rather than artificial ones has a relaxing effect and can help recovery after surgery.[23–32] Fresh flowers rather than artificial ones are better for physiological relaxation.[33–35] Even being in rooms with natural wood has a relaxing effect.[36–41] And if we can't find any real nature, even viewing photos or videos of nature has a helpful impact on stress levels, with 3D Virtual reality more helpful than 2D images.[42,43] When we connect with nature we help support our parasympathetic nervous system response, which is part of the *Soothe* system, and this helps us to be able to access feelings of warmth to ourselves and others. We are more likely to be able to find empathy when our *Soothe* system is activated and we feel connected to something bigger than ourselves.

I used to work as part of a team supporting children and adolescents with mental health difficulties, including crisis response. It was a rewarding, but high-challenge environment. On my way to work I would often be thinking about clients from earlier in the week, and sometimes worrying about whether they were safe. I began to realise that not only was it stressful when I was at work, but I was bringing that stress with me outside of work hours. I was fomenting the stress and worry before I even arrived in the clinic. I was lucky that I had to park my car fifteen minutes away from the hospital on the other side of a park. I started to bring my attention to the park as I walked into work – noticing the trees, the flowers and the birds, and allowing myself to become absorbed in the sights, sounds and smells of the early morning park. While this didn't change how stressful the role was at work, it did mean that I wasn't mentally already in work stress before I got to work. Instead, I felt a sense of hopefulness and beauty from the connection with nature. Connecting with a self-transcending experience helped me access a state of calm and warmth and to feel empathy for myself and my clients.

While nature is one example that can help generate a self-transcending experience, there are others you may prefer to experiment with; art, music or spiritual practices, as examples. I can't give you the experience of self-transcendence on this page. It is something to experiment with, put into regular practice, then see what happens.

Empathise reflective practice

Finding self-transcendence in nature

Find a place where you can connect with nature.

Start by noticing your breathing. Focus on extending your exhale, creating space for the next inhale.

Allow your eyes to wander.

Practice noticing and naming what you see.

Become aware of the sounds that you can hear.

Breathe in and notice what you smell.

Bring your attention to any physical sensations from the wind, sun or rain.

Start moving slowly with your breath, again noticing what you can see, hear, smell and feel.

See if you can find a child-like state of wonder for the beauty of nature.

Try experimenting with how you can connect more with nature...

- *Where do you feel most at ease in nature?*
- *Where is a moment of nature you could access every day?*
- *What do you notice when you allow yourself to focus on your senses when you are in nature?*

∞

Wise Action

Begin by pausing to reflect on how you are affected by working within challenging systems. Afterwards, you may wish to explore the suggestions that follow, not as prescriptions, but as support for your own discernment.

Wise Action

Reflective exercise for complex systems
Given the awareness you have brought and the empathy that you have cultivated, what wise action would be helpful for yourself or others at this time when working within complex systems?

Sometimes in challenging situations, we respond with habits that are helpful in the short term, but that may harm us in the long run. Can we also bring compassion to these responses, understand that it is a very common human experience to want to avoid suffering and that we are managing the best we can? In these situations, it may be wise to remind ourselves, if the situation is objectively safe, that we can try to act opposite to what our threat system is telling us to do.

If we feel resistance to the action, we might like to ask ourselves, is the step too big? Are we slipping into rescuing, fixing, or avoidance? Is our action wise? Can we bring compassion to the acceptance that perhaps we need to scale our action back, take small steps, for it to be wise, or remind ourselves of a longer timeline?

Sometimes we may not know what to do – the wise action may be unclear. We may need to tolerate this uncertainty. Sometimes the most helpful action is the action of non-action. This is an active non-action which includes continuing to observe ourselves and others, rather than avoidance. When our wise action is unclear or our capacity for compassion for ourselves or others is low, we may need to focus first on resourcing ourselves. We may like to consider how to call on both gentleness and fierceness to help guide our wise actions.

We may make a mistake. With all our best intentions at heart, sometimes we take an action that doesn't work out as we hoped it would. After taking action, we go back to noticing and empathy, to bring compassion for being human and making mistakes and learning as we go. We may need to generate compassion for ourselves that we are doing our best with what we know right now, and that our understanding may change in the future.

Considering the awareness you have generated, the understanding and empathy that you have connected with, what is the wise action that is helpful in this current situation?

We chronically underestimate resourcing

It can be helpful to acknowledge the strains caused by the system we are navigating. It is hard (and sometimes impossible) to sustain our emotional equilibrium and compassion capacity. The wisest action may be to make sure we first have our own oxygen mask on. As explored in Chapter 6, this goes beyond self-care, to discover what it is that helps stimulate your *Soothe* system. It can be tempting when pushing for change to lean into our *Threat* system to use fear-based energy to move us forward. But we are likely not acting at our full potential and may be causing further harm (to ourselves or others) when we come from this reactive place. Resourcing ourselves is necessary but not sufficient on its own. But before moving on to broader solutions, it can be helpful to consider the depth of resourcing necessary for the challenge you are facing.

- *Are you being generous to yourself?*
- *Do you have enough opportunity away from the system to recharge?*
- *What is truly nourishing for you?*

Sometimes we may have no choice but to stay in a system that is causing us excessive levels of stress, for economic or other reasons. The best we can do is to resource ourselves as much as possible and extend ourselves a great deal of self-compassion for managing as well as we can. We may find it helpful to reach out to others for their support. If we are in a position where we see others who are having to weather a storm of intolerable conditions, are we able to use our insight and wisdom to provide allyship, advocacy and activism on their behalf?

Take a moment to reflect...

- *What can you acknowledge about the challenges from your environment that you are facing?*
- *How can you resource yourself?*
- *Who can you offer support or allyship to?*

Finding your compassion collective

In the face of the faceless system, it can be easy to overlook the fact that it is made up of people. Compassion is about relationships – whether it is between two individuals, or groups, or from a group to an individual. When we receive compassion we conceive ourselves as worthy of care.[44] Within a tricky system, can we find connections to others? Paul offered this example of compassionate leadership when building relationships with your team.

> What enabled me to have the most success actually is weekly one on ones with all my team. I had a lot of direct reports, and it was time-consuming, but it was the best use of my time because I was there to lead. The objective of that is to take smart people and to get the best out of them. I'm not there to be the smartest person, I'm there to get the most out of the smart people. What I was trying to do was just have a regular chat centred around the person I was talking to; their friends, their families, and what they were doing at the weekend, but there would be structure to it. My first question was always the same. I was genuinely asking "How are you?", from a position of care, not just as a conversation opener. We would talk about how they are feeling, how the workload is, and how they are managing any pressure or stress. I wouldn't

> always ask the question directly – "How's everything at home?", but the conversation helped paint a full picture of who the person was. My last question was always "How can I help?", or "What do you need from me?" Starting with "How are you?", and ending with "How can I help?", was my way of saying, I care about you as a person, and I'm here to help if you want/need it, but I'm not going to force that help on you.
>
> – Paul, Senior Leader in the Financial Services Sector

Pause for a moment to reflect...

- *Who can you build a relationship with?*
- *Who can you extend compassion towards?*
- *Who can you turn to for compassionate support?*

If we are swimming against the tide. If we are taking a personal stand for the value of compassion in a system which may not perceive any value in this approach, we may feel lonely or isolated. It can take a lot of energy to keep that momentum going. To sustain ourselves, it can be helpful to find "islands of compassion" – others who view work and life through a similar lens – so we can create a compassion collective. Katerina reflected on what helps her stay grounded in her work.

> Whatever I do, I put myself out there. Inevitably, I'll find other people who get that and who connect. In various organisations where I've worked, I found others who have that burning desire to be more compassionate and human in the work that we do. That's been great. Because I've been able to connect and create networks that support each other.
>
> – Katerina Daniel, Canadian Public Service Executive

Sometimes it is the support from others that keeps us going through the challenges and helps us not perpetuate harm on others. Interconnectedness has been identified as a key theme within compassion,[45] and so forming connections with others who are trying to create compassionate change is helpful. When trying to implement compassionate change, for it to be most effective it needs to be implemented across organisational, leadership and team levels, with practices embedded across these areas.[46]

Tolerance of iterative change

It can help to examine our expectations for change. Our *Drive* for more, better, and faster may leave us frustrated and disappointed. We may need to practice both patience and persistence to keep us moving in a helpful direction, and the exercises from Chapter 6 on perfectionism may be useful.

When my husband was working for a scientific research company he was interested in improving their sustainability. One aspect he explored was whether the masks they used in the lab could be recycled or composted. He found an organisation making compostable masks that were made to high scientific specifications suitable for laboratory work. As a scientific organisation, there was naturally an interest in the credentials of their biodegradability. The product was new to the market and whilst mainly compostable, it was not 100% so. The concerns around the product not being sustainable enough meant that the company chose to stick with the existing non-biodegradable masks. The quest for perfection got in the way of iterative change. If instead more people started purchasing biodegradable scientific products, there would be increased demand that could justify further research and investment to further improve the product.

Sometimes it may be helpful to ask ourselves – what would success look like? If we can't reach 100%, what would a small improvement look like? Say we are currently 4 out of 10 for sustainability, what would 5 out of 10 look like? We can also use this reflection for our compassion capacity. If we can't be 100% compassionate, what would 10% more compassionate look like? This type of step-wise iterative change is part of agile implementation strategies that propose that successful solutions require a repeated learning cycle – of piloting, adjusting and monitoring in real time.[45] We can use the *NEW* reflective cycle for change both within ourselves and the systems in which we work. In our season of creating change, we may only see part of the solution, perhaps only one step in a helpful direction. It can be useful to shift our perspective to see that we are one piece of a greater puzzle.

- *Is the change moving in a helpful direction?*
- *Is there currently a more helpful alternative?*
- *Is the status quo more or less helpful than the change?*

Compassionate endings

Perhaps we gave a season of our lives to this role at work, but now it is time to move on. This may be a great act of compassion to ourselves, or others – like our loved ones!. We may need to acknowledge our limits, that we have done our best. If we stay too long, past the point where we could really manage, we may become resentful and burnt out. From this point, it is harder to practice leaving well. Kim shares what a difference the way the ending happened would have made to her.

> To have the redundancy communicated on a piece of paper without any acknowledgement of past efforts. Wow. It was so cold. No personal contact to talk it through.
>
> From an HR perspective, from a cost-cutting point of view, it completely makes sense. But there was no conversation.
>
> It was all very corporate, to cover their ass legally. I know they're coached legally. This is what you should say and shouldn't say, and you don't want to open yourselves up to lawsuits.
>
> Well at work you've been in a relationship. It's like being broken up with a sticky note or a text message. That's how it felt. What is the risk of a conversation, of keeping the relationship, of acknowledging that yes this time is over, *and* you've been valuable as a person? Like, how is that risky? What's the problem with that?
>
> – Kim, former Programme Manager, HR Team Services

If we are already well past our limit, and we make the decision to leave, it can be helpful to resource ourselves well for the leaving process. To see the ending as an important part of the whole experience. We are often terrible at endings; think of how you have seen endings modelled to you – the redundancy, the exasperated resignation, the bitter divorce? How many of us like to leave the party without saying goodbye, to slink away? In a good ending, we get to make space for our whole experience, to acknowledge the good and the bad, and we make space for others in the dynamic. Even if we feel that we would gladly burn the place to the ground and never see any of our co-workers again, often there is something more helpful we can take from a compassionate ending. We may be able to do this with others, or, sometimes, if the relationships are unsafe and irrevocably broken, we may need to do it by ourselves. If we find that our *Wise Action* is to leave, it can be helpful to first return to noticing – to reflect on the journey we have had, how we have felt, what thoughts we have about the situation now compared to the beginning, how we have acted or not acted, and what the impact has been on our physical health.

- *What have we learnt through this experience?*
- *What would we like to take forward with us, and what would we like to leave behind?*
- *When we look back in years to come how would we like to see ourselves handle the leaving?*

Perhaps there are still important things that need to be said, or if that isn't possible we may find it helps to express these thoughts in a letter (that isn't to be sent). Attending to the process of leaving can help bring a sense of completeness or closure that helps us move on to the next chapter.

Finding hope and purpose

Maybe paradoxically, we can find hope by acknowledging that we can't eliminate suffering. This frees us to consider instead how we can navigate suffering. It may be helpful to remember that in the broadest perspective of time, whatever we are struggling with shall pass. We focus on the things we want to change, and with our bias towards negative information we can overlook the positive changes that are happening – improvements don't get the same PR as catastrophes. In the activism space, it can be inevitable to absorb and dwell on the information about the difficulty we are seeking to resolve. We need to be mindful of what consumes our attention and make sure that we are also seeking role models, examples of change and progress so that we can dwell in the possible. Vivien, who works in senior management and governance roles, explains how connecting with her greater purpose helped guide her career:

> I have chosen to work inside those corporate organisations because that's where I saw the money and the power. Because I wanted to use my life, this time around, to make a change and to do as much as possible.
>
> – Vivien Sutherland Bridgwater, Consultant and Director

Our purpose may lead us to work for change either within or outside the system. The Activist Leader describes various archetypes for activists.[47] This is a shameless bit of nepotism as this rather brilliant book is written by my first husband's brother, Jon Miller (who I call my brother), and his business partner Lucy Parker. The book helps highlight that there is no right way, no singular way, to create change. We can use an orientation towards action that is helpful and compassionate to guide us when striving for change.

Leaders are in a unique position to be able to use their power and influence. The daily behaviours of leaders model what is expected of others in the organisation.[48] Leaders who have transformational leadership styles increase adaptability and drive innovation.[49] The power that a leader can wield is not a problem per se, it is the way in which that power is used that can be either harmful or helpful. Mary Parker-Follett, pioneer of democratic leadership approaches in the 1920s, drew a distinction between power-over approaches (dominance, control) and power-with approaches (collaborative, respectful).[50] Riane Eisler, cultural historian and systems thinker, expanded on these ideas proposing a dominator-partnership spectrum, where moving towards partnership approaches foster cooperative cultures at work.[51]

It might be helpful to take some time to ask yourself…

- *What is your compassionate purpose?*

Creating different

We may be in a position to create something different. Maybe we want to lead an organisation that puts people at the centre, that takes a compassionate approach to the world of work. It's likely that we don't have a blueprint to follow. It can be overwhelming even knowing where to start.

We can look towards others who are already pioneering different ways, creating approaches that show compassionate action in work. Compassion can look like different actions depending on the context, but is characterised by a helpfulness to reduce suffering, and often entails corporate social responsibility ideas and servant leadership styles. Here are some examples from the clothing, politics, consumables and travel industries.

Patagonia, the outdoor clothing brand, is well known for embedded practices that show care for the environment and workers through values of quality, integrity and justice, and actions such as being a founding member of the Fair Labour Association, paying a living wage, and having environmentally sound practices that include an emphasis on recyclable materials and durability.[52,53]

There are several compassion advocacy groups, including the Global Compassion Coalition, The Charter for Compassion, Compassionate USA and Compassion in Politics (UK). They all promote compassionate practices for individuals and systems to reduce global suffering. For example, Compassion in Politics (UK) advocates for a system that puts compassion at its core to transform politics with empathy, integrity and fairness. They campaign for changes in political discourse towards civility and engage in robust discussion that focuses on mental health, social inequality, environmental sustainability and democratic reform.[54]

Southwest Airlines was founded by Herb Kelleher who follows a servant leadership style. He makes taking care of employees his top priority.[55] Co-leader Colleen Barrett, who shares Kelleher's values, finds that because employees are treated well they have good job satisfaction, which means they take care of customers, ultimately positively impacting their bottom line and shareholders. Despite the volatility of the airline industry, Southwest Airlines managed 46 consecutive years of profitability until the disruption caused by the COVID-19 pandemic.

Ben & Jerry's Ice Cream was founded by Ben Cohen and Jerry Greenfield in 1978, with a focus on creating social change as a way to give back to the community.[56] The firm adopted social, economic and quality missions in 1994, and in 1999 was named number five of the Top Most Reputable Companies (US). Their success brought interest from multinationals and in 2000 they were acquired by Unilever. Buyouts of successful small businesses with high levels of corporate social responsibility bring concerns about whether these values can be maintained, and Ben & Jerry's continues to strive to maintain theirs. There is hope that Unilever will enable Ben & Jerry's to retain its core missions, especially as Unilever has its own Sustainable Living Plan where it aims to improve the health of a billion people, move to 100% sustainable resources for raw materials, halve the environmental impact of everything it sells, and double its revenue. The current mission statements for Ben & Jerry's are: Human rights and dignity, social and economic justice, environmental protection, restoration and regeneration.[57] These have led them to make significant media statements on social justice issues such as support for Black Lives Matter after the murder of George Floyd.[58] They also fund the Ben & Jerry's

Foundation, which provides support for grassroots organisations working for progressive social change.[59]

The consequences of following compassion as a value to reduce suffering are going to look different in different contexts. As leaders, we can hold ourselves in compassion, grow our tolerance for making mistakes along the way and learn from these. It's not going to be perfect and those we interact with may be struggling with the uncertainty too. Katerina shares that by holding onto our common humanity and shared values, we can find a way:

> Today I heard people expressing all kinds of hesitations and fears, and what I saw was just the human reality of going through different stages of growth. The compassion that I can bring to that is just encouraging them to keep going through that growth. Like, it hurts. It's hard. It's painful. Let's keep going. We're not alone. Let's walk it together. Let's find a better way.
>
> Because of that discomfort, it's easy to just walk away saying it's too much. That's what I wish I had more of when I was going through some of those painful times – that encouragement. I see you and I see what's happening, and I'm going to walk with you through some of that.
>
> So that's what I try to be, especially at work. I try to be there walking with people and reminding all of us that our work is about human relationships. It's not about transactional policymaking or programs or, you know, contracting or whatever different process or system that we think we're caught up in. It's about human relationships. And so always try to bring the human element back into work, just humanising our relationships and reminding ourselves why we do what we do.
>
> This has changed my work relationships and how I interact within a very old system that I work within, but I never feel like it's an old stodgy place. If I'm constantly pushing my agenda, my friends call it "Oh, you're there with your agenda". There's another way folks, let's do great work, let's be smart, let's get stuff done AND let's not leave a trail of pain and brokenness around us because we're doing that.
>
> – Katerina Daniel, Canadian Public Service Executive

∞

Over the last six chapters, we have focused on challenges for leaders as individuals, in relationships with others, and in the context of the broader systems in which we work and live. Drawing on insights from leaders worldwide, we've applied the *NEW* reflective cycle to common challenges, showing how *Fierce Compassion* can offer clarity and strength in the face of complexity. While each chapter stands alone, they also build on one another, gradually strengthening the skills needed to meet inner and outer challenges. This chapter invited us into the complex territory of systems and culture, where change is rarely fast or easy. Here, compassion becomes a somewhat radical and courageous stance, which requires us to stay grounded in awareness and integrity. When we listen inwardly and lead from insight, we begin to shift what's possible. In the final chapter, we turn towards the future to discuss how we can keep showing up for this work in ways that are effective and sustainable.

∞

Chapter 10 Summary – navigating complex systems

This chapter explored how *Fierce Compassion* equips leaders to stay grounded and responsive within uncertain, unjust and rapidly changing systems.

Notice

- Recognise when overwhelm, cynicism or detachment take hold in the face of complexity
- Become aware of systemic forces that shape behaviour, culture and burnout

Empathise

- Hold space for the emotional toll of leading within broken systems
- Extend compassion to yourself and others while facing hard truths

Wise Action

- Lead with purpose even when impact feels uncertain or progress is slow
- Choose courageous, values-aligned action while accepting limits and complexity

References

1. Crawford, P., Gilbert, J., Gale, C., & Harvey, K. (2013). The language of compassion in acute mental health care. *Qualitative Health Research*, *23*(6), 719–727. https://doi.org/10.1177/1049732313482190
2. Baker, L. R., Martimianakis, M. A. (Tina), Nasirzadeh, Y., Northup, E., Gold, K., Friesen, F., Bhatia, A., & Ng, S. L. (2018). Compassionate care in the age of evidence-based practice. *Academic Medicine*, *93*(12), 1841–1849. https://doi.org/10.1097/acm.0000000000002373
3. Anandarajah, G., & Roseman, J. L. (2014). A qualitative study of physicians' views on compassionate patient care and spirituality: medicine as a spiritual practice? *Rhode Island Medical Journal*, *97*(3), 17–22.
4. Kerasidou, A. (2019). Empathy and efficiency in healthcare at times of austerity. *Health Care Analysis*, *27*(3), 171–184. https://doi.org/10.1007/s10728-019-00373-x
5. Kerasidou, A., & Kingori, P. (2019). Austerity measures and the transforming role of A&E professionals in a weakening welfare system. *PLOS ONE*, *14*(2), e0212314. https://doi.org/10.1371/journal.pone.0212314
6. Rawal, S., Strahlendorf, C., & Nimmon, L. (2019). Challenging the myth of the attrition of empathy in paediatrics residents. *Medical Education*, *54*(1), 82–87. https://doi.org/10.1111/medu.13877
7. Roze des Ordons, A. L., MacIsaac, L., Hui, J., Everson, J., & Ellaway, R. H. (2019). Compassion in the clinical context: constrained, distributed, and adaptive. *Journal of General Internal Medicine*, *35*(1), 198–206. https://doi.org/10.1007/s11606-019-05467-9
8. Gilbert, P. (2020). Compassion: From its evolution to a psychotherapy. *Frontiers in Psychology*, *11*(11), 1–31. https://doi.org/10.3389/fpsyg.2020.586161
9. Dowling, T. (2018). Compassion does not fatigue! *Canadian Veterinary Journal*, *59*(7), 749–750.
10. Inês Laíns, Johnson, T. J., & Johnson, M. W. (2024). Compassionomics: The science and practice of caring. *American Journal of Ophthalmology*, *259*(259), 15–24. https://doi.org/10.1016/j.ajo.2023.10.006
11. Fernando, A. T., & Consedine, N. S. (2014). Beyond compassion fatigue: The transactional model of physician compassion. *Journal of Pain and Symptom Management*, *48*(2), 289–298. https://doi.org/10.1016/j.jpainsymman.2013.09.014

12. Gęsiarz, F., & Crockett, M. J. (2015). Goal-directed, habitual and Pavlovian prosocial behavior. *Frontiers in Behavioral Neuroscience*, *9*, 1–18. https://doi.org/10.3389/fnbeh.2015.00135
13. Pavlova, A., Paine, S.-J., Cavadino, A., O'Callaghan, A., & Consedine, N. S. (2023). Do I care for you more when you really need help? An experimental test of the effect of clinical urgency on compassion in health care. *British Journal of Health Psychology*, *29*(1), 59–79. https://doi.org/10.1111/bjhp.12687
14. Keltner, D. (2016). *The Power Paradox*. Penguin.
15. Levine, R. V., Norenzayan, A., & Philbrick, K. (2001). Cross-cultural differences in helping strangers. *Journal of Cross-Cultural Psychology*, *32*(5), 543–560. https://doi.org/10.1177/0022022101032005002.
16. Cha, J. E., Serlachius, A., Cavadino, A., Kirby, J. N., & Consedine, N. S. (2023). Self-compassion and compassion for others: A multiple mediation study of personal values. *Mindfulness*, *14*(10), 2417–2429. https://doi.org/10.1007/s12671-023-02202-8
17. Lackey, N. Q., Tysor, D. A., McNay, G. D., Joyner, L., Baker, K. H., & Hodge, C. (2019). Mental health benefits of nature-based recreation: a systematic review. *Annals of Leisure Research*, *24*(3), 1–15. https://doi.org/10.1080/11745398.2019.1655459
18. Wen, Y., Yan, Q., Pan, Y., Gu, X., & Liu, Y. (2019). Medical empirical research on forest bathing (Shinrin-yoku): A systematic review. *Environmental Health and Preventive Medicine*, *24*(1), 1–21. https://doi.org/10.1186/s12199-019-0822-8
19. Grassini, S. (2022). A systematic review and meta-analysis of nature walk as an intervention for anxiety and depression. *Journal of Clinical Medicine*, *11*(6), 1731. https://doi.org/10.3390/jcm11061731
20. Wang, X., Rodiek, S., Wu, C., Chen, Y., & Li, Y. (2016). Stress recovery and restorative effects of viewing different urban park scenes in Shanghai, China. *Urban Forestry & Urban Greening*, *15*, 112–122. https://doi.org/10.1016/j.ufug.2015.12.003
21. Lee, J. (2017). Experimental study on the health benefits of garden landscape. *International Journal of Environmental Research and Public Health*, *14*(7), 829. https://doi.org/10.3390/ijerph14070829
22. Van den Berg, M., Maas, J., Muller, R., Braun, A., Kaandorp, W., van Lien, R., van Poppel, M., van Mechelen, W., & van den Berg, A. (2015). Autonomic nervous system responses to viewing green and built settings: Differentiating between sympathetic and parasympathetic activity. *International Journal of Environmental Research and Public Health*, *12*(12), 15860–15874. https://doi.org/10.3390/ijerph121215026
23. Oh, Y. A., Kim, S. O., & Park, S. A. (2019). Real foliage plants as visual stimuli to improve concentration and attention in elementary students. *International Journal of Environmental Research and Public Health*, *16*(5), 796. https://doi.org/10.3390/ijerph16050796

24. Song, C., Ikei, H., Nara, M., Takayama, D., & Miyazaki, Y. (2018). Physiological effects of viewing bonsai in elderly patients undergoing rehabilitation. *International Journal of Environmental Research and Public Health*, *15*(12), 2635. https://doi.org/10.3390/ijerph15122635
25. Hassan, A., Chen, Q. B., Jiang, T., Lyu, B. Y., Li, N., Li, S., Shangguan, Z. Y., Li, Y. T., Jun, Z. L., Luo, Q., Chen, X. Y., Wang, Y. Y., Zeng, C. C., Yang, J., & Tahir, M. S. (2017). Psychophysiological effects of bamboo plants on adults. *Biomedical and Environmental Sciences*, *30*(11), 846–850. https://doi.org/10.3967/bes2017.114
26. Park, S.-A., Song, C., Choi, J.-Y., Son, K.-C., & Miyazaki, Y. (2016). Foliage plants cause physiological and psychological relaxation as evidenced by measurements of prefrontal cortex activity and profile of mood states. *HortScience*, *51*(10), 1308–1312. https://doi.org/10.21273/hortsci11104-16
27. Ochiai, H., Song, C., Ikei, H., Imai, M., & Miyazaki, Y. (2017). Effects of visual stimulation with bonsai trees on adult male patients with spinal cord injury. *International Journal of Environmental Research and Public Health*, *14*(9), 1017. https://doi.org/10.3390/ijerph14091017
28. Park, S.-A., Song, C., Oh, Y.-A., Miyazaki, Y., & Son, K.-C. (2017). Comparison of physiological and psychological relaxation using measurements of heart rate variability, prefrontal cortex activity, and subjective indexes after completing tasks with and without foliage plants. *International Journal of Environmental Research and Public Health*, *14*(9), 1087. https://doi.org/10.3390/ijerph14091087
29. Igarashi, M., Song, C., Ikei, H., & Miyazaki, Y. (2014). Effect of stimulation by foliage plant display images on prefrontal cortex activity: A comparison with stimulation using actual foliage plants. *Journal of Neuroimaging*, *25*(1), 127–130. https://doi.org/10.1111/jon.12078
30. Ikei, H., Song, C., Namekawa, T., Igarashi, M., & Miyazaki, Y. (2014). Physiological and psychological relaxing effects of visual stimulation with foliage plants in high school students. *Advances in Horticultural Science*, *28*(2), 111–116. https://doi.org/10.13128/ahs-22823
31. Park, S.-H., & Mattson, R. H. (2008). Effects of flowering and foliage plants in hospital rooms on patients recovering from abdominal surgery. *HortTechnology*, *18*(4), 563–568. https://doi.org/10.21273/horttech.18.4.563
32. Park, S.-H., & Mattson, R. H. (2009). Ornamental indoor plants in hospital rooms enhanced health outcomes of patients recovering from surgery. *Journal of Alternative and Complementary Medicine (New York, N.Y.)*, *15*(9), 975–980. https://doi.org/10.1089/acm.2009.0075
33. Song, C., Igarashi, M., Ikei, H., & Miyazaki, Y. (2017). Physiological effects of viewing fresh red roses. *Complementary Therapies in Medicine*, *35*, 78–84. https://doi.org/10.1016/j.ctim.2017.10.001
34. Ikei, H., Komatsu, M., Song, C., Himoro, E., & Miyazaki, Y. (2014). The physiological and psychological relaxing effects of viewing rose flowers in office workers.

Journal of Physiological Anthropology, *33*(1), 6. https://doi.org/10.1186/1880-6805-33-6

35. Igarashi, M., Aga, M., Ikei, H., Namekawa, T., & Miyazaki, Y. (2015). Physiological and psychological effects on high school students of viewing real and artificial pansies. *International Journal of Environmental Research and Public Health*, *12*(3), 2521–2531. https://doi.org/10.3390/ijerph120302521
36. Zhang, X., Lian, Z., & Wu, Y. (2017). Human physiological responses to wooden indoor environment. *Physiology & Behavior*, *174*, 27–34. https://doi.org/10.1016/j.physbeh.2017.02.043
37. Sakuragawa, S., Miyazaki, Y., Kaneko, T., & Makita, T. (2005). Influence of wood wall panels on physiological and psychological responses. *Journal of Wood Science*, *51*(2), 136–140. https://doi.org/10.1007/s10086-004-0643-1
38. Tsunetsugu, Y., Miyazaki, Y., & Sato, H. (2002). The visual effects of wooden interiors in actual-size living rooms on the autonomic nervous activities. *Journal of Physiological Anthropology and Applied Human Science*, *21*(6), 297–300. https://doi.org/10.2114/jpa.21.297
39. Tsunetsugu, Y., Miyazaki, Y., & Sato, H. (2005). Visual effects of interior design in actual-size living rooms on physiological responses. *Building and Environment*, *40*(10), 1341–1346. https://doi.org/10.1016/j.buildenv.2004.11.026
40. Tsunetsugu, Y., Miyazaki, Y., & Sato, H. (2007). Physiological effects in humans induced by the visual stimulation of room interiors with different wood quantities. *Journal of Wood Science*, *53*(1), 11–16. https://doi.org/10.1007/s10086-006-0812-5
41. Song, C., Ikei, H., & Miyazaki, Y. (2018). Physiological effects of visual stimulation with forest imagery. *International Journal of Environmental Research and Public Health*, *15*(2), 213. https://doi.org/10.3390/ijerph15020213
42. Igarashi, M., Yamamoto, T., Lee, J., Song, C., Ikei, H., & Miyazaki, Y. (2014). Effects of stimulation by three-dimensional natural images on prefrontal cortex and autonomic nerve activity: A comparison with stimulation using two-dimensional images. *Cognitive Processing*, *15*(4), 551–556. https://doi.org/10.1007/s10339-014-0627-z
43. Anderson, A. P., Mayer, M. D., Fellows, A. M., Cowan, D. R., Hegel, M. T., & Buckey, J. C. (2017). Relaxation with immersive natural scenes presented using virtual reality. *Aerospace Medicine and Human Performance*, *88*(6), 520–526. https://doi.org/10.3357/amhp.4747.2017
44. Condon, P., & Makransky, J. (2020). Recovering the relational starting point of compassion training: A foundation for sustainable and inclusive care. *Perspectives on Psychological Science*, *15*(6), 1346–1362. https://doi.org/10.1177/1745691620922200
45. Pavlova, A., Paine, S.-J., Amelie Tuato'o, & Consedine, N. S. (2024). Healthcare compassion interventions co-design and feasibility inquiry with clinicians and healthcare leaders in Aotearoa/New Zealand. *Social Science & Medicine, 360*, 117327–117327. https://doi.org/10.1016/j.socscimed.2024.117327

46. Amajuoyi, P., Benjamin, L. B., & Adeusi, K. B. (2024). Agile methodologies: Adapting product management to rapidly changing market conditions. *GSC Advanced Research and Reviews*, *19*(2), 249–267. https://doi.org/10.30574/gscarr.2024.19.2.0181
47. Parker, L., & Miller, J. (2023). *The Activist Leader - A New Mindset for Doing Business*. Harper Collins.
48. Kouzes, J. M., & Posner, B. Z. (2016). *Learning Leadership: The Five Fundamentals of Becoming an Exemplary Leader*. Wiley.
49. Jun, K., & Lee, J. (2023). Transformational leadership and followers' innovative behavior: Roles of commitment to change and organizational support for creativity. *Behavioral Sciences*, *13*(4), 320. https://doi.org/10.3390/bs13040320
50. Follett, M. P. (1949). The giving of orders. In H. C. Metcalf & L. F. Urwick (Eds.), *Dynamic Administration. The Collected Papers of Mary Parker Follett* (pp. 65–66). Harper and Brothers Publishers.
51. Riane Eisler. (1998). *The Chalice and the Blade*. Thorsons.
52. Shourkaei, M. M., Taylor, K. M., & Dyck, B. (2023). Examining sustainable supply chain management via a social-symbolic work lens: Lessons from Patagonia. *Business Strategy and the Environment*, *33*(2), 1477–1496. https://doi.org/10.1002/bse.3552
53. Patagonia. (2024). *Core Values*. Patagonia. https://www.patagonia.com.au/pages/core-values
54. *Compassion in Politics*. (n.d.). *Compassion in Politics*. https://www.compassioninpolitics.com/
55. Otero, T. (2020, April 6). *Southwest Airlines: Servant Leadership Creates Organizational Success*. Sites.psu.edu. https://sites.psu.edu/leadership/2020/04/06/southwest-airlines-servant-leadership-creates-organizational-success/
56. Bayle-Cordier, J., Mirvis, P. H., & Moingeon, B. (2012). Leadership, social responsibility, and projected identity: The ben & jerry's story. *Academy of Management Proceedings*, *2012*(1), 12029. https://doi.org/10.5465/ambpp.2012.12029abstract
57. Ben & Jerry's. (2025). *Our Values, Activism and Mission*. Ben & Jerry's. https://www.benjerry.com/values
58. Ben & Jerry's. (2020). *Silence Is NOT an Option*. Ben & Jerry's. https://www.benjerry.com/about-us/media-center/dismantle-white-supremacy
59. *Homepage - Ben & Jerry's Foundation*. (2024, April 16). Ben & Jerry's Foundation. https://benandjerrysfoundation.org/#

11 Embracing humanity

Fierce Compassion for leading and learning

Leaders today are facing increasingly complex local and global challenges. There isn't one answer to all of these present and future issues, but our individual and collective insights offer a way forward. While many in leadership positions are interested in fostering compassion, empathy and connection, there can be a gap between intent and action. The generosity of those in leadership who were interviewed for this book helped identify areas of leadership challenge that were explored using the *NEW* framework.

Fierce Compassion invites us into the "how"– how to grow our capacity for compassionate action. The *NEW* reflective learning cycle provides a process to follow, and tangible skills to develop, in order to support compassionate leadership. It is this cycle that helps leaders to move from compassionate ideas to compassionate action. As your context shifts, so too might the insights that resonate. Returning to a chapter with fresh eyes after a challenge, a conversation or a moment of growth, can open up new perspectives. Let this book be something you return to, not just something you finish. At the core of this book is the encouragement to try these exercises in your own life.

When we take the step into action and practice, we gain more insight into our strengths and challenges, we develop more skills and build our resilience. It feels good, like we are getting somewhere!

But then...Something happens. We find some roadblocks along the way.

We find ourselves worrying, feeling disappointment and frustration. We chew it over in our minds. It wakes us in the early hours of the morning. When we inevitably stumble, we often question ourselves.

And, here is where the problem starts.

DOI: 10.4324/9781003583080-11

> I SHOULD be fine.... after all the work I have put in! Haven't I learnt anything?! What's wrong with me? I thought I had gotten over... (insert perceived failing that you have been insightful and skilful about overcoming). I know I can easily get caught here.

You're hooked back into expectations of linear thinking:

X is a problem. I will do Y and then it isn't a problem anymore. Job done!

There is a paradox in the work of self-improvement. As we increase our awareness we become more aware of what is not going so well. We are coming off the autopilot setting. As we notice more and more, we can feel as though we are doing worse, even when we are improving overall.

Compassion helps with emotional regulation, which is an important tool for leaders, but this can lead to another problem. Somewhere along the line, we may have developed a subconscious idea that as we learn more about ourselves and gain more skills for life we will glide through life on an even keel, all the time. We desperately want to avoid the choppy waves and seek the stillness of the calm lake. But this flat line of constant emotional stability is an unrealistic expectation of ourselves and of the tools we hope will deliver it. Constant emotional stability, all the time, regardless of what is going on around us (or inside us) is only achieved by a robot. Being a robot is not a desirable outcome. We have temporarily forgotten that we are human.

And humans experience a full range of emotions on a regular basis. The complexity of life means we get thrown curveballs, new challenges and change. We have ups and downs in our emotional states, and we respond to external and internal stimuli constantly. This is the "natural distress" and joy of being human. Sometimes how we react to this natural distress causes additional suffering (see Figure 11.1).

While we may want to be compassionate, it is part of our human experience that, despite our best intentions, at times we cause suffering to others or ourselves. When we feel the pull of a strong (and maybe unexpected) emotion, can we practise curiosity and non-judgement? Can we intervene at this point and choose not to kick ourselves while we are down, or be too hard or resentful to others? A great way to kill compassion is to criticise ourselves for not being good enough at it. Some days we can also become frustrated with the skills, reflective exercises or the very idea of compassion. When we lose the compassionate ground beneath our feet can we also bring compassion to this experience?

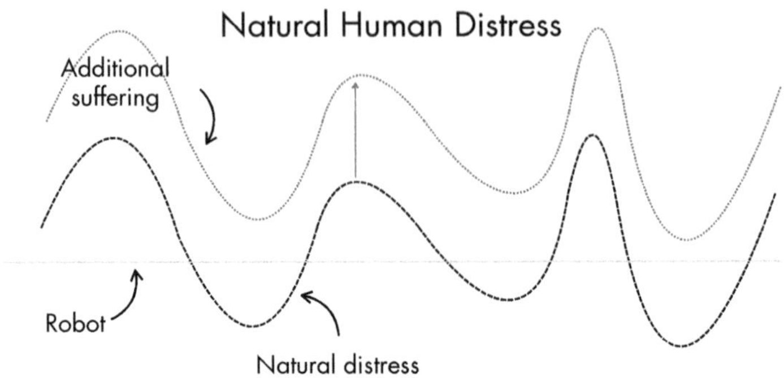

Figure 11.1 Natural human distress.

Try practising a compassionate and curious response.

- *What is this feeling? Where do you notice it in your body?*
- *What would a caring response to this feeling be (regardless of your judgement about it showing up)?*
- *Considering how you are feeling, what would be helpful to do (or not do) right now?*
- *Remind yourself that regardless of how much work you have done you are still human and it is normal to have emotional responses.*

As we compassionately tend to our natural distress, we avoid the amplification of additional suffering. The emotional waves become more manageable to navigate.

When we want to create new compassion habits, it can be helpful to start small, to link the habit to something we already do on a regular basis. Choose something you do everyday like brushing teeth or having a glass of water, and add a short compassion practice to this. It helps to reward ourselves immediately afterwards; it can be as simple as saying "well done". This acts as positive reinforcement, making it more likely that we will behave compassionately towards ourselves again in the future.[1]

If you find yourself jumping to problem-solving and quick solutions, it can be helpful to check that you are spending enough time practising empathy skills. You might like to try writing down your self-critical thoughts on one side of a page, then try to write self-compassionate thoughts on the other side. If you struggle with the compassionate side, ask yourself what you would tell a friend in a similar situation. You can also reverse this exercise to work with critical and compassionate thoughts for others. Then compare the two approaches...

- *What are the consequences of self-critical thinking?*
- *What would be the outcome of listening to the self-compassionate voice?*

It can be helpful to remember that even for large-scale problems that significant change is possible over time. For instance, in the 1970s, around the world about 20 million children died each year from the effects of poverty. Today that figure is five million.[2] There is still a long way to go to reduce the suffering from global poverty, but we can avoid the hopelessness that can lead to not taking any action by reminding ourselves of the benefits of gentle persistence.

If we find ourselves stuck and can't find a compassionate way forward, we may need to connect with others. Perhaps this means speaking to someone in your compassion collective or seeking support from a coach or therapist who uses compassion-based approaches. There are different ways to connect with others and deepen your compassion practice too. You might like to revisit the reflection exercises throughout this book as your leadership challenges evolve, or share the practices with your team or compassion collective.

While this book has focused on the use of compassion for leaders, with many examples from the work environment, we can't separate our work and private selves. Our compassion skills generalise into our home life to also support our relationships with family and friends. *Fierce Compassion* becomes a process we can lean into over and over again, even for some of life's biggest challenges. Maggie shared a personal story about how compassion helped her to navigate loss:

> When my mother died I was very out of my comfort zone, because I created a story in my mind that I was dreading the day my mother left this world. I was there when she died and it was such a new experience. There was no one there in the room with me and I felt a sort of fierce compassion. I had to really be willing to let her go. Be willing to tell her "Mum, you've done your job. As a mother you are amazing. I am fine. I know you're worried about me". I was massaging her face and stroking her face and looking in her eyes, and with her really looking at me, I was saying "You can go now". I think that

was probably the hardest but most beautiful moment in my life – to find a way of letting somebody go that I loved so deeply.

– Maggie Eyre, Director of Fresh Eyre

In a world that brings complexity, uncertainty and challenge, *Fierce Compassion* offers not an answer, but a way to keep showing up – with courage, care, and connection. It's been my great privilege and joy to hear how compassion has helped people in many different situations. We can find inspiration when we share and listen to each other's unique experiences of the compassionate journey we take together. The benefits of *Fierce Compassion* are revealed when we play with the concepts, skills and actions in our own lives. As this book concludes, hopefully, it is clear that this isn't an ending, but an invitation to continue to engage with the *NEW* reflective learning cycle to make life deeper and richer.

Pause for a moment to reflect...

- *How might Fierce Compassion help you in your leadership and life?*
- *Who will you connect with on your Fierce Compassion journey?*
- *What is the first small step that you can take today to put Fierce Compassion into practice?*

∞

Chapter 11 Summary – embracing humanity

This chapter explored the personal and ongoing nature of leadership growth, and encouraged readers to meet their imperfections, efforts and emotional fluctuations with *Fierce Compassion.*

Notice

- Acknowledge the myth of emotional mastery and the reality of inner turbulence
- Recognise moments of disconnection, exhaustion or self-doubt as natural parts of the journey

Empathise

- Respond to setbacks with tenderness and curiosity, not criticism
- Honour the courage it takes to keep learning, growing and reconnecting after missteps

Wise action

- Practise gentle, consistent habits that support emotional regulation and reflection
- Embrace self-compassion as a leadership strength and recommit to values-aligned growth

References

1. Fogg, B. J. (2020). *Tiny Habits: The Small Changes that Change Everything*. Houghton Mifflin Harcourt.
2. Dattani, S., Spooner, F., Ritchie, H., & Roser, M. (2019). *Child Mortality*. Our World in Data. https://ourworldindata.org/child-mortality

Index

Note: **Bold** page numbers refer to tables and *italic* page numbers refer to figures.

For Product Safety Concerns and Information please contact our EU
representative GPSR@taylorandfrancis.com
Taylor & Francis Verlag GmbH, Kaufingerstraße 24, 80331 München, Germany

www.ingramcontent.com/pod-product-compliance
Ingram Content Group UK Ltd.
Pitfield, Milton Keynes, MK11 3LW, UK
UKHW020008200926
475702UK00015B/2536
9781032950686